BEFORE TRANS

Before Trans

Three Gender Stories from Nineteenth-Century France

RACHEL MESCH

STANFORD UNIVERSITY PRESS
Stanford, California

STANFORD UNIVERSITY PRESS
Stanford, California

Printed in the United States of America on acid-free, archival-quality paper

LIBRARY OF CONGRESS CATALOGING-IN-PUBLICATION DATA
Names: Mesch, Rachel, author.
Title: Before trans : three gender stories from nineteenth-century France / Rachel Mesch.
Description: Stanford, California : Stanford University Press, 2020. | Includes bibliographical references and index. |
Identifiers: LCCN 2019040801 (print) | LCCN 2019040802 (ebook) | ISBN 9781503606739 (cloth) | ISBN 9781503612358 (ebook)
Subjects: LCSH: Dieulafoy, Jane, 1851-1916. | Rachilde, 1860-1953. | Montifaud, Marc de, 1845–1912. | Transgender men—France—Biography. | Authors, French—19th century—Biography. | Gender identity—France—History—19th century. | LCGFT: Biographies.
Classification: LCC HQ77.7 .M47 2020 (print) | LCC HQ77.7 (ebook) | DDC 306.76/8092 [B]—dc23
LC record available at https://lccn.loc.gov/2019040801
LC ebook record available at https://lccn.loc.gov/2019040802

Cover design: Kevin Barrett Kane

Cover photos: © Eugène Pirou / Bibliothèque Marguerite Durand / Roger-Viollet

Typeset by Kevin Barrett Kane in 10/14.4 Minion Pro

Contents

BEFORE TRANS

INTRODUCTION

JANE DIEULAFOY MIGHT BE the most famous French person you have never heard of. In 1882, Dieulafoy and her husband, Marcel, a civil engineer and architecture enthusiast, left their comfortable home in the southern city of Toulouse to travel the unpaved roads and mountain paths of Baghdad and Turkey all the way to Persia, in what is modern-day Iran. They hoped to excavate the ancient city of Susa, which British explorer William K. Loftus had located decades earlier but failed to unearth. What they found exceeded their wildest expectations: extensive palaces buried underneath the sandy, rock-strewn hills, forgotten by time and nature. After two government-sponsored missions, the couple finally returned to France in 1886 with forty tons of artifacts from the royal homes of Darius and Artaxerxes. Resettled in Paris, they were celebrated with the opening of the Salle Dieulafoy at the Louvre, leading to record-breaking crowds for the museum's new Department of Oriental Antiquities. Jane and Marcel Dieulafoy were a veritable fin-de-siècle power couple: they lectured about town, hosted an exclusive salon where they staged theatrical performances, hobnobbed with Prime Minister Raymond Poincaré, and were regularly invited to President Félix Faure's receptions.

All the while, the staunchly Catholic Dieulafoy went about in the most stylish men's suits.

Dieulafoy first appeared in men's clothing when she fought alongside Marcel in the Franco-Prussian War, just months after they were married. She returned to this practice on the voyages to Persia a decade later, never to wear skirts again—this despite the fact that it was hardly fashionable for upper-class Parisians to do so, and certainly not in her socially conservative milieu, where feminism was something of a dirty word and corsets remained the unchallenged norm. Dieulafoy and her peers recognized the intellectual capabilities of women and supported their effort to take on increasingly visible roles. But within this social sphere, women were careful not to appear rebellious, in order to avoid comparison with the menacing figure of the feminist seeking emancipation—the "New Woman," the Anglo-Saxon import who embraced professional roles and did not always choose marriage over independence.[1] Both were perceived as a threat to French traditions and values. Instead, shifts in gender roles in Dieulafoy's upper-bourgeois circles were contingent on balancing modernity with conventional notions of womanhood, career with domestic roles, and of remaining feminine in the process.[2] Nonetheless, Dieulafoy had secured a "permission de travestissement"—a pants permit from the police—for it was illegal in the nineteenth century for Parisian women to circulate in men's clothing without one. As of a city ordinance established in 1800, "any woman who wishes to dress as a man" was required to have the signature of a health official attesting to her medical need to do so. It is unclear how Dieulafoy qualified, as no record of her actual application remains.[3] She was one of only a handful of women to take this measure.

Jane Dieulafoy found a way to express her gender in a way that, to all appearances, made her comfortable and confident. But there were signs that, as she lived this unconventional life, she puzzled over who she was. She kept a notebook filled with clippings containing any mention of gender-crossing or pants permits, from current events, social commentary, or fiction. When her own name appeared in these accounts, it was underlined with a blue pencil.

The name Rachilde may have also appeared in those pages, for she too had secured the pants permit at around the same time as Dieulafoy; born Marguerite Eymery, she had abandoned her rural home for Paris upon turning twenty-one in 1881. Taking the name of a Swedish nobleman whom she claimed to have channeled during a family séance, she found her way to the

FIGURE 1. Jane Dieulafoy around 1900.

Source: Roger-Viollet. Reprinted with permission.

bohemian literary scene, eventually appearing at balls and cafés dressed in men's clothing. She had cut off her hair, stopped powdering her face, and began wearing bigger shoes as well.

While Dieulafoy was digging up ruins in Persia, Rachilde released the decadent novel *Monsieur Vénus* with an enthusiastic Belgian publisher in 1884. The book earned her a hefty fine and a prison sentence in Brussels for pornography—which she avoided by staying in Paris—while also making her the sweetheart of the Parisian literary circuit. Unlike Dieulafoy, Rachilde seemed to embrace her identity as a rebel, even to cultivate it as a reputation, while steering clear of any identification with women writers or feminism. Her calling card read, "Rachilde, Man of Letters."

But at the same time as she was building a reputation for wild antics, Rachilde felt deeply vulnerable and struggled for stability. In 1889 she surprised those who had come to think of her as an eccentric rebel by marrying the writer Alfred Vallette, choosing intellectual affinity and friendship over romantic inclination. At that point, she put her pants away and began working with Vallette to revive the famed literary journal the *Mercure de France*, becoming one of the most influential critics of the time as its chief book reviewer. Still, Rachilde continued to rail against the confines of her sex in fiction and plays that pressed hard against gender norms and conventional sexual categories. In her writing, Rachilde imagined her avatars alternately as a monster, a hysteric, an animal, a werewolf, a man.[4] She was never entirely sure what she was, but she had long been sure that the term "woman" did not describe her.[5]

In Dieulafoy's notebook, another name appears next to her own with striking frequency: Marc de Montifaud, the name by which the writer christened Marie-Amélie Chartroule de Montifaud was best known. She, too, had received official permission to wear pants. Like Dieulafoy, she wore tailored men's suits and a man's haircut for much of her life. Rachilde had noticed her as well. In her short volume *Why I Am Not a Feminist* (1928), she mentions Montifaud—misspelling her name as Montifaut—alongside Dieulafoy as another of the "women on French soil who dressed in men's clothing" like herself during the 1880s.[6]

Montifaud began her career as an art critic, and her work in that domain has recently been recognized for its "personal, materialist vision, one that

LA VIE MODERNE

Tout Paris

JOURNAL HEBDOMADAIRE ILLUSTRÉ

PLANCHE VI

Rachilde (par E. Langlois).

FIGURE 2. Rachilde on the cover of *La Vie moderne*, February 26, 1887.
Source: Médiathèque Pierre Fanlac, Périgueux. Reprinted with permission.

distinguishes itself from the conventions of the academy."[7] But it was not Montifaud's essays that made headlines in her day. She published dozens of anticlerical tales for which she was incessantly—and disproportionately—pursued by the French censors, some of whom were enraged that the writer they had assumed was a man was not. In 1877 Montifaud was charged with "offense to public decency" and sentenced to prison. (She would serve her time in an asylum instead.) The legal thrashing did not stop her from continuing to write. Despite repeated death threats, an attempted poisoning, and set-ups meant to prove her sexual impropriety, she continued to churn out controversial historical works, in addition to works of fiction that mocked the political forces out to get her. In some of these writings, Montifaud celebrated historical figures who had been persecuted for their difference or simply misunderstood, including the Abbé de Choisy, one of the gender-crossers of whom Dieulafoy had also written a historical account.

When Montifaud returned to Paris in 1882, after fleeing her latest prison sentence, she was no longer the awkward, veiled young woman described in the press accounts of her trials. She had taken to wearing men's suits, as she would for the rest of her life. With her closely cropped hair framing her broad, square jaw, she easily passed for a man, and many of her friends and colleagues addressed her with masculine pronouns. Defiant to the core, Montifaud seemed perplexed that her behavior could be anyone's business but her own. "I am myself," she wrote in 1879, "myself alone. Which is certainly not enough, but ultimately, I am me." It was a tacit acknowledgment that her life—like Dieulafoy's and Rachilde's—had no clear referent within the gender-stratified social structures of her time. This was nineteenth-century France, after all, where one of the Enlightenment's most tenacious legacies was the importance of the difference between the sexes. At the same time that the struggle for equality was hard fought, this sense of sexual difference as a value in its own right has endured in France to this day.

Dieulafoy, Rachilde, and Montifaud shared the expanding world of fin-de-siècle literary Paris, where publishing opportunities abounded thanks to a growing audience of readers and a thriving newspaper industry. In certain ways, though, these writers were worlds apart from one another. While Dieulafoy staged classical plays in her opulent living room in the wealthy Passy neighborhood, entertaining conservative politicians and academics

FIGURE 3. Marc de Montifaud around 1900.

Source: Eugène Pirou / Bibliothèque Marguerite Durand / Roger-Viollet. Reprinted with permission.

(even while she and Marcel outfitted androgynous actors in purposefully gender-neutral clothing), Montifaud's closest associations came from the world of art criticism and journalism. Rachilde circulated in a slightly different milieu of avant-garde writers such as Jean Lorrain, Paul Verlaine, and Catulle Mendès. Each was famous in her own way, but the three moved in different social circles connected to distinctly separate literary and social milieus. They were not united in any particular cause, beyond their personal rejection of gender norms, although none of them intended that her choice should serve as a model for women in general. Wearing men's clothing was just one of the ways in which they expressed their incompatibility with the gender assigned to them at birth.

In the past several years, transgender identity has emerged as an expansive designation of the nearly limitless ways to express gender beyond the binary poles of male and female. It is a category, then, that is also a means of refusing categories entirely. Rather than defining a particular identity, trans can designate a departure from assumed gender more broadly.[8] "Trans is not one thing," critic Jacqueline Rose has recently remarked. "In addition to 'transition' ('A to B') and 'transitional' ('between A and B'), trans can also mean 'A as well as B' or 'neither A nor B'—that's to say, 'transcending,' as in 'above,' or 'in a different realm from,' both." The broad category of trans can include anyone who feels misaligned with the gender attributed to them, regardless of how they identify and how they choose to express themselves. This includes those who identify as nonbinary, genderqueer, pangender, and gender fluid.

Recent scholarship has begun to consider the ways in which the trans framework can be used to shine a light on earlier figures who resisted gender norms—to explore what "trans before trans" might mean and the implications of casting back in history with a new set of critical tools.[9] "What is at stake in imagining and recovering trans experiences and identities before the modern concepts and terminology?" asks Robert Mills in his contribution to a special issue of *Transgender Studies Quarterly* devoted to "Trans* Historicities."[10] "Under what circumstances, historically, has gender's multiplicity and transformability been rendered visible?"[11] The lives of Dieulafoy, Rachilde, and Montifaud offer one set of answers to that question.

In applying the associations of the modern trans framework, I do not mean to claim that Dieulafoy, Rachilde, and Montifaud *were* trans, or that this term, which is the product of a more recent and specialized history, now supplies a definitive answer to the questions around gender posed by their lives. Instead, I want to suggest that the modern notion allows us to view the stakes of those questions more clearly: it helps us to recognize the kinds of issues they were working out.[12] It's a careful line that I am drawing but one that we are already accustomed to in other realms: for example, we think about various behaviors in the past through the lens of feminism, long before the movement existed; we speak of queerness even with the knowledge that people in earlier centuries did not think of themselves as gay or straight.[13] I am suggesting a parallel framing with trans, in order to recover a more complex history of gender identity.

Such a concept—gender identity in a historical context—is in itself anachronistic. As a result, as much as this book is about "trans before trans," it is also about "gender before gender," because gender did not exist in nineteenth-century France as a phenomenon separate from biology. Or at least, it did not exist in language: there was no way to name the difference between the body's physical markers and the cultural and social expectations of that body. English-speakers started doing this in the 1950s, the point at which "gender" moved beyond simply designating grammatical categories of masculine and feminine.[14] The shift took place much more recently in France, where an expanded meaning of the word *genre* has only come into use in the past several years. (Acknowledging that difference as a field of study is even newer in France than it is in the United States: *les études de genre* constitute a relatively marginal area of focus in the French academy compared to here.)

But as the following biographies make clear, even before there were complex ways of thinking about the relationship between bodies and gender, there were those who experienced their gender in complex ways. Without the nonbiological notion of gender, however, it was much more difficult to talk about any difference between the gender assigned to you and who you might otherwise know yourself to be. In many non-Western cultures, notions of multiple or nonbinary genders have existed for centuries, with built-in terminology, such as the Two Spirit in certain Native American tribes or the Kathoey in Thailand; perhaps those born into such cultures do not experience nonbinary gender as a problem to be solved but rather as simply a way of being.[15] Language in many ways determines our experience of the world. But in French, as in English, language has been organized in binary terms until only very recently. French is even more gendered than English, lacking our gender-neutral pronoun *they* in favor of the gendered *ils* or *elles*.[16] As a result, those who experience gender variance in these cultures have traditionally found themselves outside of language. Contemporary trans writer Riki Wilchins remembers that "language had always felt like a poor tool, one that didn't even begin to capture the ways I felt about the world or the things in my head." She was perpetually puzzled by "the million things I felt and thought that I could never say, which knowledge and categories and meaning didn't begin to capture."[17] The proliferation of new terminologies in our current culture is not a resolution of this difficulty but rather a symptom of it: a reminder of the ways in which gender variance is infinitely individual and does not readily fit into general terms. In fact, one thing that links past with present is the difficulty of finding the right linguistic vessels through which to identify oneself when the available terms feel inadequate.

In what follows, I suggest that for Dieulafoy, Rachilde, and Montifaud, stories were a way to work around the linguistic challenge of nineteenth-century gender variance. Where language works toward precision, narrative allows for depth and complexity. Indeed, stories are a way to use language to express that which exceeds language. This book attempts to piece together the story of those stories: the paths by which Dieulafoy, Rachilde, and Montifaud worked to understand themselves.

With no ready terms with which to account for gender nonconformity in the nineteenth century, contemporary commentators puzzled over the unusual presentations of Dieulafoy, Rachilde, and Montifaud as "bizarreries" or as elusive forms of hysteria—that catchall disease plaguing bourgeois women of the time. More recently, scholars have tended to see them as eccentric rebels, each one unique, sui generis, not fully explicable or comparable to anyone else. Studies of all three always mention their difference, their "eccentricity," or their unconventional behaviors (in particular their choice of clothing) as features of their identity—character traits, as it were. Yet few of these studies ever interrogate their choices as anything more than that: as not quite a choice at all but rather as an expression of self. What's more, up until this point, they have been considered rebellious women, proto-feminists challenging patriarchal structures in original ways. I propose that in order to truly understand them, we should stop thinking about them exclusively as women but rather as individuals pushing against that very identity, for whom the appropriate gender designation remains an open question.

GENDER STORIES

"Identity," writes historian Lisa Duggan, "is the story or narrative structure that gives meaning to experience." Likewise, we might think of gender identity as a set of "stories rather than labels," through which individuals forge connections between their experiences and the world around them.[18] Modern identities such as those documented in this book tend to be dynamic rather than stable; meanings accrue over time, shift, and evolve; stories of self can be told and undone, and then retold, in relation to stories and models encountered elsewhere.

As contemporary trans writers have demonstrated, for those who do not align with the gender assigned to them, gender can be the core of the identity story—a necessary and vital tale to tell. (For most cisgender people, on the other hand, gender identity as such is rarely thought about at all.) Many contemporary trans authors have shown how writing provides a way to give shape to gender identity, putting emphasis on the depth and breadth of story over any individual term or label. Despite its flaws, the television series *Transparent* was groundbreaking for that reason. Jennifer Finney Boylan recently reflected on her own writing as a necessary corollary to the medical interventions that she had undertaken: "I'm aware that the woman I have become in middle age is perhaps less the result of hormones than of a lifetime telling stories," she observed. "It was the writing of these books that, more than anything else, helped me understand the narrative of my own life, and those of other women like me."[19] Similarly, singer-songwriter Rae Spoon recounts that "more and more, I have thought of my gender as a story I tell myself."[20]

To what extent, this book asks, could gender be "a story that I tell myself" in late nineteenth-century France?[21] What kinds of stories did Jane Dieulafoy, Rachilde, and Marc de Montifaud formulate in order to make sense of selves that didn't align with familiar categories? How did they construct those gender stories, how were they able to relate them to others, and what can we learn from their process?

Recent accounts by trans writers describe an early search for both referents and narrative. "I never thought that I would see myself in the mirror," writes Joy Ladin. "Rather than embodying my identity, my body erased me, proved that I didn't, couldn't, exist."[22] When she discovered a story on transsexuality in an issue of her mother's *Good Housekeeping* magazine at around age eight, it was "the first time I had language for what I was, the first inkling that there were others like me." But a label is only one kind of affirmation. It was narrative that Boylan sought as a teen, searching "the library in vain for the story of a person I might resemble," but to no avail. "Without much in the way of dependable narrative or contemporary myth," she writes, "there were ways in which I felt, back then, as if I did not exist."[23] Leslie Feinberg wondered why "I couldn't find myself in history. No one like me seemed to have ever existed."[24] Her pioneering volume *Transgender Warriors* included Joan of Arc and the Chevalier d'Eon, both of whom Dieulafoy had also turned to as models for self-understanding.

For these modern writers, existence and affirmation came in part by telling their own stories or recovering a forgotten history. This need to construct one's gender story personally, sometimes repeatedly, as part of a transition to selfhood seems to bypass the important differences of race, class, and gender that are determinative in crucial ways that I don't mean to overlook here.[25] It is a need not resolved by terminology or common language, because each gender story is wholly unique. More than any particular identity, then, it is the call to writing that Dieulafoy, Rachilde, and Montifaud share with these modern trans writers. In what follows, I will show how writing offered a way to resolve gender difference in relation to the stories circulating around them, and in so doing, to consider why and how they found themselves outside of nineteenth-century gender norms.

All three of my subjects, in fact, were known as storytellers. Profiles of Dieulafoy describe her as a charming raconteur, both disarming and charismatic. And all three wrote as if their lives depended on it, producing many thousands of pages over the course of their lives. Dieulafoy, whose work was so often historical, was prolific, using hundreds of detailed pages to rebuild worlds that no longer existed and reconstruct lives from her vivid imagination. Her archives are populated with piles of dossiers, themselves filled with piles of writings; in addition to the seven published novels, a historical treatise, and a collection of short stories, there are dozens of unpublished stories, biographies, and plays, scrapbooks and notes, speeches and essays—her meticulous, tiny script crossed out and rewritten, cut out and pasted back in. The travelogues themselves numbered over one thousand pages; *Parysatis* is four hundred pages; her final work on Isabella of Spain is a five-hundred-page tome with notes and bibliography. Rachilde left a similar trove of paper and publications, filling dozens of dossiers in her Parisian archives. In her extensive correspondence, filled with broad, inky strokes defying all borders and boundaries, her words wind around calling cards, filling up the margins. She wrote a dozen plays and more than forty novels, continuing to write year after year, up until the end of her life at the age of ninety-three. Rachilde spoke of literary production as a kind of trance. So did Montifaud, who described her writing as a kind of compulsion—a bodily act over which she seemingly had little control. She produced, in total, two dozen volumes of novels and short stories, nine nonfiction works, and hundreds of newspaper and magazine articles.

While Dieulafoy, Rachilde, and Montifaud did not always write about gender explicitly or directly, they wrote about it constantly. They looked to history, religion, medicine, and literature for sources and inspiration as they wrote and rewrote stories about who they were and why and how they were different, and about figures from the past who were different as well.

SPEAKING OF GENDER

Stories about gender identity have appeared in the past decade in nearly every form of modern media: books, magazines, social media, online writings, photography, television series, and film have all played a role in the development of modern trans discourse, providing a forum for discussion, as well as endless points of reference through which a new generation of individuals has come to understand themselves. In some ways, nineteenth-century France was not all that different, as Dieulafoy, Rachilde, and Montifaud searched for stories to fold themselves into and measure themselves against. It's no coincidence that this era was characterized by the explosion of the

FIGURE 4. Trading card commemorating the Dieulafoys' discovery of the Frieze of Lions, included in a box of Lombart chocolates. The frieze is on display in the Louvre.

mass press; in the years between 1880 and 1900, the publishing industry expanded in nearly every sector of its market. Newspapers multiplied in number, driven by an increasingly literate public, looser laws on freedom of expression, and a competitive marketplace. Circulation skyrocketed from a combined total of one million in 1870 to five million in 1910. Whereas in 1882 there were 3,800 periodicals printed in France, within ten years that already sizable number had tripled.[26] Other forms of mass culture were growing as well, as new forms of entertainment emerged every week in the Parisian capital, where all three writers spent their adult lives. Long before our current obsession with reality TV and breaking news, city dwellers were fascinated by anecdotes about everyday experiences and human-interest

FIGURE 5. Postcard of wax statues of Jane Dieulafoy and Jules Verne in the Musée Grévin wax museum.

stories, sending readers hurrying to the kiosks for morning and evening editions. New forms of social community developed through a sense of shared entertainment and sources of knowledge that often crossed class lines. As crowds filled museums, department stores, and the new vehicles of public transport, everyone was likely to be talking about the same scandals, if not the latest art exhibition or the newest trends in fashion. In addition to their appetite for reading, Parisians collected photographs and postcards of celebrities, which they compiled in albums or traded with friends. By the late 1890s, one could come across a card-size image, suitable for trading, of "Madame Dieulafoy, the famous explorer," in packs of chocolate or boxes of rice (figure 4). Eventually, her wax effigy was installed at the famous Musée Grévin wax museum (figure 5).

Whether or not there was a word for it, gender was everywhere in the new mass culture. Parisians were consumed with the shifting roles of women in society, as well as with a perception that French men were not quite living up to social expectations. The devastating loss of the Franco-Prussian War in 1870 fueled a growing sense that the French family was in crisis, failing to produce enough healthy boys to keep the country safe.[27] Men were perceived as not strong enough, women as not committed to their traditional maternal roles. Against this backdrop, women were assuming increasingly public roles, in part as a result of educational reforms that dramatically increased women's access to education. Divorce was legalized in 1884, provoking a flurry of debate about the possibility of further reform to what had been a rather strict model of marriage.[28]

With these social shifts came a vigorous backlash. In the urban center in particular, population growth and new modes of circulating through the city meant that people from different walks of life increasingly came into contact with one another, pushed close together on the new mass transit vehicle known as the omnibus, making their way through department stores, or sitting next to each other at cafés and restaurants.[29] This inspired endless commentary about the various kinds of women one might encounter. In the emerging media, there was much talk about the so-called New Woman—a figure of modern femininity seen as a threat to family structures. The New Woman was herself a kind of sequel to the much-reviled *bas bleu*, or bluestocking, the denigrating term for a French woman writer. The artist Honoré Daumier had devoted a whole series, in the 1840s, to mocking her in the newspaper *Le Charivari*, where she was presented as a man-hating hag, quick to leave her husband and children in the lurch. As the press continued to expand in the second half of the century, women began publishing in record numbers, threatening to overshadow men's contributions in this sphere—following the pants-wearing George Sand's notorious example. To make matters worse, the feminist had joined the scene as another model of modern femininity threatening the patriarchal establishment, even though contemporary French feminists tended to link their activism to support for traditional family structures. Between 1892 and 1913, six feminist congresses took place in France, in which women advocated for child welfare, marriage reform, and social equality.[30] The writer, the feminist, and the bluestocking were often conflated in the public imagination, variations on the perceived threat to the traditional French family.[31]

Not only was gender a hot topic in the political and social sphere; it extended as well to science in this golden age of French positivism. In the emerging field of medicine, a great deal of attention was devoted to discerning just what separated women and men from a biological vantage point. As women entered professional roles, there was much at stake in proving that they were fundamentally different from men: less intelligent, more prone to illness, and especially prone to madness. The hysteria diagnosis that became a household word in the second half of the century was documented by lengthy scientific tomes explaining the fundamental difference of the female body from the male one. Using the brain was thought to damage the uterus directly; reading novels was only second in danger to writing them.[32] In the latter part of the century, experts in the nascent field of sexology made the study of sex a science and worked to demarcate categories of sexual behavior, laying the groundwork for the taxonomies and hypermedicalization that would come to stigmatize gender-variant and queer subjects for the next century.[33] Even so, there was as yet no term to describe the experience of being assigned a gender at birth that did not match one's internal sense of self. Gender nonconformity was linked to sexuality through what was known as the inversion model: an effeminate man who was attracted to men or a mannish woman was considered homosexual.[34] The distinctions between gender identity (who you are), gender expression (how you present yourself), and sexuality (who you are attracted to) had yet to be theorized or articulated. Androgyny was the stuff of myths, while hermaphroditism was tied to physiology. The closest approximation of transgender identity in French appeared with the 1895 French translation of Richard von Krafft-Ebing's *Psychopathia Sexualis*, where he presented the case of a patient "who feels like a woman in a man's form" as a form of mental illness.[35]

Gender questions circulated in artistic and literary circles as well. New schools of painting pushed back against long-standing academic rules about how and in what context women could be portrayed as sexual objects. Manet nearly caused a riot with his *Olympia*, the unabashedly naked prostitute on display for all to see. The school of painting that would come to be known as Impressionism offered endless scenes of women engaged in the activities of modern life. Whether on the boulevard or in the music hall, they were far from the cloistered rigidity of academic portraiture. In the literary realm, it would be hard to overstate the presence of gender as a theme. As early as the 1840s, the French novel was preoccupied with gender-crossing, as exemplified by Théophile Gautier's *Mademoiselle de Maupin*, the story of a woman who disguises herself as a man and seduces a man and a woman; George Sand's play *Gabriel*, which tells the story of a girl raised as a boy in order to inherit the crown; and Balzac's castrato Sarrasine in his novella of the same name, who performs as the female La Zambinella. The drama of Balzac's story is in the discovery—for both the reader and the main character—of his "true sex."

Fiction about gender subversion was even more common in the second half of the century, sometimes appearing as short stories in daily papers; Dieulafoy included at least one in her notebook. Naturalist and decadent fictions from the 1880s and 1890s were fascinated with notions of sexual depravity and perversion: Jules Barbey d'Aurevilly, Joris-Karl Huysmans, and Catulle Mendès depicted femme fatales who were all the more troubling for their masculine traits. Writers from the poet Baudelaire to novelists Adolphe Belot and Emile Zola fantasized in their work about sapphic desire between women.[36] In fact, when "the creations of French writers" were cited in American obscenity trials in 1892, Balzac and Belot were mentioned by name.[37] In cataloging the various forms of female deviance, late nineteenth-century French writers were obsessed with science, and scientists were in turn indebted to literature. The physiologist Dr. Charles Richet famously cited Flaubert and other authors in his writings on hysteria, while Flaubert, Zola, and many of their peers studied medical sources to most accurately depict their subjects' physical responses.[38]

Dieulafoy, Rachilde, and Montifaud worked to understand themselves in relationship to these current ideas, searching for points of similarity through which to form their own gender stories and reject those that were imposed upon them. It was hardly a simple time to be a woman writer, and each faced off directly against the *bas bleu*. Their narratives reveal an awareness that the images of modern femininity they encountered could not fully account for their self-perception, perhaps especially because these images were so dominated by negative stereotypes.

In terms of living models of gender-crossers (as opposed to literary fantasies or medical case studies), there were few public personalities with whom they might compare themselves. The legendary George Sand had died in 1876, but she was in many ways of a different era.[39] They would have heard of Rosa Bonheur, the celebrated painter, who, like them, had acquired a pants permit and to whom Dieulafoy—also celebrated—was often compared. But Bonheur lived with her female partner in the French countryside, mostly out of the spotlight. The actress Sarah Bernhardt, a beloved Parisian celebrity, often dressed in men's clothing, but as a kind of performance associated with her work in the theater. One is hard-pressed to find well-known men who wore women's clothing during this time, although certain male writers such as Jean Lorrain and Pierre Lôti would occasionally cross-dress for entertainment.[40]

Within a few short years, there would be more points of reference—more women publicly modeling alternative gender and sexual identities, with more of a sense that boundaries were regularly traversed. In 1907, Colette would appear nude on the French stage with her lover, the Marquise de Belbeuf, who wore her hair cropped short and dressed in men's clothing. Known as Missy, the marquise is surely an example of "trans before trans"; she and Colette mingled with the writers Nathalie Clifford Barney, Lucie Delarue-Mardrus, Renée Vivien, and Liane de Pougy, several of whom were romantically involved with each other at various times.[41] This group would become known as "Sapho 1900"—but not until 1900 had long passed.[42] The gender stories of Dieulafoy, Rachilde, and Montifaud take place mostly in the 1880s and 1890s, just before this vastly different landscape for gender-crossing would emerge. Bookended between the more famous lives of George Sand and Colette, they showcase the private processes of self-analysis in relation to shifting models and possibilities, just before the dawn of the Belle Epoque would become, in some ways, the Queer Epoque.

Dieulafoy, Rachilde, and Montifaud's stories reveal the complex interplay between internal drives and external influences by which their nontraditional gender identities took shape in the last two decades of the nineteenth century. Each figure mapped herself onto the pages of stories that demonstrated the profoundly individual nature of gender consciousness and identity formation. While there may have been a notion of a "third sex" circulating during this time, as Laure Murat has argued, it does not seem to have played much of a role in their explorations, perhaps because of its association with deviance and perversion. Certainly, myriad literary precedents paved the way for them to engage with themes of gender and sexuality in their novels, and Rachilde and Montifaud cite the influence of Naturalist and Decadent writers on their work. But these precedents do not fully account for the unique course of their individual explorations or for their stark differences from one another.

Dieulafoy, a devout Catholic, largely ignored literary trends. Instead she turned to Christian lore, comparing herself to the model of the so-called transvestite saints. She retold the story of Joan of Arc in her own image, introducing references from her travels to Persia. Rachilde was influenced by popular medical accounts. She feared she might be a hysteric—a diagnosis covering any female behavior seen as deviant. Montifaud, on the other hand, was outraged by the endless commentary in the press on women writers; while initially she resisted pressure to explain herself, she later offered the gender-crossing seventeenth-century nobleman François Timoléon de Choisy as a model for the celebration of gender defiance.

These are not the only narratives they defended or attacked. The chapters that follow describe the deeply personal, unpredictable path of gender exploration for Dieulafoy, Rachilde, and Montifaud, each of whom moved away from the category of woman in various ways. The questions raised by this process are just as important as the lack of answers to these questions. Why should one person see themself as a hero and another as a deviant? Why didn't they seem to identify with images of the "third sex" suggested in popular fiction, or seek to create community with others like themselves? They certainly knew of each other. But if it occurred to any of them that their desire to dress a certain way might bind them together in a deeper, shared struggle, there is no evidence that they ever reached across social lines to attempt any sort of meaningful contact. It would not have been difficult, for they had numerous friends and acquaintances in common. Or perhaps precisely because it had occurred to them, they chose to eschew this association.

Dieulafoy's notebook of press clippings serves as a vital testament to the process of gender exploration in the late nineteenth century. A compendium of gender reference points, the tattered, overstuffed volume offers a glimpse into her efforts to discern where her own example might fit in. Should she be appreciated through an article about "The Society of Feminists Congress" (June 14, 1892) and another on "The Assembly of Women" (May 13, 1892)? Should she identify with a piece on "Lady Lawyers and Doctors" and women at the Académie française? Or was she better understood as one of the "Men-Women and Women-Men" troubling the Parisian boulevards, those disparaged "All as men!" (September 23, 1894) in an article comparing Dieulafoy to a man recently arrested for wearing women's clothing? Did her use of men's clothing enhance her marriage through "an unbroken companionship" ("Uses Hubby's Wardrobe"), or did it render her "an object of curiosity"—akin to the "the bearded woman" and "several other people who would be ridiculous in the clothing of their sex" mentioned in "The Replacement of Men by Women"? Dieulafoy did not respond to these pieces directly, but her written efforts—two novels about girls who become boys, published during the same time period, and speeches about a brand of feminism that allows for conventionally masculine roles—clearly represent an attempt to make sense of herself in relation to the accounts and commentaries that she zealously collected. While Rachilde and Montifaud did not keep similar notebooks or journals, they reacted to depictions of themselves in essays and letters; their own gender stories—the ways in which they thought of themselves—come into sharpest relief against the narratives in which they felt implicated or judged.

The biographies that follow thus document the disparity between the public view of Dieulafoy, Rachilde, and Montifaud and their own view of themselves—between the stories told about them and the stories they told about their own lives. Recovering that disparity is crucial to this project, for I am arguing that the writings of Dieulafoy, Rachilde, and Montifaud clearly show how they have been misunderstood. The chapters that follow consider the ways in which they rejected (or sometimes repurposed) the terms put forth to describe them. These three did not fit readily into the nineteenth-century categories available for describing women who defied convention. As a result, they were most often considered either feminists (an association they mostly rejected) or eccentrics. The former categorization misreads their behavior as advocacy on behalf of women, while the latter dismisses or pathologizes it. Modern critics, on the other hand, have more or less repeated the error by considering their subversion of gender norms to be a form of early feminism, regardless of the different motivating forces behind some of those challenges.[43] The complexity and volatility of their own gender identification are rarely acknowledged. Despite their masculine gender expression, the current scholarly literature is too often limited to considerations of their presumed femininity.[44]

To be sure, Dieulafoy, Rachilde, and Montifaud exhibited many behaviors that were not inconsistent with feminism, and they attempted to seize privileges denied them because of their assigned sex. But the details of their lives and writings reveal a persistent, overriding set of concerns that, while sometimes overlapping with their marginalization as women, found their impulse elsewhere. We know that their gender-crossing cannot simply, or only, be attributed to feminism because feminism did exist, in many forms, during their lives, and they mostly rejected it, in particular their affinity with women as such. Women's rights, emancipation, suffrage, and marriage reform were ideas freely circulating in the late nineteenth century, but these were hardly the issues that interested Dieulafoy, Rachilde, and Montifaud. Moreover, all three of them identified with gender-crossers whom we might describe as "trans feminine": men who dressed as women or identified with femininity. This shared affinity suggests an awareness that their difference in gender expression was not an expansion of the ways in which they could be women. Rather, its determining feature was the departure from assigned sex. Again, Dieulafoy's notebook offers a certain kind of evidence: feminism was one way of understanding her, but not the only way.

And yet, to the extent that these writers are known at all, it is thanks to feminist criticism, which has rescued them from obscurity along with many other women writers of their time. We might thus describe their legacy in scholarship as the result of a certain confirmation bias: the inherent assumption that every enigmatic aspect of their writing or life stories can be explained by the (assumed) fact of their being female. Through this limited prism, every subversive act translates as a "kind of early feminism"—whether or not they explicitly rejected that label.[45] Wearing pants has been almost entirely subsumed by this analysis.[46] There is no historical term for masculine-identifying women who might not have identified as women had they lived in our day but who faced their lives as women, often in tension with the patriarchal constraints placed upon them.[47] The trans framework helps us recognize these figures and thereby recover a dimension of gender history that is otherwise obscured by the overlapping fields of women's history and feminism.

And what about sexuality? Another error that earlier scholars have made in considering Dieulafoy, Rachilde, and Montifaud has been to assume that their difference must be a sign of same-sex attraction and to explore this possibility without also considering gender identity.[48] In the cases of Dieulafoy and Rachilde, there is simply no evidence to support this conclusion (aside from Rachilde's short-lived ambiguous relationship with the female artist Gisèle d'Estoc); indeed, for these two, their attraction to men while also identifying with masculinity was a crucial aspect of what they were attempting to understand. This may help explain why they were married—and for Dieulafoy, quite happily so. That said, marriage was not so much a choice for women in the nineteenth century as a necessary pathway to adulthood and enfranchisement, without which they could not own property or circulate easily in public places. In any case, all three were apparently comfortable in what appeared to be a heterosexual paradigm—another reason why their contemporaries struggled in their efforts to categorize them. There was no point of reference, medical or otherwise, for separating gender and sexuality in this way. Thus, Rachilde imagined her gender-crossed avatar in *Monsieur Vénus* as mentally ill and unable to speak the terms of her desire for a man, as a man. Montifaud, on the other hand, was attracted to women as well as to men, which she may have understood as being connected to her masculine gender expression. Their stories reveal a complex relationship between gender and sexuality that cannot be easily delimited by modern terminologies.

Comprehensive, book-length biographies of Dieulafoy and Rachilde exist (and have been tremendous resources for my own work); there are also a few shorter biographical accounts of Montifaud's life.[49] The three stories that follow offer correctives to those efforts by demonstrating how these figures' sense of their gender difference played a central role in their lives and in their writings. In the process, they recover the work of gender identity as a dynamic, variable, years-long process of creating meaning through recognition and differentiation. The essays that follow are constructed with the aid of photographs, archival ephemera, novels, letters, treatises, and poems, evidence collected across the disparate paths each writer took—from Persian travels to pornographic writings. But the way in which this evidence is treated requires its own critical approach. Just as queer theorist José Muñoz argues that "queerness is often transmitted covertly," the same can be said, historically, for "transness." "Instead of being clearly available as visible evidence, queerness has instead existed as "innuendo, gossip, fleeting moments, and performances," notes Muñoz.[50] Similarly, the evidence for these gender stories is not always explicit, and sometimes the clearest evidence is a lack thereof.

In what follows, I do not engage in traditional scholarly criticism; instead, my work privileges narrative over argument. In the absence of a shared theoretical language, it is not my intention to supply missing vocabulary or to try to define these figures through the designation of labels. In telling their stories, I only rarely refer to modern terminologies or debates; for the most part, the modern trans framework offers a paradigm shift through which the stories I relate come into clearer focus, often through an effect of layering and accumulation. What we now know about the specific and expansive challenges of gender variance—and perhaps especially, the difficulty of translating it into words—allows us to more deeply comprehend these three writers, all of whom struggled to find the terms through which to understand and express themselves. That said, we must also take care not to impose our own constructions on what was not yet articulated. The newer language brings us in some ways closer to these historical figures, but it also threatens to misread their experiences through our own modern filters. Such is always the risk with historical work, no doubt. As I use the new language as a reference point for our modern eyes, I hope to also bring to light a certain kind of freedom we no longer have: that of not having to precisely name the terms of gender variance, and thus being able to craft one's own story in its place.[51] It is those stories—the creative ways in which Dieulafoy, Rachilde, and Montifaud interpreted their own lives—that I seek to highlight here.

Had they lived in our time, perhaps they would have chosen different names for themselves, and perhaps different pronouns. Rachilde experimented with masculine grammar forms for a time in the 1880s, and some of Dieulafoy's novels, with their gender-crossing protagonists, make gestures toward this possibility. Many of Montifaud's friends addressed her in the masculine, and she often wrote with masculine grammatical forms, under the assumption that her audience would assume that she was a man. But in the absence of a means to describe themselves otherwise, all three deferred to or continued to use female pronouns for most of their lives. In 2006, Leslie Feinberg explained that despite identifying herself as transgender, she found the pronouns "she/her" to be appropriate in certain settings, so as not "to resolve the social contradiction between my birth sex and gender expression and render my transgender expression invisible."[52] In using female pronouns to designate Dieulafoy, Rachilde, and Montifaud, I seek to maintain a similar contradiction, preserving the historical nature of their lived experience. At the same time, I realize that at times the female pronouns may feel jarring. Even so, given the personal nature of pronoun choice and the ambiguity of their identifications, I did not feel it was appropriate to choose alternative pronouns on their behalf.[53]

A NOTE FROM THE FIELD

My own effort to understand Jane Dieulafoy, Rachilde and Marc de Montifaud led me beyond my scholarly comfort zone into a rich and complex field that had not been part of my gender education but through which the lives and work of these writers came into much sharper focus. As a scholar, I had taken seriously Joan Scott's famous delineation of gender as a "useful category of historical analysis." And yet I had understood that category in chiefly binary terms. If being a woman in nineteenth-century France was all-determining in ways that my work had long sought to expose, being gender variant added a different, complex layer that my own fields of French literature and history have largely overlooked, even in their explorations of the history of sexuality. I hope this book can be the beginning of a reckoning in French studies, leading to more explorations of what "trans before trans" might mean in postrevolutionary France. I am certain that any future work will only complicate and enrich my own. More fundamentally, I hope there will be a new generation of trans scholars to lead the way.

Indeed, the more I have immersed myself in the field of trans studies, the more I have questioned my right to do so. As Julia Serano argues in *Whipping Girl*, too many academics and writers have exploited transgender issues for their own purposes over the past several decades. As a result, writes Serano, "those who do attempt to speak as our proxies, who claim to understand our bodies, our issues, or our identities, necessarily push us further into the margins."[54] This has happened even as trans has come into the cultural spotlight in recent years with renewed sensitivity: the television series *Transparent* failed to cast any trans actors in its first season; the cisgender Eddie Redmayne played the protagonist in the film *The Danish Girl*, and Scarlett Johansson was compelled, amid controversy, to give up her role in a film in which she was cast as a trans man. There's a difference, of course, between writing about gender variance and taking a role as a trans person in a major motion picture. But the question of who has the right to tell a certain story is a legitimate one. I am deeply aware that there are those whose lives are determined and made vulnerable by the questions considered in this book. Rather than pushing gender-variant voices into the margins, I hope that by amplifying the stories of these three writers, this book will make more room for them and others like them to be heard.

PART I

JANE DIEULAFOY: MASCULINITY FOR GOD AND COUNTRY

1 A SOLDIER IS BORN

IN 1871, JANE DIEULAFOY POSED for a portrait. She had only just returned with her husband Marcel from the battlefields of the Franco-Prussian War. After the grueling experience of war—and the humiliating French defeat—Jane and Marcel had resettled in Toulouse, where it would take the diminutive Jane months to recover from the conditions that she had endured. Without a particularly hearty constitution himself, Marcel was also debilitated, and Jane remained devoted to him, concerned about his health and well-being while he took on new administrative obligations.

Years later, Jane would take hundreds of photographs of sites far from home in Baghdad, Persia, Spain, and Morocco. But at this point, she did not yet own a camera, much less know how to use one. She had not yet written any novels and perhaps did not even realize that she was a born writer. Yet there was an impulse to record herself as a soldier, in order to memorialize a fleeting identity just as she was expected to enter into a bourgeois life—an effort to document her heroism and the persona that she had briefly inhabited.

In the portrait, she stands against a landscape of shadowy movement, the silhouette of another soldier on horseback blurred in the distance (figure 6). Leaning against a rock, she is dressed in what appear to be riding clothes: brown boots, black bloomers. While the image was meant to capture her as a soldier, her rifle is not pictured; she holds a riding whip instead. Her hat

FIGURE 6. Portrait of Jane Dieulafoy from 1871, artist unknown, located at the Hôtel Dieulafoy, Paris. Photograph by author.

rests on the table, as if to make clear that no flowing locks hide underneath; rather, her hair is cut in a boyish pouf.

This tableau is old before its time—referencing an academic tradition long out of fashion. In it, Dieulafoy looks like a young man from a different era, and her stance is tentative and understated. The cliché of the composition is offset by the fact that she is returning from the battlefield not as a young man, as the genre would dictate, but rather as a young bride, so the outmoded genre is unexpectedly subversive. It ironically depicts a modern woman in the form of a conventional young man, hinting at the constructed and unstable nature of gender norms, which can mean such different things in different contexts.

La Vie Heureuse

FIGURE 7. Dieulafoy's 1870 portrait on the cover of *La Vie Heureuse*, April 15, 1913. Source: Bibliothèque Marguerite Durand.

It hints, too, that Dieulafoy's shift to a different kind of gender expression was already under way, despite her having recently returned to skirts and domestic duties. Years later, this image would resurface on the cover of *La Vie Heureuse*, one of the first women's photographic magazines to be published in France (figure 7). Dieulafoy would play a central role in this publication as part of the Belle Epoque female literary elite that the magazine promoted, despite the fact that she seemed to break all the rules of its hyperfeminine milieu; in a crowd of women in corsets, she seemed hardly a woman at all. In 1913, editor Caroline de Broutelles would ask her if she might feature the image of Dieulafoy in uniform in order to promote Dieulafoy's advocacy for the role of women in combat. By that point, it would be nearly impossible to imagine the world-famous Jane Dieulafoy in anything but a well-tailored men's suit.

So much had happened in the course of those forty-two years: Dieulafoy had become a fixture on the academic lecture circuit, famous for her archaeological missions; she was a novelist, playwright, and public intellectual. The events of her life are fairly well documented.[1] What follows here, however, is a more private narrative, almost entirely overlooked. This is the story of Jane Dieulafoy's gender and of the imaginative work that allowed her to accept her difference from other women and men.

When Jeanne Paule Henriette Rachel Magre married Marcel Dieulafoy in 1870, she seemed to fall straight into the only kind of marriage conceivable for her: a lifetime commitment to a husband who would view her as an intellectual partner, trailblazer, and confidant. As a child she was full of imagination, dreaming of adventure and longing to follow in the footsteps of the heroes she had read about in books.[2] Marriage to Marcel set her on that unlikely path.

Jane, as she was known, had recently returned to her hometown of Toulouse after receiving eight years of religious education in the neighboring convent of Auteuil. Marcel was a brilliant young engineer who had grown up in the same neighborhood. He had just returned from Algeria, after overseeing infrastructure repairs as a government appointee. He came from a similar background, particular to their region: his Catholic family belonged to the well-to-do upper bourgeoisie, conservative in values yet also republican, which in this context meant being devoted to the principles of a democratic society. The ambitious young man, with a passion for architecture and travel, promised his new wife a life of adventure and exploration that she eagerly embraced.

That life of adventure began perhaps more quickly than anticipated. Just months after their marriage, in the summer of 1870, war broke out with Germany. While Marcel was not drafted, he was compelled to join up once Prussian forces overtook Paris, as prominent Assembly member Léon Gambetta rallied volunteer armies from neighboring regions to come to the aid of the French. Jane was not content to wait on the sidelines; when Marcel was appointed a captain, she accompanied her husband to the front.

Jane wanted to become a soldier, but women were not allowed to enlist as members of the army. The young bride, twenty years old and inexperienced, was determined and stubborn. She was unwilling to demean herself in the ancillary domestic role of *cantinière*—bringing food and water to the soldiers—assumed by other women who followed their husbands. Instead, she exploited a military loophole, becoming a *franc-tireur*, or sharpshooter, who was not directly subject to the rules of the French army. As a volunteer, she was able to travel with Marcel's troops, wearing the traditional white blouse and gray pants of the sharpshooter. She faced the brutality of war alongside the other soldiers, demonstrating unflinching courage in brutal conditions in a way that made a lasting impression on those around her. A letter from a former general who visited Marcel's troops during the war described how Jane did "what few women had ever done before" even when she had to sleep in the snow or ride horseback through day and night.[3] Fiercely patriotic, she found the work immensely satisfying. It was Jane Dieulafoy's first time in men's clothing, and it seems likely that it was also the point when she began to understand her potential place in the world.

Losing the Franco-Prussian War would be felt for decades in French society. Being trampled by the Germans was experienced as a veritable crisis of masculinity, and writers and politicians fretted over the absence of healthy young men to defend the country for years to come. Shifting gender roles and women's increased visibility in the public sphere only added to this anxiety, increasing fears about a waning population. But these worries would not become part of Dieulafoy's own life narrative. She had experienced the war as a triumph.

Two decades after rising to battle, Dieulafoy would recount a version of her remarkable months as a soldier for France in the historical novel *Volunteer (1792–1793)*, set during the French Revolution. The novel was published in installments in the highbrow intellectual journal *La nouvelle revue* in 1891 and was later released in Colin's historical fiction series, where it is listed alongside Gustave Flaubert's *Salammbô*. Writing would become a crucial way for Dieulafoy to make sense of her unusual fate. In this and other stories, she developed characters who mirrored her own gender expression, creating narratives in which gender-crossing was not only justified but celebrated. She set her tales in remote historical contexts, even when this led to unfavorable reviews, and buried her subversive storylines in the most conventional, sentimental prose.[4]

Volunteer tells the story of young Paule Marsig, who secretly follows her father into a volunteer army. Paule borrows one of his old uniforms and cuts her hair short. Soon she is fighting alongside men, and no one seems the wiser; all that is noted is the young soldier's tenacious courage. As Paule valiantly protects her father, she earns the respect of her fellow soldiers and, when her true identity is revealed, the love of one of them, Guillaume Briez. While initially she refuses Guillaume's overtures because of her devotion to the cause, he persuades her to be both his comrade-in-arms and his fiancée.

Of course, gender-crossing would never be so simple in revolutionary times—nor one hundred years later—and that is likely why Dieulafoy invented a conflict at the heart of their relationship. Midway through the novel, Paule discovers a troubling family secret. Guillaume's mother is accused of a past affair with Paule's father, making the couple siblings, or literally, "brothers-in-arms"—a phrase used repeatedly to describe their relationship as soldiers. It is no coincidence that Dieulafoy invented a form of sexual transgression as a plot device. This unlikely twist served as a decoy for the transgressive relationship between Paule and Guillaume: that of a man in love with a woman who passes as a man. Happily, Paule discovers the evidence to disprove the scandalous accusation and legitimize their relationship. The story ends with a celebration of their marriage, with Paule's heroism reconfirmed and the enemy brutally punished. The subversive gender questioning that drives most of the novel is carefully neutralized through this happy ending. Even as Paule rejects conventional feminine norms, the French family emerges not just intact but refortified.

The resonance of the novel with Jane Dieulafoy's own life story is plain: a girl assumes a masculine role to serve her country as an army volunteer and, despite her seeming rebellion against gendered social structures, falls in love with a man and marries him. Paule's decision to go to battle is described as an impulse that cannot be ignored, as she follows her feelings of devotion for a man that she loves. It takes no great leap to transpose Paule's fictional story of filial devotion into Jane's decision to volunteer alongside her new husband, Marcel. Inspired by compatriot Paule Mink, who commanded her own volunteer army to fight off the Prussians at Auxerre, Dieulafoy assigned her protagonist one of her own middle names, Paule, and a surname resembling that of her family, Magre.[5] In other parallels, Jane's father died shortly before she married Marcel; and Jane was frequently assumed to be Marcel's son during their later travels in Muslim lands.

Throughout the novel, Paule expresses feelings of gratitude toward her country, the cause for which she was drawn into battle. But the French word she uses for "country" is not *pays* but *patrie*, containing the Latin root for "paternity," and the story is indeed one of filial devotion: that of a daughter who becomes a son in order to serve her father and her fatherland, situating herself firmly within a masculine tradition. It is a story of rebirth that effectively writes out the woman's traditional place, replacing the maternity that was meant to define the young wife's role in the world with paternity and patrimony. *Volunteer* thus also begins to offer a glimpse into Jane's relationship with Marcel. Like Guillaume and Paule, the couple were bonded as brothers-in-arms: like-minded partners who were best friends. They were never to have children, for reasons that may or may not have been medical.[6] Little correspondence remains between the two, for the simple fact that they were nearly always together, beginning with Jane's first act, as a new wife, of following Marcel to battle. She would go on to join him in travels throughout Europe and the Middle East, accompanying him to Morocco in 1914 to serve France once again during the Great War. Marcel himself encouraged these choices: he not only enjoyed having Jane by his side but admired her deeply—not to mention that he benefited from her fierce intellect. He delighted in her later accomplishments and worked to secure her proper honor. Jane, in turn, relished the all-male environment associated with their shared work—in combat, on their journeys to the Middle East, and in academic settings later on in Paris.

There is little doubt that Jane's role in the Franco-Prussian War was a formative experience and a crucial time in her life, and that clothing—dressing as her male peers—had something to do with it. In *Volunteer*, Dieulafoy invests the soldier's uniform with a transformative power over the girl who is wearing it for the first time. It is the blue uniform that leads directly and explicitly to the "new life" for which Paule is immensely grateful. Dieulafoy's language is dramatic as she presents Paule's change of clothes as the impetus for a complete transformation of character, from exterior to interior. The clothing allows Paule to "overcome her initial destiny"—a remarkable formulation referring to the female life that she abandons—and leads in turn to more changes. Paule's body "hardens" and her personality, once expansive, becomes rough within its "new envelope."[7] In other words, this was no simple costume change.

If Dieulafoy was anything like her heroine, the uniform facilitated her self-actualization as well. The war was likely an early moment in which the possibility of a "new life" opened up before her.[8] Something may have shifted inside Dieulafoy as she faced the world in this "new envelope" and was suddenly received in a totally different and deeply affirming way. But it also seems likely that she experienced an exterior alignment that finally felt comfortable and allowed her to be properly seen. Masculinity and patriotism were inextricably linked for Dieulafoy ever after, and clothing was one crucial way in which she expressed these dual identifications. Decades later, she would stroll through Paris in a three-piece suit, her red badge of the Legion of Honor proudly displayed on her lapel (figure 8). As a soldier, she was awash with feelings of pride and glory, and in the years that followed, she would seek out those feelings whenever possible, in every exploit she embraced.

Dieulafoy's fictional retelling of the experience in battle also allowed her to compensate for the possibilities that were never fully open to her during the Franco-Prussian War. She was able to address the injustice faced by her heroine, a volunteer like herself, who was excluded from enrolling in the army. Once Paule's bravery is proven, Dieulafoy writes, the need for her recognition as a true soldier becomes evident:

> How much greater would her influence be if she were part of the regular army! Her bravery would become an incomparable aid, her presence would inspire the patriotism of the new recruits, those who, because of a lack of education, experience, and discipline, have no other motivation. In order to keep up with her, the nervous conscript would gain courage; to surpass her, the experienced soldier would find his stamina. It's more important to do something than to make proclamations; for a country in distress, no instrument of salvation should be disparaged.[9]

Note the gender-neutral language used here: there are no appeals to feminine traits or rationalizations for lack of masculine ones. What Dieulafoy

FIGURE 8. Portrait of Jane Dieulafoy by the female artist Amélie Beaury-Saurel, 1890, at the Hôtel Dieulafoy, Paris. The red Legion of Honor ribbon can be seen on her lapel. Beaury-Saurel has also given Dieulafoy a hint of mustache above her lip.

describes in these passages is a talented soldier who rises above the rest: a soldier without a body, a pure "instrument of salvation."

Dieulafoy returned to the scene of battle repeatedly in her fictions. It was always a place of emotional connection and satisfaction, often linked to the hypermasculinity of the milieu. Being a soldier meant, after all, being surrounded by men and being treated as one. Later, on the eve of World War I, she would come to be known for her patriotism and lifelong devotion to the cause of women in the military. "If you allow women the great honor of participating in the National Defense," she wrote in a letter published in *Le Figaro* in March of 1913, "I would ask you the favor of being called up first." She was sixty-three years old at the time. While the motivation for her activism has often been viewed in feminist terms, the designation proves problematic, given Dieulafoy's unique understanding of the term. She did not actively support other causes in the name of feminism and was not really advocating for full equality in this one. Rather, her support of female soldiers came from something more specific and more personal. Not all women should go to war, she argued; but some women soldiers were as good as any men.[10]

In fact, according to Dieulafoy's own "feminist theories" presented in academic lectures in the 1900s, the true woman was both mother and warrior, and true women were few and far between.[11] Modern French society had lost sight of this ideal, whose models she identified chiefly in historical figures hearkening back as far as the medieval and even the biblical eras: Deborah, Jael, Joan of Arc, and Catherine the Great. It's worth noting that these women were also unlike all the other women of their time. Dieulafoy's feminism was a far cry from the prevailing ideologies of the late nineteenth century espoused by so many of the women who joined her in journalism and fiction writing. Her female ideal embraced both masculine and feminine traits, unlike the New Woman, who rejected family structures entirely and was often pictured wearing pants and smoking cigarettes.[12] But neither did Dieulafoy's figure align with the more politically neutral *femme moderne*, or "modern woman." This alternative image adhered to traditional ideals of femininity—far from the battlefield—while pursuing new ways to balance achievements of family *and* career. The *femme moderne* was promoted in the popular women's magazines *Femina* and *La Vie Heureuse* to allay anxieties around rapidly shifting gender roles. Modernity didn't have to be threatening, they demonstrated, with images of writers and artists who also tended babies and dusted breakfronts. Behind the glossy photographs, however, these publications did important feminist work, establishing the first literary prize distributed by an all-woman jury, of which Dieulafoy was a founding member.[13] That prize, originally the Prix Vie Heureuse, became the Prix Femina, which is coveted to this day.

While Dieulafoy agreed to be featured in these publications, she did not see herself as a modern woman. In order to advocate for a better future, she always turned toward the past, where she found a handful of examples of a less rigid model of femininity. In the process, she rationalized her comfort in what was almost an entirely male milieu and reconciled it with her conservative values: it was not that she rejected femininity, her writings suggest; it was that she rejected current models of it. If she was not a modern woman, then, Dieulafoy fancied herself an ancient one. Through a historical paradigm developed over the course of her life, Dieulafoy eventually came to understand that she was exceptional because she was born in the wrong time period. It was a creative solution, to be sure, fostered by her innate sense of confidence. Dieulafoy rejected the models of femininity available in her own time and place, without rejecting her association with womanhood or identifying fully as a man, which was not really an option. Rather than believing that the problem lay in herself, she put the onus on a society that could not accommodate her. Over the course of her life, Dieulafoy constructed her own gender story, a consistent and repeated narrative that either ignored or rejected the cultural norms of her peers and which we will trace through her novels and writings. Through this story, she situated her masculine identifications in a broader context and affirmed them as natural.

The Franco-Prussian War was a crucial step in the development of Dieulafoy's self-awareness, as it forced her to recognize her difference from other women. Conscious of her own courage, she also sensed her right to a full existence despite this difference, through an understanding of what she might have to offer to France as "an instrument of salvation."[14] And so she likely began to cultivate an essential part of her lifelong personal narrative. As a conservative and a devout Catholic, Dieulafoy would allow herself the distinct pleasures that masculinity afforded her to the extent that she was acting in service of a higher cause. She seemed to have discovered on the battlefield that assuming a masculine identity could be a way of serving France. In her pseudo-autobiographical novels of gender-crossing and in the later travelogues from her missions to Persia, this is the story that she constructs for herself over and again: that of a woman who passes as a man for the greater good, who is ultimately recognized and affirmed as a new kind of female hero by everyone around her without having to relinquish her masculinity.

Dieulafoy's repeated story carefully displaces the lens from the "what" of her gender—the innate sense of self that likely drove these identifications and determined her life path—to the "why." She never wrote about her self-image directly, even while she collected articles in her notebook that described her as a "Femme-Homme." But she spent a good deal of time telling stories about why those who began life as girls might not continue to present themselves as female. In the process, she relied on a starkly conservative vision of what French citizenship should be: service to country above all else, together with a deep belief in the cultural superiority of the French nation. If her own difference suggested a tension with this vision, she never acknowledged it. Instead, her Catholic background and unflagging patriotism provided a stable framework and set of narratives in which she seemed determined to fit herself. Marcel's support—and perhaps tacit understanding—may have also had something to do with it.

Dieulafoy's story is wonderfully optimistic, and it is nearly always told with a happy ending. Her ability to see herself as part of a wider cultural narrative may well have been the reason that she enjoyed, by all accounts, such a happy and fulfilling life. But it was an uncommon story for a proper married woman from a respected family who had no intention of causing any scandal. It would take time to formulate its threads and weave them together into a coherent whole. When she returned from battle in 1871, she was not yet ready to introduce this new version of herself to the public view.

2 UNEARTHING JANE

IN THE ARCHIVES of the National Institute for Art History in Paris, Jane and Marcel Dieulafoy's personal albums are stored in a private collection, large cardboard books filled with sepia-toned prints glued onto thick pages. The albums are a rare material relic of French Orientalism—evidence of the personal pleasures of travels to the East and the face-to-face encounters between natives and the Europeans who were fascinated by them. For so many of those Europeans—the Dieulafoys included—it was not enough to catch a glimpse of other worlds or even to live among the natives for a while; they wanted instead to bring the contact with otherness home—through writings, painting, and photography.

In the past several decades, France and other colonial powers, together with those who study them, have begun to grapple with this legacy, surveying the irreparable damage caused by these encounters—from the frequent brutality to the racist cultural histories built upon false narratives. But in the late nineteenth century, there was hardly any hint of the reckoning to come. Orientalism was a cultural pastime, a source of delight fueling a nascent mass culture. The imagined differences between France and this part of the world were divided into an appealing binary. France represented civilization and all of its burdens—knowledge, work, and responsibility—whereas the Orient was wild, lazy, and free—the id to the French superego. Far from the demands of French society, the Orient was conceived largely as a playground for sensual fulfillment, adventure, and mystery.[1]

Thumbing through the Dieulafoy albums, one sees this contrast between France and its Others. There are haunting portraits of natives in turbans and headscarves, set against desolate landscapes, near crumbling structures that gesture toward an absent civilization. But every once in a while, Dieulafoy herself peers out from an image, a reminder of the person who took these photos and the complex journey she had undertaken. This was no typical Orientalist.

In one such photograph, Dieulafoy lies against the dusty weeds of the Turkish shoreline (figure 9).[2] She is a few kilometers away from an archaeological excavation site at Susa. The year is 1885, and she and Marcel are on a mission funded by the French government and the Ministry of the Arts to excavate the long-buried palace of Artaxerxes before the ravages of nature and neglect would take a permanent toll. The mission was conceived as rescuing a forgotten history, which, if successful, would bring glory to France, weakened in the recent war. It would allow the country to demonstrate its archaeological prowess—a symbol in turn of multiple strengths, both physical and intellectual.

This particular photograph is striking for many reasons. It captures a moment of unguarded intimacy, as a relaxed Jane lounges beside an improvised wooden shelter, resting her head on her left arm. Her right arm lies against the curve of her hips and her legs are stretched out in the grass. She gazes serenely toward the camera, her face resembling the neutral canvas of Impressionist subjects as she looks up from a book propped open against a metal can. The pose is a feminine one, playfully alluding to her time and place: it is that of the odalisque, the Oriental woman as sexual object and sexual desire. This was a favored trope of European painters: an implicit demonstration of power over the entire foreign culture, which was coded feminine in relation to the virile European culture. The reference to the odalisque is all the more relevant here for the proximity of the scene to the Dieulafoy excavation site, where ancient palaces and harem rooms have already been unearthed. Like Eugène Delacroix's "Women of Algiers" (1834) or Jean-Auguste-Dominique Ingres's "Odalisque with a Slave" (1839), the figure pictured here is at her leisure, surrounded by a clutter of domestic objects: a kettle and bottle on a nearby box serving as a table, with books strewn about. Like the voluptuous

FIGURE 9. Photograph of Jane Dieulafoy in Persia, from the Dieulafoys' personal albums, 1885.
Source: Bibliothèque de l'Institut national d'histoire de l'art, Collections Jacques Doucet, 4 PHOT 18 (5).

images, she reclines not on furniture but close to the ground, on a tapestry that might also serve as her bed. It is a space of intimacy, of bodies and earth, and indeed Dieulafoy's face appears grimy with dirt. A vast distance is the only backdrop, locating her in the wide-open terrain of the neglected land to which the camera pans out to show another familiar Orientalist trope: that of a lost civilization.

For European painters of Dieulafoy's generation, the sexual availability of the Oriental woman was suggested by the figure's passive indolence as well as by the visual context, the depiction of the interior space, the Oriental boudoir, and billowing folds of clothing loosely wrapped around bodies ready for the taking—if there was clothing at all. But this figure is no odalisque, and her pose is not really sexual. She is fully dressed, and she is wearing a man's collared shirt, button-down jacket, and trousers. Two rifles flank the entrance to the shelter, and Jane Dieulafoy has already proven that she knows how to use them.

This stunning portrait—a self-portrait, in fact, for Jane was the photographer on their mission and likely arranged its composition and developed the print—is an important artifact from the most significant period in Jane's life. This was the period in which she came to accept her masculine persona for good, having learned to navigate the dangers of the Middle East by acting as a French man—protected along with the rest of her team by the long arm of the French government.

When Jane returned with Marcel from the Franco-Prussian War in 1871, her passion for adventure had only just been kindled. For several years afterwards she satisfied herself by channeling her interests through Marcel's work, supporting him when, as a city engineer, he toiled in the wake of the devastating floods that afflicted the Garonne region.[3] Always socially adept, Jane played the bourgeois housewife in their hometown of Toulouse, having returned to women's apparel and let her hair grow once again. But she also seized every opportunity to travel with her husband and flee the stifling boundaries of her domestic world. Later, she would write of how she had baffled everyone with her willingness to do so: when she left for Persia, her friends wondered why on earth she would have renounced "the most attractive pleasures" of her domestic chores along with the simple delights of the provinces: municipal concerts, local preachers, and the comradery of her female peers, with their gossip about pregnancies, raising children, and looking pretty.[4]

Fortunately for both Dieulafoys, within a few years of returning from war, Marcel was charged with the oversight of historical monuments under the direction of Eugène Viollet-le-Duc, the renowned architect who had just completed his restoration of the Cathedral of Notre Dame. An influential if controversial figure, Viollet-le-Duc nurtured Marcel's curiosity about the East and encouraged his interest in the comparative study of Muslim and Western architecture. Over the next few years, Marcel and Jane traveled to Egypt and Morocco and all over Europe. Finally, in 1879, Marcel was granted the leave from his government post that would send them to Persia, a land that had long captured Marcel's interest. Persia, he suspected, would hold the secrets to Western architectural history. Jane was delighted to come along for the ride.

In preparation, Jane studied Persian history and Farsi; she took a course on photography and studied first aid. Her principal responsibility during the expeditions would be secretarial: she would keep detailed travel diaries chronicling their journeys and document their trip in photographs. Jane packed lightly and strategically—her photographic equipment and a few changes of clothing. Those clothes were pants, as she returned to the masculine attire of her brief stint as a soldier.

Had she dreamed of this moment, longing for the return to the kind of clothing worn during those terrifying, exhilarating times, a decade before? There would be no hint of such feelings in her meticulous journals. Instead, she simply explained that assuming a male appearance allowed her to ride on horseback more easily, as well as to travel openly with the rest of her caravan. Muslim women were not allowed to travel with their faces exposed. For this reason, Jane is often remembered in the context of other nineteenth-century female travelers who sought adventure in far-off lands and wore pants in order to move more freely.[5] Yet unlike Isabella Bird, Gertrude Bell, and Isabelle Eberhardt, each of whom returned to feminine clothing when back home or even at their own encampment, Dieulafoy was never to wear skirts again. She would appear only in masculine attire for the rest of her life: meticulously tailored men's suits, complete with waistcoat and cravat, and—rumor has it—a cardboard panel that smoothed over any hint of bosom.[6]

In the travelogues published throughout her journey and then compiled upon her return, Dieulafoy's accounts are dense and filled with a sometimes excruciating degree of detail: from precise descriptions of flora and fauna to the architectural features of buildings down to their dimensions and number of bricks. Along with these notations, she also recounts the peripatetic adventures of European explorers in a largely unwelcoming foreign land, revealing her own ability to withstand hard conditions and terrifying obstacles.[7] But reading closely, one discovers another narrative that perhaps she did not realize she had included. As she recorded her travels through Persia, Dieulafoy ended up recording her shifting sense of self. This parallel narrative reveals how she developed a framework for understanding her difference from other women. Within her travelogues, we find a story within a story, fittingly enough: a veritable Persian tale that is also an early narrative of gender transition.

HOW CAN ONE BE PERSIAN?

Persia had long captured the French literary imagination, as an exotic land with strange customs and veiled women. One hundred and fifty years earlier, Enlightenment philosopher Charles Louis de Secondat, Baron de Montesquieu, had become famous—well before formulating his views on the social contract—for his satire about imaginary Persians traveling to Paris. In his *Persian Letters*, part epistolary novel, part philosophical treatise, the characters Usbek and Rica describe the strange sites and practices of the French people. Through their adventures, Montesquieu treated his French readers to a playful window onto themselves, while also providing drama in the Persian seraglio to push the plot forward. Usbek, the philosophizing Persian, turned out to be something of a despot, and the colorful depiction of his wives' conflicts with the eunuchs charged with controlling them pitted Persian gender roles against French ones. But the enduring legacy of the novel lies in its straightforward interrogation of cultural relativism. After noticing Rica in his unusual garments in the middle of Paris, a baffled onlooker asks: "How can one be Persian?"[8] Ever since, French thinkers have evoked this question in order to acknowledge the difficulty of engaging with those perceived as other.

With her travelogues, Dieulafoy offered her own set of answers to Montesquieu's famous question, while asking it anew at every turn. How can one be Persian?, indeed. She recorded their travels in detail, with descriptions of their heart-stopping adventures as infidels alongside dry scientific accounts of archaeological wonders. The travelogues were published in installments in *Le Tour du monde*, a "new travel journal" that fed upon the European appetite for adventure and exoticism. Later, the wildly successful series was collected in bound volumes. As historical documents, they tell us the story of the Dieulafoy mission: the discovery of ancient monuments and the dangerous process of excavation and transport. As biographical documents, on the other hand, they offer something far more compelling: Dieulafoy's first and most personal published writings. Over the course of hundreds of pages of narrative, they reveal how Dieulafoy found her own voice through her encounter with these unfamiliar cultures. At the same time, they document the complex ways in which she sought to avoid scrutiny, presenting the story of someone thirsty for knowledge and understanding who did not want to be known herself. At least, not at first.

The first entries that appeared in *Le Tour du monde*, based on the journals Dieulafoy kept during their first mission, maintain a scientific distance, even as she describes harrowing encounters, Marcel's illness, and her own physical challenges. In these early entries, Jane matter-of-factly establishes a gender-neutral voice for the three hundred pages that follow. She notes early on that "the only way to pass unnoticed and to circulate freely is to adopt Muslim garb: a most repugnant sacrifice for a Christian."[9] Otherwise "a curious crowd" invariably gathers to witness a woman without a veil. Like her male colleagues, Dieulafoy dresses in the "Muslim garb" of the natives in order to see without being seen, despite its supposed offense to her as a Christian. That this is men's clothing is slipped in without comment. Jane soon recognizes that the operative term for Europeans is *farangui*, or non-Muslim; France is referred to as Faranguistan (land of non-Muslims), which refers to Europe more broadly. This is the identity that distinguishes her from her surroundings, and when she must conceal herself, it is her Frenchness rather than her femininity that threatens her success. As with her transition from women's to men's clothing in wartime, culture takes precedence over gender as the lens through which her difference will be understood.

And yet, Dieulafoy's distance from gender norms and the conventions of femininity is insistently palpable, layering the text with meanings that she refuses to directly acknowledge. Relying on an expectation of the same curiosity about otherness that Montesquieu's fictional Rica noted with the Parisians, Jane does not train her lens on the locals alone. Instead, she shows how these nonfictional Persians repeatedly marvel at the strange habits of their French visitors, so that French conventions come to appear as odd and arbitrary as Persian customs. Moreover, Jane recounts how they perceived *her*—which is not a simple narrative, given our gender-crossing tour guide. For Jane does not offer herself up as an explicit example of the strangeness the Persians are encountering but instead guides her nineteenth-century readers to look through her rather than directly at her. In the process, she implicitly refuses to become the object of analysis. In other words, Jane assumes the role of Montesquieu himself where one might expect her to become the counterpart of his traveler Usbek: rather than take center stage as a fascinating character in her own right, she stays out of focus as an invisible narrative voice.

Toward the end of their first month abroad, Jane and Marcel travel with a caravan of Muslims on pilgrimage to Teheran. Bringing up the rear in their own wooden travel compartment, a group of wives is supervised by "a young man whose rosy cheeks and intelligent look drew my eyes." What captures Jane's attention is that the young man moves comfortably among the women, chatting and attending to their needs.[10] As it turns out, this young man *is* a woman, a *pichkhedmet* whose shaved head and men's clothes allow her to "go out with her head uncovered without causing controversy" (figure 10)—a description that is tantalizingly close to Jane's own self-description. The *pichkhedmet* is thus able to stay close to the women, whom she both guards and attends. Dieulafoy does not pause on the figure of the *pichkhedmet* longer than on any other object of interest. Before the reader has had a chance to absorb the intriguing mention of this fascinating, unfamiliar type of person, or to reflect on the similarities between the doubly gendered *pichkhedmet* and the narrator herself, Dieulafoy has moved on. In the next paragraph, she quickly steers us to look past the *pichkhedmet* to the group of women under her care, whose "hidden beauties" she attempts in vain to glimpse. Nonetheless, the pertinence of this episode will accrue over time, as Dieulafoy is the only member of her team permitted to visit the harem and meet with the women. Indeed, the very reason she is able to recount the story is her own ability to move freely, with her cropped hair, between genders and to "pass" as either one.

Several months into their journey, the French doctor Joseph Tholozan, who had recently treated Marcel for an illness caught on his travels, introduced the couple to the shah, for whom he served as personal doctor. The dramatic scene of their meeting replays in reverse Jane's appraisal of the *pichkhedmet*: this time, she is the object of curiosity. Upon being introduced to "Monsieur and Madame Dieulafoy," the king startles. "What, this young man is a woman?" Tholozan assures the shah that the Dieulafoys are welcome guests: they have arrived on the recommendation of mutual friends, with a letter from the French ministry. The conversation proceeds, and Jane reports the dialogue, again without commentary. Asked why she does not wear the clothing of European women, she responds: "Because I can travel more freely and always pass unnoticed. Your Majesty is aware of how, in Muslim countries, it is difficult for women to appear in public with their faces uncovered."[11] Using here the same explanation that she had offered her readers in the story of the *pichkhedmet*—in order to "pass" unnoticed—as well as her signature charm, Dieulafoy reestablishes the logic of her own narrative while carefully avoiding the appearance of self-advocacy. She deftly redirects the lens, focusing the question on Persian women rather than herself. The shah then agrees that hers was the right decision, remarking that, indeed, women

FIGURE 10. The *pichkhedmet* as depicted in an etching from the travelogues. Source: Dieulafoy, *La Perse, la Chaldée et la Susiane.* This image accompanies the entry from April 22, 1881.

cannot travel with their faces uncovered in this country without inciting a riot. The shah's comments are woven seamlessly into her reportage, and as with the *pichkhedmet*, Jane offers no further editorial.

In the process, Jane leaves her readers with an apparent series of lenses onto gender that is really a hall of mirrors. Remarkably, the shah has given Dieulafoy permission to be both a French woman and a Persian man—both of whom can travel freely, face unveiled. And this, to some degree, is the pretense of her appearance: the way she dresses allows her to maintain some semblance of female identity while still presenting as masculine. According to the logic of her own storytelling, she is unrecognizable as female only because of the difference in dress between Persian women and French women—itself a revelation for nineteenth-century readers, confirming what Enlightenment fictions had predicted. When Persians fail to recognize her as a woman, she can say that it is because she's a *French* woman. Never mind that she bears no resemblance to French women at this point, as the only image of her in this volume will make clear.

The illusion of presenting oneself while in fact offering very little was to be Dieulafoy's signature rhetorical move. If Montesquieu's text had showcased femininity, with its eunuchs and seraglio drama, as a prime object of study in Persia, in Dieulafoy's version the femininity under discussion was certainly was not going to be her own. Throughout her travelogues, the utter contrast between French and Persian gender roles reminds readers that femininity is a function of culture rather than biology. One is not born a woman, Simone de Beauvoir would later instruct, but rather becomes one; and this process of becoming is a function of the culture into which you happen to be born. But as Dieulafoy repeatedly teaches this lesson, she manages to quietly divert attention away from the fact that her own gender expression did not conform to either French or Persian standards. With her knowledge of cultural expectations, she was learning how to create a space for this expression in whatever culture she happened to find herself.

There is evidence that Dieulafoy was aware of what she was doing—that she was hardly oblivious that the *pichkhedmet* was related to her own way of being. When the Dieulafoy rooms opened at the Louvre in 1888, a writer from the Paris newspaper *L'Univers Illustré* began to ask pointed questions about her own unusual appearance. Dieulafoy replied by telling the reporter about the *pichkhedmet*. The story had evolved, however: Jane recounted that the young woman passing as a man was being mistreated by the Persian in charge, who was making his pilgrimage with the whole harem because he had been unable to conceive a child. In manipulating this narrative over time, Dieulafoy—known for her gifts as a storyteller, as the reporter duly acknowledged—distracted the journalist from his interest in her own ambiguous gender. Offering the *pichkhedmet* as a window onto heterosexual practices (the man who cannot get his wives pregnant), she avoided becoming an object of focus in her own right. Instead, she subtly steered her interlocutor to look through her rather than at her with this strategic pivot.

Dieulafoy's subtle self-effacement distinguished her from nearly every other nineteenth-century female explorer who traveled to the East. Throughout the period, this kind of travel had allowed European and British women to comment playfully on their own femininity. Gertrude Bell and Isabella Bird were photographed in the alluring feminine costumes of the places that they visited, as were Dieulafoy's writer colleagues Myriam Harry and Marcelle Tinayre several years later (figure 11). But throughout these essentially playful acts of dress-up, each of these travelers affirmed her Western identity along with her femininity. For most nineteenth-century traveling women, the interest of the foreign costume was in its difference from their "normal" Western dresses—and corsets, in some cases. The striking contrast served as a reminder that ultimately they were really just "normal" Western women.

Dieulafoy, of course, was not just a "normal French woman," nor was she a typical Orientalist woman writer in any sense. She was working hard to shape a different kind of voice in her writing: that of the traditional male Orientalist, a purely scientific observer who would erase himself from the picture, the better to establish his own perspective as objective fact. As Linda Nochlin and other scholars have demonstrated, the male Orientalist sought to report while helping a European audience to forget who was doing the reporting. The goal was both immediacy and scientific accuracy. This Dieulafoy, author of the first volume of travelogues from their first mission to Persia, would never pose as a pseudo-odalisque before the camera. Her sense of power and control was exclusively tied to her position behind it.

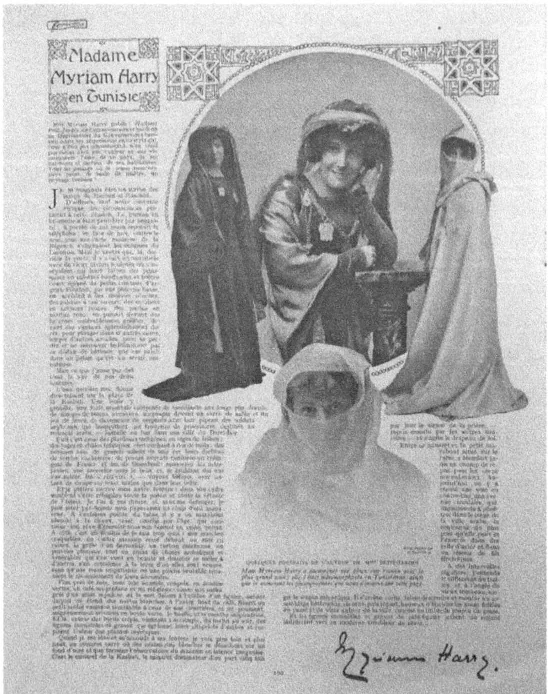

Madame Myriam Harry en Tunisie

Myriam Harry.

FIGURE 11. An article on Myriam Harry in Tunisia, describing how she would transform herself into a Tunisian woman when traveling.
Source: *Femina*, February 15, 1910.

There is one illustration of Dieulafoy in the first travelogues: a sketch by Emile Bayard, supposedly based on a photograph of which there is no record, in the fifteenth installment of her travelogue for the *Tour du monde*, dated August 23, 1882 (see figure 12). While many of the other sketches have a near-photographic quality, this one is merely suggestive, perhaps even cartoonish—a gesture toward the voice animating these accounts but not yet a realistic likeness. In it, Jane appears as a distant, otherworldly hero, recalling Napoléon himself as depicted just a few years earlier by the celebrated Orientalist painter Jean-Léon Gérôme. The artist imagined Napoléon in Egypt, on horseback, against a backdrop of empty land, as if one were standing below him. Dieulafoy is depicted from a similar vantage point: perched atop her own horse, riding astride rather than sidesaddle as a woman normally would, in command and in control. While many of Dieulafoy's female counterparts

FIGURE 12. Dieulafoy on horseback.
Source: *Le Tour du monde*, August 23, 1882.

took pleasure in trying on the clothing of the Other—playfully donning veils that they would never be forced to wear, as an affirmation of their own French femininity—this image suggests a different cultural reference point, one in which she likely would take far more comfort. Unlike her female peers, Dieulafoy did not need to overcome her culture in order to subvert its gendered demands. Rather, in this instance and so many others, she was able to find the models *within* the culture by which to fashion her own image. Why not Napoléon himself?

INSIDE THE HAREM

At the end of Jane and Marcel's first journey in January of 1882, they were on the cusp of reaching their true goal of Susa, having confronted a series of challenges, from mosquitos and illness to thieves and unforgiving roads.

They had traveled six thousand kilometers from northwestern Iran to the Persian Gulf through Baghdad to reach their destination, and their health was deteriorating as they approached Susa. Now that they were close to a goal they had never been certain of reaching, they were forced to stop for several days at Dezful to wait out a spell of rainy weather that would prevent safe passage. To fill the days that seemed unbearably long in the absence of "a more useful task," using Dieulafoy's words, the couple found topics to chat about with their hosts. It is abundantly clear that Jane was hardly interested, so many difficult months into their journey, in finding out more about Persian culture, let alone about the harem. If there were just a break in the clouds, she writes, she would sneak out onto the terrace to get a view of the tumulus, the ancient burial ground just a few kilometers away.[12]

In this final chapter of their first mission, as they wait for the sky to clear, Dieulafoy takes us inside the harem once again. In this moment, her physical presence comes into focus as never before, as she allows us to see her—and her gender ambiguity—through the eyes of Persian women, a vantage point, she quickly reveals, that she found tiresome. In a series of episodes, Dieulafoy asks once again "How can one be Persian?" while leaving herself more exposed and visible than ever before. She allows the Persian women, presented as ignorant and uneducated, to voice an uneasiness with her appearance that her French peers would be just as likely to express.

The first Persian woman believes, seeing Dieulafoy's closely cropped hair, that French women must not be able to grow their hair long. When Dieulafoy explains that it would be bothersome to have to brush it every day while traveling—offering, then, a new explanation for her masculine appearance—the woman wonders why anyone would brush their hair every day when once a week would be sufficient. It's a punchline French readers would be sure to appreciate, and one that makes clear it is the Persian who is strange and not Dieulafoy herself. In the next harem, or *andéroun*, she is asked whether she finds a bare head inconvenient, as "our prophet forbids an exposed head." Jane's reply is quick: "I'll keep your advice in mind when I become a Muslim. Until that happy day, come to Europe and you will see what people think of exposing your naked breasts, belly, and legs every time you move."[13] With her sharp tongue, Dieulafoy reserves her right to dress as she pleases. But her response to the curious Persian woman conceals the fact that her way of dressing was also different than that of her French female peers. It is another strategic pivot that keeps the focus on the strangeness of the Persian women rather than the unconventional nature of Jane's own appearance.

While never acknowledged directly, Dieulafoy's gender-ambiguous perspective is a fascinating part of her travelogues. She could pass as both man and woman—and was accepted as both—a fact that gives her a privileged position with access to more than any other foreign visitor: she can visit with kings and dignitaries as well as with the women of the harem. Her double vantage point gave her a wider view than any other Orientalist, as she could glide freely between subjects without the hint of sexual impropriety. It functioned, remarkably, as a sexless eye, and therefore as a fantasy of scientific omniscience. She too seemed sexless, a gender refugee we might say, uncomfortable with any acknowledgment or appraisal of her femininity.

When she was first given the opportunity to live out the Orientalist fantasy, to look behind the veil, as it were, Dieulafoy seemed to mock the French reader's potentially torrid investment. "European minds get overly excited at the mention of the word *andéroun* or harem, and in order to visualize these locked residences, they love to evoke the splendors of stories like the *Arabian Nights*," she wrote dismissively.[14] To satisfy these wild fantasies, she offered merely a map and architectural details.

Several months and a few hundred pages after that, Jane offered a bit more, when she was introduced to one of the beautiful wives of a Muslim pilgrim, a woman named Zika Khanoum. A dramatic portrait of this woman appears in the travelogues: standing, one hand on her hip, she wears an embroidered headdress that covers her hair while exposing her breast, in one of the very few images from the travelogues in which women are sexualized in any way (figure 13). Of all the images in the travelogues, this one has received the most attention in previous studies that seek to demonstrate, more often than not, that Dieulafoy must have been sexually attracted to this woman and others.[15] This simplistic reading, based on a facile presumption of same-sex desire, could not be further from the truth. It's true that Dieulafoy seems to embrace the male Orientalist perspective, describing how fortunate any painter or sculptor would be to have such a model pose before him. And just as Gustave Flaubert wrote in his diaries from Egypt, Dieulafoy commented on the irony of this partial exposure: "Is it due to heat or to coquetry that they lack the gauze blouse meant to cover the bust of Persian women?"[16] But rather than stop there, taking in Zika's lovely appearance, Dieulafoy proceeds to engage in conversation with her, devoting the next several pages to an interview in which they discussed Zika's travels with the shah's harem—before she was given as a gift to one of his friends—and the leader's views about Europe. They continue with a tour of the home and the courtyard. As a chronicler of Persian culture, Dieulafoy is not distracted by the sexual possibilities of the harem, as were so many male Orientalists before her. There is something else at stake for her here.

Sex is hardly present in the harem visits at the end of their first journey, as Dieulafoy reveals a bit more of herself. In one episode, she describes how she allowed the members of the harem to play with the white pith helmet that she and Marcel always wore as protective covering. As they handled the strange object, the women sought glimpses of themselves in a fragment of mirror inlaid in a "superb mosaic of cedar and ivory."[17] During these brief moments, the dazzling architectural details of the harem recede so that the animated scene may be described. In the process, we catch glimpses of Dieulafoy in that shard of mirror: the woman who is unrecognizable as a woman both in France and in Persia, with her shorn hair and man's helmet. In true Persian form, there is a story within this story, another kind of mirror fragment within an intricate frame. Sure enough, this section is subtitled "Persian Tale," and the narrative refracts Dieulafoy back to us indirectly through the words of the Persian storyteller, just when we are seeking her honest voice.

Mateb Khanoum, the woman who had asked Jane about the inconvenience of her hair, has a sole male heir, Messaoud, who at ten years old is said to be a genius. Asked to share a story, he obliges. The tale is of a sultan who is trying to avoid paying local fishermen the price demanded for their bounty. If the fish is male, the sultan's adviser tells the fisherman that they pay only for female fish, and vice versa. A fisherman arrives and is asked, "Is your fish male or female?" Wisely, however, the fisherman responds, "O king, eternal wisdom, my fish is male and female: it is a hermaphrodite." Praised for his acumen, the fisherman is made a new adviser to the king.[18]

FIGURE 13. Portrait of Zika Khanoum.

Source: *Le Tour du monde*, September 5, 1881.

As with the tale of the *pichkhedmet*, the meeting with the shah, and many other anecdotes, Jane proceeds without commentary, simply noting the boy's charm. But before she can leave, Mateb Khanoum asks her whether her bare head makes her cold. "Are you mocking me?" Jane retorts, with unusual sharpness. Is the question intended for Mateb Khanoum, one is left to wonder, or for her young son, whose tale hewed a little too close for comfort? Or did Jane perhaps identify with the boy, presented as a brilliant raconteur trapped inside all day with these frivolous women? For here was a child with an eye keen enough to recognize that the stranger was foreign not for her Frenchness but for a different kind of difference: the kind, the story proves, that transcends culture. What's more, it is a difference that, once recognized, allows others to affirm one's greatness. Was Mateb Khanoum really the one who offered the story of the hermaphrodite, one is left to ask, or might Dieulafoy herself have planted it there for her readers? Was the embedded story of the hermaphrodite Dieulafoy's own version of a Persian tale—a commentary within the commentary, subtly pointing back out to the gender-ambiguous author?

The following day, the French group sets out for Susa, the sky having cleared. They arrive at the Tomb of Daniel—of the lion's den—and find a vast plateau stretching for several kilometers. Many uneven mounds protrude from it, surrounded by broken columns and bits of ancient stones. There is clearly so much history buried beneath the landscape, but Jane and Marcel would not discover it this time around. They are soon beset by fever once again, as well as punishing rains that make travel nearly impossible. Despite the work that remains, there is no choice. Fighting illness and short on funds, it is time to return to France.

3 EXCAVATING THE SELF

SHORTLY AFTER THE COUPLE'S RETURN from the first mission, Dieulafoy's vivid travelogues were published in *Le Tour du monde*. It's no wonder that readers were fascinated by her exotic stories, which made her a celebrity of popular culture in ways that Marcel would never match. Her accounts were included among those of the great explorers of the nineteenth century: this was the journal that featured Darwin, Burton, and Livingston. For his part, Marcel published the definitive volume on Persian art and architecture, *Persian Art*, in 1884; it remains an invaluable historical resource to this day, as many of the finds that he documented have since been destroyed.

Upon their arrival in France, Jane and Marcel had no plans to return to the Middle East. Sick and exhausted, they considered themselves lucky to have survived. Months later, however, they confided to their friend Louis de Ronchaud, chief curator of the Louvre, that they were dreaming of Persia once again. He persuaded the couple to continue their mission, this time under the auspices of both the Ministry of Fine Arts and the War Ministry. Impressed with Marcel's engineering prowess and archaeological acumen, Ronchaud was also deeply enamored of Jane's work. In 1882 he secured her nomination as an Officer of the French Academy, the famed Académie française, a bastion of conservative values, through a direct appeal to the Ministry of Fine Arts. This is not to be confused with being elected a member of the Academy, a privilege from which women were excluded. In 1886, Ronchaud followed suit with Dieulafoy's nomination to the Legion of Honor, after receiving a letter from Marcel detailing why it was merited.[1] Later, he would devote a book of poetry to her.

The Dieulafoys were determined this time around to embark on the excavation of Susa. Backed by financial support, arms, and munitions that included several warships, a team of supporters, and diplomatic connections, the couple also added two new members to their group: the young biologist Frédéric Houssaye and an engineer named Charles Babin, both of whom would become lifelong friends of the Dieulafoys.

Persia beckoned not just for the treasures left behind. There remained a different sort of work to accomplish. In Persia, Jane had come tantalizingly close to the identity of fearless explorer that would eventually define her in the public eye, but she had not yet put that version of herself on display. Over the course of those many months, she had kept her voice—and herself—carefully hidden from view, while she benefited from her ability to move freely in Persian society. There was much more to discover—not just in buried Eastern lands but in her own layered self.

Back in France, as she let her hair begin to grow again, the prospect of returning to a feminine identity, to corsets and dinner parties, must have been daunting. Returning to Persia meant a return to work as well as to comradery, to a sense of place as part of a team of men. It also meant that Dieulafoy could continue to wear men's clothing.

On November 28, 1884, less than a month before they were scheduled to leave, Jane and Marcel had their photographs taken in the studio of Eugène Pirou, one of the most popular portraitists of the day. The resulting image would become her new author's photo, replacing the tentative horseback sketch from the travelogues, which was removed from the 1887 volume of the dispatches when they were published by Hachette upon her return. Pirou's portrait would accompany nearly every profile of Jane in the mass press for decades to follow. Taking turns posing before the camera with Marcel, perhaps she already had in mind a new ambition: to be seen as equals, and to do so by actively claiming her masculine identity, owning it, and affirming it. Marcel likely believed the same: he had written to Ronchaud requesting that she be nominated for the Legion of Honor. He was devoted to his wife and seemed to understand what she needed. In his letter to Ronchaud, Marcel described Jane not only as a loyal companion but as "the most useful and the most entirely involved collaborator in my work and in our discoveries."[2] Notably, he used the male form *collaborateur* rather than *collaboratrice*.

Her hair closely cropped, Jane posed for the photograph wearing a black redingote, loose tie, and pants. Her outfit was the generic costume of nineteenth-century masculinity, and it was the exact same outfit that her husband wore (figures 14 and 15).

PARADISE FOUND

Confident in her abilities and supported by the Parisian elite, Jane returned to the Middle East with her journals and camera—and most likely a new sense of purpose. Her travelogues from this second mission show the change in disposition, charting the transition between Jane's desire to hide her gender from view—to remain a vehicle for others to look through and thus free from any clear gender of her own—to a desire to be seen alongside her male colleagues. It's the distance, then, between a willfully neutral scientific voice and a confident one that embraced its masculine traits and celebrated men and maleness. If she had wanted to pass unnoticed in the first mission, by the second she very much wanted to be recognized and appreciated along with the rest of her team. It is impossible to know exactly when each dispatch was written or what kind of editing took place after the fact. But given the level of detail and the fact that the entries are corroborated by information shared on the same dates in certain letters written home to France, it seems likely that the vast majority of these hundreds of pages were recorded in real time during their journey.

In Dieulafoy's writings from this period, masculinity is no longer a means to an end; it has become part of her identity. Here she is ready to broadcast that identity quite deliberately: in the stories she tells, she situates herself firmly within her male cohort and reminds her readers repeatedly of the masculine role that she plays. The dispatches from the second mission represent a crucial moment in Dieulafoy's life as she proudly assumes her new identity—recouping the sense of glory she had experienced on the battlefields of the Franco-Prussian War. The archaeological dig thus becomes a fitting metaphor: in Susa, Jane journeyed through her own psychological layers in order to excavate a long-buried version of herself.

FIGURE 14. Jane Dieulafoy by Eugène Pirou, 1884.

Source: Bibliothèque nationale de France, Société de géographie. Reprinted with permission.

FIGURE 15. Marcel Dieulafoy by Eugène Pirou, 1884.

Source: Bibliothèque nationale de France, Société de géographie. Reprinted with permission.

In one entry, Dieulafoy refers to her new colleague Houssaye as "my bearded double"—a seemingly off-hand yet striking admission about how she saw herself and did not mind being seen: as the mirror image of her male peers.[3] There is visual evidence of this as well, and the images from the second mission complement the written narrative in ways they do not in the first volume. They offer a visual story for which Jane herself did not yet have the words. Facing the December 5, 1885, entry, for example, is a full-page image of the group of four in their tent: Jane, Marcel, Houssaye, and Babin (figure 16). It is a sketch based on a blurry photograph that the Dieulafoys kept in their private albums. In the original, one can hardly make out the figures. In the published travelogues, however, the pen-and-ink version is much clearer, revealing the four colleagues, with Jane's masculine contours in full relief. Jane is indeed the clean-faced double of Houssaye, who would remain a close friend and confidant long after the mission was completed. She sits hunched over, chin resting on hand, facing Houssaye, with Marcel and Babin in the background. This is not the image of a woman in "Muslim costume" or one seeking to hide her face. By rights the picture should be shocking for its suggestion that she slept in close quarters with these fellows. Instead, it normalizes Dieulafoy's presence among men, assimilating her with the group.

This second mission lasted through two winters in 1884 and 1885–86. It began with a journey aboard the vessel *Tomkin*, including a terrifying fire on board, which was followed by frustrating negotiations upon Persian soil to secure workers and food sources. They needed to ensure their safety from the suspicious natives, who were convinced that the foreigners were bringing bad luck by disturbing the souls of the dead. The team persevered by promising to steer clear of the Tomb of Daniel. In any case, it was the palace they had their eyes on.

Within a few weeks, they were mounting a huge operation, with hundreds of Persian workers digging trenches. After confirming, as Loftus had suspected, that the site contained remains from the Achaemenid palace built by Darius, later repaired by his great-grandson Xerxes, Marcel's team began to make exciting discoveries: a series of bulls' heads representing the towering columns that had lined the structure, and the colored enamel stones of the stunning Frieze of Lions (figures 17 and 18). The team worked for a few months to excavate as much as possible, knowing that these discoveries

FIGURE 16. Jane, Marcel, Babin, and Houssaye, in *A Suse: Journal des fouilles*, p. 240.

would likely be their legacy but also that they were racing against Mother Nature. With the punishingly hot weather about to arrive, they packed up as much as they could for transport back to France: fifty-five massive cartons of artifacts. The plan was to return the following season with the equipment to transport the giant bulls' heads. Thrilled with their discoveries and hopeful for a rapid return, the team made their way to the shores of the Karkheh River on the Turkish border, where they found themselves with two extra days to relax while awaiting passage to France.

This rare moment of respite ("two days of laziness deliciously savored") was a chance to take stock and creates a pause in the breakneck speed of the second travelogue.[4] More important, in these entries Jane reveals her emotional investment in her work for the first time, as she describes her attachment to the place they had once fled. "Adieu, deserted Susa! Adieu, my dear burial grounds!" she writes plaintively, noting that this was the place where she had experienced her greatest challenges but also "unparalleled joys."

In this moment Jane bids farewell not only to the excavation site; she also says goodbye to a part of herself that is inextricably connected to all

FIGURE 17. The Frieze of Lions as it was being put together.

Source: Bibliothèque de l'Institut national d'histoire de l'art, Collections Jacques Doucet, 4 PHOT 18 (5).

FIGURE 18. The bull's head on display in the Louvre, with the Frieze of the Archers in the background.

that it represents. She describes her identification with Darius and Xerxes as an emotional, personal one: where she found faithful friendship, poetry, and discovery:

> I had identified with the past that you represent, and I lived a life made up of Darius's and Xerxes's dreams, those heroes of yesteryear, friends who could not be unfaithful to me. Disappear, vanish into thin air; but the happiness of recovering paradise lost will never allow me to forget the poetic charm of your rocky paths, the lovely mysteries of your solitude, the sublime harmonies of a natural landscape of which I had been ignorant.[5]

Dieulafoy does not mention here the appalling conditions, the head lice and the mosquitos, the drenching rains and the hot sun; rather, Susa is associated with the happiness of finding "paradise lost," poetic charm and unique pleasures. This passage of her writing, in exposing her own feelings, reveals a deep shift. Absent is the dispassionate scientific observer of the previous series. Dieulafoy has become a character in her own drama, fully alive in the text; she has finally allowed herself the complex emotional palette she will later give to her fictional characters.

While in a few years Dieulafoy would turn to the past to recover female heroines in figures such as Isabella the Great of Spain and Joan of Arc—figures who combined conventionally masculine traits with feminine ones—for now her story contained no such women heroes. With Darius and Xerxes in mind, she sketched out the story line, still somewhat tentative, that would offer her a framework for recognizing her gender-nonconforming self. Friend to heroes past, she wrote of her deep pleasure in the "glory of reviving the dead." The term "glory" is significant, the very word she uses in *Volunteer* to describe Paule Marsig's service to her country and in all likelihood how she understood her own role in the war. On the second journey Persia's emotional weight seems connected to Dieulafoy's retrieval of this sense of self. Among the buried souls that she brings back to life in the tumulus, or burial ground, is very much her own: the masculine persona that provided her with the most edifying experiences of her life. This discovery of self began in the war, which she described throughout her life as a kind of "paradise lost." Indeed, the most challenging, arduous experiences turned out to be the most precious and the most meaningful.

"I am not leaving you entirely," assured Dieulafoy as she addressed the desolate landscape. "Some fragments of my soul remain attached to your shrubs." As she waited for the ships to transport them home, everything was at stake. They needed to successfully transport their excavations to France and prove their importance in order to receive more government funds to finish what they had started. Some of the most important discoveries were still buried underground; the team had caught glimpses of them but needed better equipment. More important, the greater their discoveries, the greater the chances for maintaining her masculine persona as scientist, adventurer, and, especially, hero. She would need to come back not just to retrieve the artifacts but to retrieve these parts of her identity. Dieulafoy's personal journey maps onto the troubling agenda of French imperialism in this unexpected way. To prove her masculinity, she would need to conquer the Orient; the rescue of these objects was fundamentally about saving herself.

Jane's rare moment of verbal reflection by the Turkish waterfront is matched by a rare moment of photographic intimacy. In fact, we can actually match this window into her mind-set with the photograph in which she poses against her improvised shelter, odalisque style. In the image, Jane seems to embody the French expression *bien dans sa peau*—comfortable in one's skin. She appears at ease in her rugged clothing, surrounded by the everyday signs of her daily life. If the image recalls paintings of the odalisque, it recalls another work of art with which she was also likely familiar: Manet's 1863 *Luncheon on the Grass*, in which a nude female figure is pictured alongside two fully clothed men lounging on the ground. As Dieulafoy meets the viewer's gaze, she mirrors the nude woman's blank stare, even as her clothing links her to the men.

The photo is one of a series taken outside of the tent, all of which show her relaxed, comfortably situated in the domestic chaos of the lean-to against the stark landscape. They depict Jane the explorer as a seasoned traveler taking a break, showing mastery of and comfort in her foreign setting—and more than a little playfulness as well. In that sense, they suggest a distinctly modern effort to capture the "real" Dieulafoy, with the casual mess of her surroundings as evidence of the interruption of her improvised domestic space (figure 19). Taken together, this series of images suggests a deliberate effort to capture Jane's sense of ease in her temporary home: proof of her

FIGURE 19. Photograph of Jane Dieulafoy in Persia, from the Dieulafoys' personal albums.

Source: Bibliothèque de l'Institut national d'histoire de l'art, Collections Jacques Doucet, 4 PHOT 18 (5).

new persona made possible through this new technology. The photographs represent another way to ensure that she could bring her Persian self home with her.

Unlike the hundreds of photographs taken of the land and its inhabitants, these photos of Jane were never published—perhaps because they represent so vividly her embrace of a masculine persona, unlike many of the images that circulated in the media, which enhanced her image with contoured cheekbones or pink lips. In the context of Dieulafoy's gender evolution, the Persian photographs might be compared to the posttransition images that have become central to modern transgender identity as the concrete affirmation of a fully realized gender expression.[6] In the context of the Orientalist explorer, however, these photographs have their own significance. With the camera, a tool used to capture new sights and to document images never seen by European eyes, Jane trains the lens on this new version of her body instead, as if to register its discovery.

BOYS ON FILM

Most of the time, Dieulafoy's camera was not aimed at herself. She took hundreds of photographs, and the majority of them—especially in the later dispatches—were of people. Many of these images are haunting: Bedouins with vacant eyes, listless children, thickly veiled women. Dieulafoy's photos reveal a sensitive and distinct eye for the human body in all its variety. Vivid portraits capture both the richly detailed costumes of the inhabitants and their excitement and vulnerability in being photographed for the first time.[7] While her travelogues give voice to her movement between genders, these photos provide an important further dimension to Jane's development. They dramatically belie the repeated scholarly claim that Dieulafoy was particularly invested in the women that she encountered.[8] While she documented many interactions with Persian women, Jane was far more fascinated by Persian masculinity. These ethnographic images startle the modern eye. There is little visual context for taking in their subjects, and one is left to imagine the troubling imbalance of power that the camera imposed; these are classic examples of the Western viewer rendering the Oriental subject for their own purposes. In this case, that purpose seems to have been deeply personal.

As Dieulafoy waits with the team on the Turkish shoreline, her images of Persian boys become particularly evocative. They present a visual meditation on masculinity that mirrors her new willingness to write about herself. On the facing page to Jane's reflections on leaving the tumulus from late April 1885, for example, there is a full-page image of "an Arab boatman" (figure 20).[9] Clearly, the picture is posed: rather than lounging by his anchored boat, the young man stands upright, hand on his hip, his right foot turned out in the tradition of academic portraiture. While he wears the same style of clothing as scores of other male figures in Dieulafoy's volumes, he wears them differently. The image is charged with eroticism. The boatman's toga is open, revealing his skin. Indeed, the loose fabric forms a feminine V at the waist, exposing a defined chest and a hint of nipple; the sketch thus evokes the women from the harem from the previous volume. He holds a thin oar in his right hand, and his skin gleams against the sun as he gazes directly at the camera.

This photograph suggests a fuller investment with masculinity than Dieulafoy's more cerebral written reflections, literally fleshing out this period in the travels as being rife with emotion—and with feelings of all sorts. Indeed,

Batelier arabe (voy. p. 92). — Dessin de Bida, d'après une photographie de la mission.

FIGURE 20. "An Arab boatman."

Source: Dieulafoy, *A Suse: Journal des fouilles*, p. 182.

this photographic accompaniment suggests another, sensual dimension to Jane's fear of leaving "paradise lost," as if she were freer here not just in her gender expression but in her sexual desires. So free that she can act out—unthinkingly, perhaps—colonial fantasies of sexual mastery, once again exploiting the existing culture to carve out her own place, in keeping with its more disturbing traditions.

The conservative Dieulafoy never wrote of sexuality directly, and it is unlikely that as a devout Catholic she acted upon these fantasies. We know only that her male-identified female fictional characters always fell in love with men, and that sometimes the desire that they expressed was both lustful and forbidden. In a story line that echoes that of Paule Marsig in *Volunteer*, Dieulafoy's novel *Brother Pelagius* tells of young Marguerite, who disguises herself as a monk during the Crusades. Like Paule, she embraces a male identity that changes her both internally and externally. But she is also racked with troubled, physical longing for her former fiancé, Fortunat, who is unaware of her new identity; she cannot reveal her identity to him, for to do so would betray her gender violation. Marguerite is ravaged nearly to the point of death by the impossible choice between maintaining her new and gratifying identity as a monk and giving in to her heart's desire. In the erotically charged images from Persia, we can recognize a hint of the question that would be posed more fully in that novel (and to which we will return): how does the male-identified woman love?

The suggestive sensual elements of these images were never articulated within the published travelogues. Rather, in some cases they were flatly denied by accompanying captions that did not even acknowledge that there were people pictured, as if to insist on their scientific work in an archaeological narrative separate from the human one. In the full page "Funerary Urns," for example, a Persian boy stands next to a human-size urn, arm resting against its rounded mouth (figure 21).[10] His absence from the caption suggests that he is there only to show the scale, but the image is all light and shadow, curves and musculature: the boy and urn form a gorgeous and inseparable pair. Leaning against the artifact, his right arm rests on his hip, while the left foot pivots across the right leg in a classic pose of European male portraiture. The boy's stance mirrors almost exactly that of Jane herself in the 1871 postwar portrait (figure 6).

FIGURE 21. "Funerary Urns."

Source: Dieulafoy, *A Suse: Journal des fouilles*, p. 151.

Unlike Jane in the portrait, however, the boy looks down, his eyes shaded; his feminine belted garment opens in the same suggestive V as the boatman, but his heart-shaped faced looks more delicate. The waves of the boatman's hair peek out from his turban, but the boy with the urn has a short haircut like Jane's. Next to the hourglass-shaped urn, his stance is more odalisque than warrior: he is the girl-boy to her boy-girl. If the boy is pictured next to the urn to demonstrate its scale, perhaps that is because masculinity now serves as an important unit of measurement for Jane—the very standard against which she measures herself during these formative months in Persia.

The placement of "Funerary Urns" at this point in the travelogues suggests that we are at a key chapter in Dieulafoy's personal narrative: her gender story. This is the moment in which she reconnects with the masculine iteration of herself that emerged during the war and reengages with her own malleable gender. In both the stories that she tells and the photographs that she takes, we can see her attempting to work through her own gender expression and its meanings. These images show us that her travels in Persia allowed Jane to contemplate the possibility of gender-crossing and a looser understanding of the bounds of masculinity and femininity. Behind the emergence of a joyful and proud embrace of masculinity, she began insistently to search for models, for others like her. She did not find many who had entered the world as female and taken on male attributes, but she would later study many men who adopted a female persona: the Abbé de Choisy (1644–1724), whose mother dressed him as a girl until the age of eighteen, after which he resumed the practice at the urging of Madame de Lafayette; the Chevalier d'Eon (1728–1810), who used his androgynous features to disguise himself as a woman and spy for France, and who claimed to have been designated female at birth; and Stuart, the American opera singer who presented as female. She would compose histories of these figures with Marcel that at one point they intended to publish. It's unclear why they changed their minds.

The images of Persian masculinity in Dieulafoy's travelogues should be understood in this light, along with the scrapbook of contemporary discussions of gender-crossing. They can be seen as part of Dieulafoy's lifelong effort to recognize herself in other human forms, to find her gender-fluid kin, and perhaps even to imagine herself as an object of desire. In addition to sultry men gazing into the distance (figure 22), there are those with shapely legs

FIGURE 22. Muslim negotiator.

Source: Dieulafoy, *A Suse: Journal des fouilles*, p. 206.

and, in the final pages, a slew of androgynous figures draped in loose-fitting fabrics.[11] While never acknowledged in writing, the significance of these figures and of the gender-neutral clothing would endure: Marcel and Jane would reinvoke the androgynous looks of the boy with the urn and the boatman years later in their theatrical salons—where "classical" costumes allowed men and women to play interchangeable roles, and where the sensual was again present and evocative but never acknowledged.

HOSANNA!

Jane and Marcel did succeed in returning to Persia to complete their mission, after spending the summer in France. Their reentry was enabled in part by the French coast guard, who lent them a warship to secure their safe travels in the Persian Gulf—a fact that served to renew Jane's affinity with a military role. In the introduction to the final leg of their mission, Jane devotes admiring paragraphs to this vessel and notes her own newfound interest in cannons, rifles, and the deployment of the Hotchkiss.

Images of men fill the last pages of her travelogues, alternating between portraits of individual Persians and depictions of groups at work. From afar, these groups look like a small army, and Dieulafoy frequently used military analogies to describe them as they worked in trenches.[12] As if to confirm that the intimacy shared in the tent with her colleagues was akin to that of soldiers in a platoon—brothers-in-arms, as it were—there is more than one sketch of the group from a distance, perched on horseback, guns pointed toward some threat far away.[13] Dieulafoy is among these troops of men, but there is no way to determine which silhouette is hers.

And then there is the most famous image of all, the one that would become an enduring iconographic record of her prowess, associated with Dieulafoy's celebrity for years to come. It was featured in the *Tour du monde* and would populate collectible inserts in chocolate wrappers and rice boxes celebrating "Madame Jane Dieulafoy, explorer of Susa" (figure 23). In the image, Jane wields a pistol aimed at several bandits who are coming toward her with spears. As the accompanying narrative recounts, Marcel and the others were retrieving their boat while she guarded their precious cargo. Realizing that their cartons of artifacts were at risk, she was terrified but able to think on her feet. Digging deep for her "strongest voice," she yelled out at the eight spear-wielding aggressors:

FIGURE 23. Full-color insert depicting Dieulafoy defending her treasures against bandits, in the Famous Explorers series, based on the incident of December 3, 1885.

"I have fourteen bullets at my disposal. Go find six more of your friends."[14] The terrified bandits ran off. While there could not have been a photograph of this moment, Marcel recorded it in his sketch book.

The second Dieulafoy mission soon proved successful beyond anyone's expectations. Not long after their final return to Susa, Marcel's team made a stunning discovery: a section of Darius's palace that remained buried below Xerxes's own estate. "UNEXPECTED DISCOVERIES" read the breathless telegram sent from Basra in February 1886, urgently asking for a warship capable of transporting twenty thousand kilograms of artifacts.[15] The Dieulafoy team had discovered the central hall (Apanada) of the palace believed to have been built by Darius and restored by Artaxerxes, its stunning friezes still gleaming with deep shades of blue and green.

In a chapter titled "Hosanna!" written just after Christmas in 1885, Dieulafoy joyously recounted her role in this "miraculous discovery." "So many things have happened, so many joys, so many hopes realized!" she writes.[16] As she tells it, the fate of these forgotten artifacts rests entirely on her abilities—a fact confirmed by Marcel and later reports.[17] She finds herself believing ("Ô extremities of fate") that if she were to leave, the "gold mine would suddenly collapse";[18] that were it not for her, the mysteries of the tumulus could not be solved. In fact, she had a special talent for making sense of the puzzle of broken pieces. She writes, playfully, that though she had not brought a magic wand to Persia, "I have a special recipe for figuring out where the enamel fragments belong."[19] She leaves the pieces in front of her as she falls asleep at night, and when she wakes up in the morning, they seem to fall magically into place.

What Marcel has discovered and Jane helped reconstitute is the Frieze of the Archers—a series of muscled warriors carrying bows and arrows rendered in dazzling enamel work ("with beautiful lines, beautiful shapes, beautiful colors") in greens and blues on a scale beyond what they have previously excavated (figure 24).[20] Dieulafoy's excitement comes through not only in the journals but in letter after letter that she writes to friends and family, detailing the joys of this discovery. In those letters, and throughout the rest of the travelogues, she refers to the archers—poignantly and gleefully—as her *fils*, her sons. In a letter to Ronchaud, she describes their discovery as a kind of birth, for she watched the figures appear part by part: "A warrior's head appeared, another one's beard and hair."[21] At the same time, she wrote to her friend the Countess of Castellane about the "miracle" that her "sons had escaped without suffering more from the flames that had destroyed the palace and from the iconoclastic hands of Artaxerxes, who exploited his ruins as if they were a quarry of building materials."[22] After carefully removing the soldiers in pieces, she describes taking them to wash and clean, and then carefully packing them up for transport home. As a woman in the nineteenth century, having sons would be a way for Dieulafoy to channel her own ambition in a world with so many gender barriers. But she did not need sons to break through these barriers for her; she broke through them on her own, while coyly embracing the conceit of motherhood with this terminology.

A few entries before the Hosanna chapter, on Christmas Eve, Dieulafoy had meditated on her sense of closeness to the Nativity from her position on a landscape that mirrored the one in which Jesus was born. Retrieving the archers was also a way of resurrecting them—reviving the dead—and in writing about them, her patriotic pride mapped onto a religious discourse. She designated her archers not just as her sons but as "the Immortal ones"—a term used by historians and archaeologists of this time period, but also one that coded them as divine and further elevated her role in bringing them

FIGURE 24. The Frieze of the Archers currently in the Louvre Museum.

back to life. What's more, the term *immortel* linked them to a great French institution, the Académie française, to which Marcel would be elected in ten years. Thanks to his work in Persia, he would become an *immortel* himself, as its members were known.

The archers were a way for Dieulafoy to be part of both the Greek past and the French future, and a means of linking nationhood with religious conviction. Two of the novels that she would go on to write weave these themes of glory, nation, and church together in order to describe the accomplishments of a girl who became a man. While in *Volunteer* the gender-crossing heroine helps ensure the birth of the French Republic, in *Brother Pelagius*, set in medieval times, the young protagonist is depicted as an anointed ancestor to Joan of Arc, perhaps the greatest French hero, and thus *immortelle*, of all. Is it a coincidence that Dieulafoy named her Marguerite, meaning daisy, the very flower she so admired on her archers' uniforms?

Jane was emotionally bound up in the process of restoring the warriors, eager every morning to "run to my new loves and bring back to life the Glorious past of the Great Kings with my own hands."[23] Might this affinity have also been linked to the fact that the warriors were bedecked in ornamented uniforms that challenged gender distinctions? She describes these sartorial features in detailed awe: white robes covered in flowers or stars, skirts embroidered alternately with geometric patterns and blue and green daisies, their "ears and wrists weighted with golden rings and bracelets."[24] She retraces these details, the sky-blue brodequins and the yellow and white flowers, in her letters to both the countess and to Ronchaud. The only clear marker of the archers' masculinity was their matching beards. Like the figures whom she documented in her unpublished histories and the Persian boys whom she photographed, Jane's attachment to the archers likely stemmed from a point of identification: she saw in these figures another affirmation of an existence beyond the binary poles of masculinity and femininity. Years later, she would become friends with Pierre Lôti, a writer who was elected to the Académie française along with Marcel and thus also an *immortel*. Like her, Lôti had traveled to the Middle East, and he would often wear gaudy jewelry and other fashion accessories gleaned from his travels atop traditional men's clothing; in other instances, he would don exotic costumes. In a letter to Lôti from 1912, Dieulafoy alluded to the fact that he had once dressed as her beloved archers: "Know that in wearing one night the Immortal Ones' uniform," she wrote, referring to her Persian discoveries, "you have earned constant favor in the eyes of their archaeological mother."[25] Linking herself to Lôti and her ancient sons, she suggested her own creative genealogy, in defiance of place and time.

As Dieulafoy prepares to leave Persia for the last time, she notes with satisfaction, "In an hour, we will leave Susa, happy, triumphant, masters of the opulent bounty of vanished centuries."[26] She emerges here very much the master of her own past, ready and willing to own her gender variance and its long history, having reclaimed her identification with French glory. Her final reflections recall the images of the battlefield and the grueling, dangerous work that she and the team had faced. "The relics of the Achaemidian palace were not taken out of a superb palace, but resuscitated from the greedy entrails of the earth and conquered at the peril of our lives,"[27] she notes on the last page of her journal. As the historiographer of this great accomplishment, she writes: "I must speak strongly and without false modesty." And that she does, remarking: "The Susa mission launched a desperate battle, and with the help of divine Providence, it returns victorious." Dieulafoy ends the travelogues with this proud voice, seeming certain of a personal narrative that will allow her to walk "strongly and without false modesty" into her future. Conflating her discoveries of the Achaemenid past with her own self-discovery, resuscitating her masculine persona from her own past as a soldier, she confirms in these statements her right to live a different kind of life.

FROM PERSIA TO PARIS

Thanks to the urging of Marcel and Ronchaud, Jane was awarded the Legion of Honor shortly after her return to Paris in 1886. In his letter to the government ministry, Ronchaud anticipated the resistance to giving a woman the honor normally reserved for men. Addressing the committee, he compared "the intrepid traveler" to the painter Rosa Bonheur, a recent recipient who had also discovered "glory and fortune in culture." Famed for her images of animals, Bonheur had secured a pants permit in 1857, under the guise that it would enable her to paint more freely. (Notably, her permit did not allow her to appear at public events in men's clothing.) Bonheur lived a secluded life in the French countryside with two different female companions; when she traveled to Paris, she preferred to wear a dress.[28] Well known to the Parisian public, she was often cited alongside Dieulafoy in the accounts of pants-wearing women included in Dieulafoy's notebook—a model, then, against which Dieulafoy likely measured herself. In referring to Bonheur, Ronchaud does not mention the shared masculine presentation explicitly; rather, he underlines their contributions as a positive reflection on their country. He also mentions Marcel's own wish that his "devoted and indefatigable wife" should be recognized for her service.[29]

Dieulafoy's achievement, announced in *Le Journal officiel* in August of that year, caught the attention of the press, who reported extensively on her honor (figure 25). The ceremony took place in the Louvre's antiquities wing, where the Persian artifacts were in the process of being classified and restored in preparation for permanent display. Reporting on Dieulafoy's accomplishments, the press noted her bravery and talents, including both her archaeological aptitude and her linguistic skills in Persian, which enabled her

1. Tombeau de Fatma à Koum. — 2. Tombeau de Darius à Persépolis. — 3. Taureaux androcéphales. — 4. Mme Dieulafoy en excursion. — 5. Portique de l'Apadana de Xerxès

Mme DIEULAFOY, RÉCEMMENT DÉCORÉE DE LA LÉGION D'HONNEUR POUR SA MISSION EN SUSIANE.

(Dessins de M. VUILLIER. — Photographie de M. PIROU.)

to oversee hundreds of indigenous workers. "The exceptional appreciation held for this young explorer," noted one journalist, "is compensation for her devotion to science." Of course, the journalist did not fail to note her clothing, for at the reception she had been dressed in a man's suit, described as "more practical and appropriate to the lifestyle that she has adopted."[30] But the author went on to assure readers that when Dieulafoy did wear women's clothing, "she lends a new charm to their elegance, and the intrepid traveler becomes once again an exquisite Parisienne." Another article noted that, while one might imagine Dieulafoy as "one of those indomitable viragos," she was so delicate that she fell ill as a result of the pomp and circumstance surrounding her award. In other words, the intrepid traveler, fiercely brave and talented, was still a woman after all.

Dieulafoy may have chafed at these equivocations as reminders of her difference from the men on her team. In the second set of travelogues, she expresses anxiety about how she might be perceived upon her return. Toward the end of their final journey, after the episode of fighting off eight spear-wielding bandits, she had settled with relief in her bed, ready to welcome sleep. Instead, "an unexpected image" came to mind: that of a woman who had confronted her before she left Paris to embark on the second mission. Dieulafoy pauses here in order to underline the vivid nature of this memory. It's as if the elegant woman, with her copper hair and distinguished wrinkles, were actually there before her in the tent, speaking in a charming voice not unlike that frequently attributed to Dieulafoy herself. *You know*, suggests the woman, *your travels could be of interest not just to scientists but also to fashion houses.* She then proposes that Dieulafoy, with her expensive jewels and dresses, serve as a go-between who would market French women's clothing to wealthy Persian women. It's worth pausing for an instant on this oblique reference to the way Dieulafoy must have looked in earlier years—a conventional feminine presentation of which there is scarcely any record. She had willingly sold some of her pearls during their first mission to pay for needed resources.

Dieulafoy recounts this memory with shock and frustration, as if the conversation with the stranger had taken place in Susa rather than years earlier in France. Her troubled reaction makes plain what was at stake, as

< **FIGURE 25.** Dieulafoy featured in *Le Monde Illustré*, November 20, 1886.
Source: Bibliothèque nationale de France. Reprinted with permission.

she angrily enumerates her actual accomplishments—in stark opposition to what the red-headed woman would have liked to emphasize:

> Cross the Mediterranean, the Red Sea, the Indian Ocean, the Persian Gulf, and the deserts of Elam three times in less than a year, spend entire weeks without changing clothes, sleep on the floor, fight day and night against thieves and bandits, cross rivers without bridges, endure heat, rain, cold, fog, fever, fatigue, hunger, thirst, bites from all manner of insects; live this harsh and perilous life for no other reason than to bring glory to your country, and then someone tells you, you would make a really presentable fashion model![31]

The frustration here is palpable, suggesting an underlying anxiety: that after all that Jane had done alongside Marcel and his team, she would not be recognized alongside them as a fearless explorer. After all, Marcel would never be asked about his jewelry. The subtext seems clear: to do all of this and still be seen as a woman? Reader, she seems to caution, whatever you do, do not make this mistake.

The second set of travelogues was published in 1887, a few months after Dieulafoy was granted the Legion of Honor; the publication had been announced with anticipation in the newspaper reports of the award. One has to wonder if Dieulafoy was conscious, in compiling these documents, that they represented another opportunity to present herself to the French public in the way that she wanted to be seen. In recounting the dream of the red-haired woman, was she also speaking obliquely to those journalists who had continued to view her this way? Did she consciously set out to represent herself definitively in a masculine framework, and to efface her femininity from the public record?

Not long afterwards, in 1888, Hachette published the lavishly bound two-volume edition of the travelogues, just after the dispatches from the second expedition had appeared in *Le Tour du monde*. (The bound first volume edition had already appeared in 1887, at the same time as the second set of dispatches were being published in serial installments.) Numerous features alerted readers that the author was not a conventional woman in any sense. In the introduction, Jane shared a new story about her original decision to accompany Marcel on his travels. It is the story of the skepticism of her female companions, who had tried to remind her of the domestic pleasures of knitting and gossip when she left Toulouse all those years before. "I somehow managed to resist those temptations," she writes, her voice dripping with sarcasm. It is a telling story, placed retroactively in her narrative—after all, it was not there as a prologue when the first dispatches were published in the journal in 1884. In 1888 it has a different context, as the story of a woman who had already traveled to the world's ancient sites and returned to Paris with its booty, a woman celebrated by the French ministry and the Louvre. In other words, these were the words of a woman who had already been recognized as someone who was not really a woman—at least not in the contemporary sense of the term—and who expected her readers to be in on the joke. If there was feminism here, it was of a different order. Dieulafoy did not advocate on behalf of what women could do but rather suggested that she should not be seen or judged as one.

Several other details in the volume conveyed implicitly to readers that she should be definitively associated with masculinity. Another version of the Pirou portrait (figure 26) appeared on the opening page, revealing her boyish short hair in profile and framed to reveal only the bust, with no sign of residual femininity. The frontispiece introduced her as a knight of the Legion of Honor and laureate of the Académie française, two elite patrimonial distinctions hardly ever given to women. And in the epigraph to the volume, Dieulafoy alluded to the Iliad: "I don't pay attention to the birds or the shadows. The best of fortunes is combat for one's homeland." The narrative voice of this volume, then, is that of the French soldier and epic writer all in one, pursuing patriotic work in the name of France, reviving dead fellow-heroes and bringing them home. It is nearly impossible to imagine the person to whom this voice is attached lending elegance to any women's clothing, or hobnobbing around town as an exquisite Parisienne.

When the Dieulafoys originally left Paris, they had hoped at best to persuade Ronchaud to include some of their discoveries in existing installations at the Louvre. Instead, he devoted several rooms to the Dieulafoy discoveries, which included the enamel friezes that Jane herself had been instrumental in excavating and arranging. After two years of anticipation, the Salles Dieulafoy, or "Dieulafoy rooms," opened to great acclaim in June 1888, prompting one reporter to muse about the shock of such bustling crowds in the quiet

halls of the national museum. The Assyrian wing of the Louvre, the reporter noted, was suddenly subject to the excitement of a great department store sale. The guard stationed there must have rubbed his eyes like the chairman of the guard when Sleeping Beauty awoke, wrote the reporter, wondering what sort of miracle had occurred to bring these hordes of visitors to its sleepy chambers.[32]

Jane appeared at the opening to the Salles Dieulafoy in what would become her signature men's suit (figure 27). Unlike the earlier articles about the Legion of Honor, these press accounts did not mention her femininity. From this point forward, she was Madame Jane Dieulafoy, "the intrepid explorer who wears men's suits"—the words almost invariably came together. The opening presented to an eager Parisian public not just the exotic, recovered history of ancient Persia, but also the full realization of Dieulafoy's gender expression.

Jane and Marcel received a hero's welcome at this opening. The artifacts that the couple retrieved from Persia were stunning—and remain so, drawing crowds to the Assyrian wing to this day. The Dieulafoys fed the growing fascination with Orientalism with these improbable finds. Admiring art from the "less civilized" world of the East gave French citizens an easeful sense of superiority while they enjoyed their aesthetic and intellectual pleasures. The Dieulafoys' achievements had a potent extra significance after the humiliating defeat of the Franco-Prussian War, a persistent source of pain for the Parisian public. Their achievements demonstrated that, despite the loss, France remained a powerful force on the world stage. Contemporary newspaper reports boasted of the Dieulafoy success: "All the great museums possess objects that come from ancient peoples of the Orient . . . but none yet have galleries with objects from high antiquity Persia."[33] "Monsieur Dieulafoy," noted another article, "had succeeded where the English Sir W. Loftus had failed."[34] But Marcel did not receive all the credit. One of the most intriguing parts of the story was the role Jane had played. Reporters noted the painstaking work that Madame Dieulafoy had conducted during the excavations, as well as her "virile energy." "Dressed as a man, riding a mule, bearing a rifle," she faced dangerous terrain and hostile tribes. Madame Dieulafoy was depicted as a larger-than-life hero, not only courageous and strong but

< **FIGURE 26.** Dieulafoy in another pose from the 1884 Pirou session.

FIGURE 27. The inauguration of the Dieulafoy rooms at the Louvre, depicted in *L'Univers Illustré*, June 16, 1888. The bull's head, the Frieze of the Archers, and the Frieze of the Lions are clearly on display. Jane Dieulafoy is leaning over the table in the center of the engraving, speaking to a woman.

brilliant—her skills in Farsi allowing her to communicate with the natives. She commanded and organized the workers and directed the operations.

In these accounts, Parisians seemed decidedly untroubled by Dieulafoy's appearance. It wasn't just her clothing after all. She wore her hair closely cropped—unheard of for a woman at the time. A journalist from *L'Univers Illustré* noted, admiringly, that "the men's suit that she wears so comfortably"—the one that she supposedly wore in Persia to ease her travels—dated back to the Franco-Prussian War, when she "put it on for the first time."[35] Never mind that her finely tailored three-piece suit bore little resemblance to either the loose-fitting pants for Persian travel or the blue-and-white sharpshooter uniform. The journalist had adopted Jane's carefully cultivated narrative. The other article did as well, noting her military debut as a soldier in 1870. Like her earlier role in the Franco-Prussian War, the work that Jane accomplished in Persia, supported by the War Ministry, confirmed her enduring image as a French soldier.

Was it Jane Dieulafoy's service to the nation that prevented those who encountered her from stopping too long on the incongruity of it all: the woman in the suit, lauded in the most conservative academic circles, where gender roles were rigid and women were almost entirely absent? Explanations were as many as they were varied—the former soldier, the Persian past, "out of habit," "out of eccentricity"—but the inclination was to rationalize and deflect rather than to criticize. Dieulafoy was celebrated by the highest echelons of Parisian society—academic and political—and journalists seemed to go out of the way to give her the benefit of the doubt, accepting an explanation that made little sense under scrutiny: that Dieulafoy wore Parisian suits out of Persian habit. Was it the fact that she was a national hero above reproach, married to fellow hero Marcel, that allowed her to get away with it, despite her defiance of social structures? Or was it because Dieulafoy's gender expression somehow made sense to the Parisian public, simply because it seemed to make sense for her? It was impossible to imagine her any other way.

While Jane had her own tactics for discouraging too much attention, the Dieulafoys' discoveries, it turns out, were distracting enough, only increasing the interest in Jane's travelogues and in the couple as celebrities. Perhaps that is why Jane developed the habit of launching into digressions on Persia everywhere she went. The writer Laurent Tailhade described the tiresome way in which Jane never forgot, whether in the middle of dinner or at a ball, "her identity as explorer," taking credit for Xerxes "like a man who had gotten him his start."[36] Similarly, Adolphe Brisson remarked that if Dante would also be associated with the return from Hell, in every exclusive salon in Paris Jane Dieulafoy was always coming back from Susa.[37]

4 FICTIONAL TRUTHS

AFTER RETURNING TO PARIS, it seems Dieulafoy never looked back, making her way in the upper echelons of Parisian society in her beautifully fitted suits, side by side with Marcel. She was a mainstay on the lecture circuit, speaking about archaeology and the Persian expeditions, but also about theater and social issues, and eventually feminism and women in combat. Her audiences seemed willing to overlook her unusual attire, given the nature of her conservative messages and her devotion to both her husband and her country. But there is evidence that her own gender questioning continued—that she continued to work to try to make sense of herself. For Dieulafoy, what it meant to be a woman was entangled with what it meant to wear men's clothes, and she devoted much intellectual energy to weaving the two narratives together. In addition to studies, treatises, and lectures, Dieulafoy wrote novels. In these, the cold intellectualism of her erudition was humanized, literally fleshed out through full-size personas. And in these novels the various strands of her ruminations come together, offering a prism through which to understand how she likely thought about herself.

Only about a year after publishing *Volunteer*, in which she addressed gender-crossing explicitly for the first time, Dieulafoy published *Brother Pelagius* in 1893. This novel was in many ways the sequel to the previous one, as a continued meditation on the passage from girlhood to masculinity through a retelling of the legend of Joan of Arc. The setting for this historical novel is the Middle Ages, but it is also a kind of memoir: in it, Dieulafoy seems to resolve all the puzzling contradictions of her identity as warrior, devoted wife, Catholic, and a woman who was more comfortable in men's clothes. It was not lost on some readers that this was a personal story, one in which she argued "with considerable feeling, the cause of the transvestism that she enjoys."[1]

Both Jane and Marcel were born into Catholic families. Their pride of country was matched with adherence to its most enduring religious system, which left little room for gender nonconformity. In addition to offering a framework for precisely that, the Joan of Arc story let her connect her gender-crossing to her place within both the French patrimony and the church. "I will wear pants as long as it pleases God," Joan of Arc famously declared. One can imagine Dieulafoy arriving at the same conclusion.

The protagonist of *Brother Pelagius* is Marguerite of Carcassonne, described as an ancestor of Joan of Arc, whose namesake's story provided another proof that she could not have been the only one of her kind. It is no surprise that Jane drew from Catholic legend. She had spent eight happy years in the convent, after all, and still maintained friendships with some of the nuns. In their biography, Eve and Jean Gran-Aymeric surmise that Dieulafoy's parents sent her to the religious school because they realized that their precocious, fiercely intelligent daughter would be a handful to raise. They also wonder how the future explorer could have thrived within the convent's rigid structures, and how she maintained such warmth and fondness for her former teachers over the years.[2] But it is a mistake to assume that those who come from traditional backgrounds will necessarily reject those traditions when they find themselves at odds with them. For some, the depth of attachment leads them to find a way in nonetheless, to force the tradition to make room for them rather than be chased away. Dieulafoy's success in a world that seemed ill suited to accommodate her can be explained by her ability to find models for herself in that very world. Rather than experience the church as a place of painful strictures that denied her freedom, Jane found in Catholicism a way to understand herself: the histories of the saints offered a remarkable variety of female role models and of gender-nonconformists; and Catholic tradition offered a way to sublimate her sexuality—to the extent that she may have felt alienated from her physical body—without denying her humanity.

There was no better example of this than Joan of Arc: brave warrior for France, whose feminine identity and refusal of its limits only added to the heroism of her legend. Joan of Arc, whose cross-dressing allowed her to take on men's roles, and who refused to change her clothing even when she was put on trial, so fundamental was it to the identity she held in God's name. In 1936, Vita Sackville-West would write her biography, the first of many gay writers to recognize a forebear in the Catholic heroine; the contemporary trans writer Leslie Feinberg devoted a chapter to her in the 1996 anthology *Transgender Warriors*. To this day, both French Catholics and conservatives celebrate her as a figure of national pride.

The legend of Joan of Arc, and the multiple so-called transvestite saints who preceded her, enabled Dieulafoy to tell her own story explicitly, without shame, inscribing it in a familiar tradition of heroism and martyrdom. Like Joan of Arc, Dieulafoy's Marguerite is celebrated as a war hero, martyr, and virgin—each one a way to think about how one could live out a different sort of gender expression in the nineteenth century. With her balance of male and female traits, she offered precisely the image of true womanhood that Dieulafoy imagined had existed more readily in the past.

The plot of the novel is somewhat complex: When her village comes under attack, Marguerite of Carcassonne silently offers her virginity to God in exchange for victory over the Moors. Once the town is liberated from infidel fighters, she accepts an offer of marriage from the heroic Fortunat. On her wedding day, however, she is unwilling to betray her divine promise, and she flees her fiancé and her family, who remain unaware of the vow she promised never to reveal. After shedding her cumbersome skirts and cutting her hair, Marguerite becomes a monk in a neighboring monastery, while also battling Muslim forces. Later, Marguerite's sister Florette is exiled to the same monastery and fails to recognize her own sibling in the form of Brother Pelagius. Marguerite/Pelagius is devastated to discover that Florette is in love with Fortunat, her own former fiancé, and that he is in fact the prisoner she had unwittingly injured in battle, having mistaken him for a Saracen. She ultimately releases both of them, and later, ill from the emotional turmoil of keeping her identity a secret, reveals her "true" identity on her deathbed to her father, sister, and Fortunat. The novel closes with her sacred marriage, as the divine presence calls upon her as his chaste fiancée and tells her that "Jehanne la Lorraine" (another name for Joan of Arc) will be born from her.[3]

While Marguerite's gender-crossing is based on Catholic tradition, this story is an extension of the one that Dieulafoy told about Paule Marsig, the heroine of *Volunteer*, where the Joan of Arc legend is also relevant. In that text, the young woman takes on a soldier's uniform to protect her father, already in combat. Wearing the "blue uniform," she transitions from an unknown "little girl" to the bold, fearless hero who rescues her father and France. The love story in that novel plays out through these masculine and familial roles—Paule marries Guillaume, her "brother in arms," while embracing for herself the roles of devoted brother and son. Like *Volunteer*, *Brother Pelagius* is a drama of reclaimed brotherhood, in which Dieulafoy reworks and expands on the theme of gender transformation, pausing this time to recount its emotional dimensions in remarkable depth. Dieulafoy gives voice to Marguerite's feelings about renouncing her femininity in great detail, making clear how difficult it was and how necessary. She describes how the young woman, now living as a man, is briefly seized with doubt after her hurried choice in the woods to change her appearance, for this is no simple costume change or disguise: wearing men's clothing is presented as an emotional and meaningful act. For Marguerite, dressing in this way is terrifying as an explicit rejection of conventional femininity and potentially of God's will. "Is it really you wearing this man's garment?" she asks herself in fear, as she wonders whether her new appearance is a betrayal of her religion. In these passages, Dieulafoy reveals her intimate understanding of the significance of the transition to men's clothing.

Dieulafoy's portrayal of Marguerite's doubt also allowed her the opportunity to emphasize the multiple, clear "signs of celestial will" that steer her protagonist's behavior and thus give her permission to make this change.[4] She soon comes to realize that "God had allowed her virilized soul to gain sovereignty over her woman's nature."[5] This is a remarkable sentence, which recognizes both the possibility of gender misalignment and the possibility of overcoming it through religious fervor. By presenting Marguerite's gender shift as a direct response to a higher calling, Dieulafoy evokes this shared fantasy. To be sure, the religious narrative places Marguerite alongside other Catholic female heroines—Deborah the prophetess, Saint Theodora and Saint Marina—all of whom, according to legend, "gave up their women's clothing"[6] in order to accomplish their miracles. In fact, Joan of Arc made the same claims at her trial, declaring that the decision to wear pants was made not by her but by God.[7]

The religious frame allows for a dramatic—and welcome—transition to masculinity. With the saintly predecessors attending her in spirit, Marguerite bids goodbye to the "sweet, pale, trembling girl" that was her former self.[8] She has undergone significant physical changes that permanently alter her appearance: a more rugged body and cropped hair. The narrator pauses for Marguerite to marvel over her reflection in a pool of water: "A few days of misery, a few ounces less of fabric, short hair and a beret instead of the veils that surrounded her braids, had all of this been enough to transform her to this extent?" she wonders in awe.[9] Later she is startled by the sound of her own voice, which is now deeper. When her family discover her locks of hair in the woods, alongside her ripped-up wedding dress, they interpret them as evidence of her death. And in some sense, the girl whom they know *has* died, as Marguerite herself articulates more than once.[10]

As with the gender-crossing heroine of *Volunteer*, the resonances of Marguerite's journey to masculinity with Dieulafoy's own life story are striking: the exotic medieval setting is a stand-in for Persia, and Marguerite's dangerous journey through the woods parallels Dieulafoy's travels in the wilderness. Like Marguerite, Dieulafoy had cut off her hair and marveled at a physical prowess that she did not know she had; having faced death numerous times, she returned home a changed person. Through Marguerite's story, Dieulafoy once again reworked her own life narrative, reiterating the link between gender-crossing and service to a higher cause. Moving beyond the patriotism of her earlier claims, she seems convinced here that her life was divinely inspired. Remarkably, Dieulafoy casts Marguerite's tale not as a story of begging God to change her sex; rather, it is a story of being chosen by God to do so.

MARRIAGE PLOTS

Perhaps unsurprisingly, no matter how much her protagonists seem to have embraced masculinity, when it comes to love they see themselves as women. In *Volunteer*, for example, Paule's "true" identity is quickly revealed to her love interest Guillaume, and they end up together in a marriage much like Dieulafoy's own. Marcel and Jane were a model couple, deeply enamored of each other and quite nearly joined at the hip: they were often sighted on the streets of Paris arm in arm. *Volunteer* depicted a similar partnership, one that seemingly preserved the heteronormative paradigm of marriage between a man and a woman, even if that woman defied feminine conventions in every way. In *Brother Pelagius*, on the other hand, the solutions were less elegant, depicting what appeared seamless in Dieulafoy's own life as a troubling challenge. How does one reconcile love and family with gender-crossing?, the novel asks, reformulating the questions around eros that had arisen in the Persian photos. *Brother Pelagius* suggests that Dieulafoy may have struggled with love more than her easeful marriage revealed.

The stakes of this inquiry could not have been higher. This was a time when marriage laws were in flux: divorce had been reinstated in 1884, while the controversy around it endured. Many literary publications in the early 1900s would weigh in, directly and indirectly, on the question of divorce, dramatizing the new life paths made possible from this change in the law. A series of plays performed in Paris at the turn of the century capitalized on the controversy, drawing crowds as they dramatized the potential ramifications of this major social shift.[11] While the institution of marriage itself was perceived as being under attack, Dieulafoy became an outspoken supporter and a self-proclaimed "enemy of divorce"—a position that put her at odds with many feminists and progressives.[12] Her own views on the topic would first be made explicit in her 1897 novel *Decline*: "Only indissoluble marriage can achieve nature's commandment of the Alliance between man and woman as the ultimate goal," she wrote. "Stable families are formed under the shelter of indestructible homes, and it is stable families who make up strong nations; it is strong and wise nations who are happy nations."[13] Marriage between a man and a woman, she argued, was connected to religious and national duty; to reject it would also be to reject Catholic and republican obligations. Dieulafoy's hostility toward divorce was linked to her nascent feminist theories. The family was meant to be the center of women's lives, she believed, and with the legalization of divorce it was women who became vulnerable: "Divorce is against women; it annihilates them, degrades them, removes their prestige and honor," she asserted.[14]

Dieulafoy's sense that women were dependent upon marriage for their own protection is surprising, to say the least, given her own independent nature and seeming self-sufficiency. Might she have credited Marcel—the husband who was her devoted partner through it all—with her ability to succeed? It is true that without him she would never have had the opportunity to travel the world. But that never seemed to be part of her narrative, fictional or otherwise. She, along with her heroines, proudly took credit for her accomplishments. At the same time, she was proud of her marriage to Marcel, which defined her, in part, as a woman in the public eye and protected her from scorn; their marriage was what most clearly demonstrated that her male presentation was not meant to be socially subversive. Dieulafoy's unexpected critique of divorce thus underscores the extent to which her unconventional gender expression might have potentially threatened her core social and religious values. While she had found love and partnership with Marcel—someone who loved her for who she was, even while she embraced masculinity so completely—she seemed deeply aware that it might easily not have been so. Was she concerned that other women who realized these things about themselves only after marrying might find themselves abandoned? Or was she excluding herself from this equation, worrying instead about the feeble modern French women who did not share her strength and will?

The ending of *Brother Pelagius* answers some of these questions. Marguerite is separated from Fortunat, her original betrothed, precisely because he cannot see the connection between her new existence and her previous one. In a dramatic final scene, Fortunat discovers "Brother Pelagius" lying against Florette's chest and launches forward jealously, still not realizing that his supposed rival is actually his former fiancée. Once the secret is revealed, the dying Marguerite blesses the union of Fortunat and Florette, and she is then welcomed by the voice of God as "my chaste fiancée," from whom Joan of Arc will descend."[15] This is a different version of the happy ending that Dieulafoy had imagined for Guillaume and Paule, brothers-in-arms who end up living happily as husband and wife. With Brother Pelagius, Dieulafoy proposes an alternative union—a marriage of sorts, but one situated just outside the bounds of the real. How happy, then, could such an ending really be?

Dieulafoy seems willing, with this fictional scenario, to acknowledge some of the ambiguity that her complex identity suggested. The revelation of Marguerite's original identity follows just after the abbé has welcomed her as "my son" and she is deemed worthy of death while wearing the habit of the "sons of Benedict."[16] If her father had not recognized her, she was eager to be accepted as the son of "my Father in Jesus Christ," rather than as his bride a few minutes later—a bride from whom "saintly seed" will spill, alluding to the male reproductive role rather than the female one. The matriarchal role that Marguerite plays is also strangely patriarchal: no product of immaculate conception or genealogical metaphor, Dieulafoy ultimately links Joan of Arc to Marguerite through an allusion to the physical *male* body. This language suggests an even deeper identification for Dieulafoy with masculinity and gives expression to a more involved fantasy of bodily gender-crossing. At the same time, the character of Brother Pelagius / Marguerite is a version of the kind of gender fluidity Dieulafoy embraced: masculine, but still a woman. The divine voice accepts Marguerite as his sacred bride and announces her as the matriarch to "a virgin, a female warrior, a female martyr" who will be inspired by her example. These triple denominations marry conventional masculine roles (hero, warrior) with feminine roles (virgin, fiancée) as well as more gender-neutral roles (companion, martyr) and are tied to the legends of Saints Michel (m), Catherine (f) and Marguerite (f), respectively.[17] Joan of Arc, in her own gender ambiguity, linked as it was to the supernatural and celestial will, offered a helpful precedent in this regard. By claiming this saint as her hero/ine's ancestor, Dieulafoy redefines her in ways that unsettle the pure binary opposition between male and female. In so doing, Dieulafoy betrays a desire for an identity that combines both genders but is defined by neither, even if she ultimately calls that identity female.

THE WOMAN KING

Dieulafoy's protagonist is a realization of the "true woman" that Dieulafoy would describe in her feminist writings in the 1900s. The modern French woman, argued Dieulafoy, had forgotten her earlier sense of self; she had become complacent, even confused, and had inadvertently relinquished the power that she used to yield, giving up her rights in the process. "Remember that you were the woman *king*, and a king should never abdicate!" she admonished in one lecture from 1910. "What has happened to that matron who was so strong, so powerful, so honored? What has become of that woman who knew how to join the tenderness of the ardent mother to the bravery of the warrior? She is daydreaming, she sleeps on a bed of flowers offered to her for her beauty, cradled by the pride of her successes, of her triumph. She is asleep and she has allowed all the barriers that protected her home, her children, her dignity, and the future of the race that she carries in her flanks to be carried away!"[18]

Rather than doubt her own femininity, then, Dieulafoy redefined the meaning of the word. Fighting in wars and working alongside men did not make her less of a woman but rather more of one; it was her peers who had somehow lost their way. The past, argued Dieulafoy, offered evidence of a gender-fluid ideal, when roles were more malleable and it was not unusual for women to be heroes—or even kings. Dieulafoy did not seem bothered by the fact that the examples she offered were not of average women but those remembered precisely for their unique, unfeminine contributions: Deborah and Jael, the two Catherines of Russia, Isabelle the Great, and, of course, Joan of Arc.

In the 1900s, Dieulafoy preached to her audiences about a return to earlier epochs when women like this were possible. At the end of her thirty-two-page speech, she concluded hopefully but also with a touch of anger: "The time will come without a doubt when Woman will find herself the way she is supposed to be in the social order; she will take back her rights that have been misunderstood and will stand up from the kind of humiliation that the centuries seem to have given her, and that by virtue of being usurped has degenerated into a natural order, passing as a natural state." This speech is telling in a number of ways, as it suggests that Dieulafoy found conventional French femininity to be a form of "humiliation." The only way to identify with it was to redefine what it meant to be female entirely. We find in these writings evidence of the healthy narcissism that made Dieulafoy's potentially solitary existence bearable: she saw herself as normal; it was the rest of her sex who were not.

It is unclear when, exactly, Dieulafoy formulated her ideas about the true French woman lost to history. By the 1890s, feminism was a hot topic in France, with assemblies taking place all over Europe advocating for women's emancipation, their rights within marriage, their right to higher education and professional opportunities, and their right to full participation in public life. This new advocacy allowed Dieulafoy to identify with other women in ways she seemed unwilling to in the travelogues and after her initial return; what's more, within this framework she could continue to be recognized as female without denying her accomplishments. While her own belief system was unique, grounded as it was in erudite historical knowledge, Dieulafoy followed the proceedings of feminist assemblies and congresses throughout Europe starting in the 1890s; the success of these ventures, she might have reasoned, would surely lead to more women like her. While her feminist speeches are not recorded until the early 1900s, novels like *Volunteer* and *Brother Pelagius* suggest that she was analyzing these notions much earlier. Marguerite's story is an early iteration of the pangender ideal that Dieulafoy linked to earlier forms of femininity—a keen example of how, long after returning from Persia, she continued to turn toward history to extract clues for self-understanding.

With the legalization of divorce in 1884, the new feminist activism at the fin de siècle was perceived by some as a threat to the most traditional French institutions, which were already considered to be in crisis. As much as the legal and social reforms advocated by feminists (including suffrage) elicited anxiety, the increased visibility of women in the public sphere led to the sense that the French family was changing. In response, beginning in the early 1900s, the women's magazines *Femina* and *La Vie Heureuse* offered a new kind of feminism, although they initially avoided the term for fear of appearing too political. Through their carefully constructed images of the modern French woman, these successful publications imagined women achieving in professional spheres while still adhering to their traditional roles as wives and mothers. They published photographs of women lawyers and editors, doctors, and artists. Dieulafoy published in these magazines and was frequently featured in them beside the most popular women writers of the day: Marcelle Tinayre, Gyp, Daniel Lesueur, and Myriam Harry. Jane and Marcel were celebrated as models of the new marital ideal: marriage as a form of partnership between devoted collaborators (figure 28). Jane was also a member of the all-female jury established by the magazines in order to grant their own literary prize.

On the one hand, Dieulafoy stood out in this hyperfeminine milieu for her appearance, for part of the work of these magazines was in showing how

M. ET Mme DIEULAFOY, DANS LEUR CABINET DE TRAVAIL, A PARIS.

Mme Dieulafoy est pour son mari la plus dévouée et la plus active des collaboratrices. Après l'avoir suivi dans tous ses voyages scientifiques, elle continue à l'aider à Paris dans ses nombreux travaux, ce qui ne l'empêche pas d'écrire des romans émouvants et aussi des drames, comme cette Parysatis *que l'on va applaudir aux Arènes de Béziers.*

FIGURE 28. Monsieur and Madame Dieulafoy in their home office in Paris. *Femina*, August 15, 1902.

lovely women writers could be, as opposed to the man-destroying hags they represented in the popular imagination. But even in her tailored suits, Dieulafoy did not seem to pose a threat, because of her adherence to conservative values and her association with the most conservative elements of French society. An image of her from 1902 shows the diminutive Jane in front of her elegant fireplace, etched with fleur-de-lys, that runs to the high ceiling—a visual reminder of her deference to French tradition (figure 29). The novelist Camille Marbo, a candidate for the Vie Heureuse prize, recounted how the pants-wearing Dieulafoy told her, "I didn't vote for you. I don't like people who stray from tradition."[19]

The new, more conservative feminism offered up the kind of achieving woman with whom Dieulafoy could identify and with whom she shared a certain set of values. Even so, the feminism promoted by Belle Epoque women's magazines—in which corsets were still celebrated—could not quite account for Jane Dieulafoy. In her archives, in the same dossier bulging with her "feminist theories" is the notebook in which she collected articles about feminist congresses, women entering professions from which they were previously excluded, and anything having to do with gender-crossing.[20]

The contents of Dieulafoy's archives suggest that the ultimate alignment with womanhood that enabled her to speak as a feminist required some complex psychological gymnastics. She had to work to make sense of her masculinity while also wishing to acknowledge her affinities with women and advocate on their behalf. In the process, feminism and gender-crossing were often intertwined. But wearing pants was never about seizing male privilege in the interest of equality, as it was for some feminists and suffragettes of her time or as it had been for George Sand, for example. Rather, it was about aligning the internal with the external. Gender-crossing was a deeply personal, emotionally wrought psychological challenge that she grappled with throughout her adult life. Part of this struggle likely stemmed from a feeling of being torn between male and female identities.

Again, *Brother Pelagius* offers a certain kind of evidence. Marguerite is caught between genders, unwilling and unable to relinquish either identity until she is quite literally dying from the struggle. The drama of the last third of the novel takes place around Marguerite's secret, as she finds herself in a psychologically devastating double bind stemming directly from her desire

FIGURE 29. Madame Dieulafoy in her living room in Paris. *Femina*, August 15, 1902.

to maintain her double identity—to be both Marguerite and Brother Pelagius. For if Marguerite were to reveal herself as female, she would also reveal herself as not Brother Pelagius; and to be recognized by her family would be to admit that she has lied to her religious order, throwing that masculine identity into jeopardy.

As Marguerite wanders in the fields searching for penitence and clarity, she has a sudden sensation of relief that evokes a fantasy of disembodiment: "It seemed to her that she peeled off her carnal envelope like a light piece of clothing, that her liberated spirit discovered a new rapture, that her hopes had been realized."[21] This dream of escaping gender and its burdens—a violent fantasy of leaving one's skin—has been since expressed in numerous modern transgender memoirs, as Jay Prosser catalogues in his book *Second Skins*. For Marguerite, the feeling was fleeting: she discovers seconds later that "her soul, freed for a moment, was once more reunited with her body"—the very body that hides her secret.[22] This theme casts the novel's ending in a new light, for as Marguerite is celebrated as a hero and martyr and ascends to the heavens, her "mortal shell" is all that remains—the skin from which she has finally detached. A happy ending after all?

Marguerite's conundrum goes beyond the limits of her body, however; this is also a story about the challenge of articulating an identity that is beyond language. It's worth noting that the novel alternates between her names (Marguerite and Brother Pelagius), as well as between masculine and feminine pronouns, as if uncertain how to maneuver around and through the linguistic obstacles to nonbinary gender—a question quite evidently still being negotiated to this day. Despite its difference in tone and genre, we will see that it asks very much the same questions raised by Rachilde's *Monsieur Vénus*. Indeed, their titles are mirror images of each other, reflecting gender-crossing in different nineteenth-century idioms. At the novel's close, Marguerite is literally speechless for days as she wanders around trying to figure out what to say. When she finally returns to the abbé to confess, the text does not give us her words, only noting how long it took because of the intermittent gasping, weeping, and emotional breakdowns.

The French proverb *L'habit ne fait pas le moine*—"Clothing does not make the monk"—is not referenced explicitly in the novel but is ever present nonetheless, rife with double meaning. Appearances can be deceiving precisely because in some cases the clothing *does* make the monk. The etymology of Marguerite's assumed name as Brother Pelagius—"Frère Pélage" in French—actually points to this. In French, *un pelage* (albeit without the acute accent) can mean either the fur of an animal or the peeling of skin, from a piece of fruit or even a face. Marguerite's disguise is at once a new skin and the peeling off of an old skin, pointing to the drama of hidden identity that plays out in the novel's final pages. When Marguerite's fiancé arrives, he cannot recognize her in this new form of self that is both a realization of her true identity and a denial of it. Marguerite's name connotes, then, both masking and unmasking. It points toward the complex relationship between outside and inside. Gender transformation means the realization of some hidden core identity, but it can also involve painful dissimulation and the fear that self-revelation will mean irrevocable loss.

Appearing before her former fiancé Fortunat in her Benedictine hood, wanting to reveal herself but unable to do so without renouncing the masculinity identity in which she feels so comfortable, Marguerite poignantly wonders: "Does one live a whole life behind a mask?"[23] What, we might ask, is the mask in this case—the masculine disguise or the feminine identity that cloaked the true version of Marguerite realized by the disguise? Which form of *pelage* obtains? This is indeed the underlying tension of the novel: true identity is realized through the costume change, and so to reveal her origins (Marguerite's biological femininity) is to risk denying the crucial transformation that has taken place. Ultimately, just like *Volunteer*, this is not a story of hiding one's true identity under a "new envelope"[24] but rather of discovering one's true identity *through* this new envelope and then needing to be recognized as both changed and the same.[25]

This is Jane Dieulafoy's story as well, and looking closely at her writings, one realizes that she tells it repeatedly. Over and over again, her writing allowed her to make and confirm her discovery that in order to be herself, she needed to dress as a man. These stories were crucial to Jane's sense of self, and some of them she repeated from one text to the next, with their meaning crystallizing over time. At the end of *Brother Pelagius*, the buffoonish character Pancrace reacts in shock to Marguerite's gender revelation, with an exclamation that directly echoes the words of the Persian shah: "What, this young man is a young woman?" he declares before running off in horror.

In another echo, Marguerite reflects on her relationship to feminine norms in ways that recall the anecdote related by Dieulafoy in the introduction to the travelogues, when she described how friends tried to dissuade her from embarking on her travels by warning her that she would be forsaking the joys of domestic femininity. From the perspective of the seasoned explorer, Dieulafoy wrote mockingly of the alternative life that her peers urged her to embrace: "I would invent new marmalades and coulis; the next day I would direct, as sovereign ruler, battles against flies, the hunt for mites, the darning of socks." Similarly, from the distance of her new role as Brother Pelagius, Marguerite recognizes the ways in which, as a girl, she had simply assumed the role that was handed to her: "Within the strict paternal home," Dieulafoy writes, "her mind and body had slumbered in a detachment as weighty as the clothing around her body." She had never thought to question the life set out for her in the domestic world. "Such was the want of custom, and she had obeyed its age-old tyranny, never thinking to question it."[26]

These passages suggest that gender is socially constructed, that is, created and naturalized by "custom." They also suggest that Dieulafoy might not yet have fully formulated what she later cast as "feminist theories," including her belief that in times such as the era in which Marguerite lived, women could more readily act as both warriors and wives. This notion of an ideal woman that no longer existed allowed Dieulafoy to see herself as a woman, even if her idea of what a woman should be was different from that of nineteenth-century France and different from that of other French women advocating for women's rights. By insisting on her female identity and speaking on behalf of other women, by rejecting divorce and celebrating her marriage with Marcel, she held on to her own origin story, even in her masculine persona. This female point of origin may have served as a comforting reminder that, like Marguerite, she was still the same person she had always been, even if she appeared to be different in many ways.

5 LOVING MARCEL

AND WHERE IS MARCEL DIEULAFOY in all of this? Serious, academic, less likely to attract the spotlight, Marcel returned to the civil service upon their return to France. Like his wife, he lectured regularly about his discoveries in the Middle East, and in 1895 he was elected to the Académie française, the most prestigious honor for a French intellectual and one for which Jane was not a contender owing to her sex (the first woman was elected in 1986). There is little written record of Marcel and Jane's relationship, in all likelihood because they nearly always traveled together.

Visually, we have a few indications. They were said to be frequently seen walking the streets of Paris in perfect tandem, always a well-matched pair.[1] In one well-known image, they look like they could be father and son: a gray-bearded Marcel faces his wife, both wearing identical three-piece suits and white ties (figure 30). They are at ease, arms resting near each other, although Marcel appears to be standing below the seated Jane. Still, the image is striking, a sketch that was likely based on a photograph, and one that makes absolutely no effort to feminize Jane's appearance or reassert heterosexual norms. The two are meticulously dressed, dapper and straitlaced, and hardly the image of the highly gendered marital relationships of their peers and associates. They are far more "Monsieur et Monsieur" than "Monsieur et Madame." Indeed, the image appears in Leslie Feinberg's 1996 *Transgender*

FIGURE 30. Jane and Marcel Dieulafoy in Uzanne, *Figures contemporaines*, 1901.

Warriors with the caption "A female to male trans person with husband. Are they a heterosexual couple? Two gay men?"[2]

In the context of the sense of crisis around the institution of marriage, it is all the more striking that the Dieulafoys were held up as a model of conjugal bliss, even as an example of a new kind of marital partnership more in line with the new roles that French women were eager to take on. In the article from *Femina* in 1902, Jane is described as "her husband's most devoted and energetic (active) collaborator. After following him on all of his scientific travels, she continues to help him in Paris on his many projects, which does not prevent her from writing touching novels."[3] But plaudits were not limited to the women's press. Another article describes with admiration "that brave double life, hardworking and productive, of Mr. and Mrs. Dieulafoy."[4] Lest we assume that it was just the French who had become accustomed to this unique couple, with their particular legacy and cultural significance to their homeland, it should be noted that the Dieulafoy marriage captured international attention as well. The *New York Morning Journal* reported the following, under the headline "Uses Hubby's Wardrobe":

> Madame Dieulafoy, the noted archaeologist, always wears the clothes adopted by men as best suited to her needs and convenience. She goes much into society with her husband, but never changes her way of dressing. Her husband approves, and they study and make their archaeological researches together. They agree that a common dress enables man and wife to submit to the same conditions and share the same pursuits. One can go where the other goes in bad weather. Vicissitudes of travel and arbitrary social rules that make distinctions for petticoats all are effaced. It permits an unbroken companionship. It makes possible one life where now there are two lives.[5]

The *Philadelphia Public Ledger* similarly noted that "Madame Dieulafoy, the archaeologist, now wears masculine attire altogether, and her husband thoroughly approves of it. They study and make archaeological researches together, so that their sympathies have in no way become bifurcated by Madame's dress reforms."[6]

Their public image, then, confirmed a sense of comradery and partnership, without a hint of impropriety. To be sure, there was criticism as well. An image from the satirical newspaper *L'Assiette au Beurre* from 1905 shows Marcel with his pants missing, his wife having taken them (figure 31). But even that image is not particularly vicious, and in general the couple was celebrated in the most privileged sectors of society. Their marriage was held up as a more complete realization of the institution, rather than as a threat to it, bringing husband and wife closer together in "unbroken companionship."

The bonds of Jane and Marcel's relationship were clearly visible, but they were anything but typical. They appear to be homosocial bonds, and perhaps one might even think of them as homosexual ones, as two male-identified individuals who loved one another. While we know little about their private lives together, we do have a record of their shared interests and passions through the work that they did, stretching far beyond the Persian adventures. These collaborations leave reason to believe that Marcel may have understood his wife best of all.

Both devotees of classical theater, Jane and Marcel began staging performances in their salon beginning in the late 1890s, adapting scripts from medieval Spanish romances and classical plays. In 1900, they coauthored a volume titled *Private Theater*, in which they presented those texts. Athens

FIGURE 31. A less than favorable depiction of the Dieulafoys in the satirical newspaper *L'Assiette au Beurre*, August 19, 1905.

and Jerusalem, they write in the preface, offer enduring wisdom and beauty that work directly against the ennui and malaise of present-day society, where people are always looking for a panacea in the modern.[7] Classical theater, they suggest, is an antidote to the ills of modern life. *Private Theater* comprises a theatrical version of the biblical *Song of Songs* and a poem by Theocritus, two medieval farces, and a forgotten early nineteenth-century comedy.

The volume also contains detailed instructions and suggestions for how to perform and stage these plays in one's salon. Perhaps not surprisingly, gender played a central role. Regarding the costumes, the Dieulafoys assure the reader that all that was needed could be found in every household and that these clothes were unlike the elaborate "barbarisms" misconstrued on the modern stage. They had insisted on these "simple forms," they wrote, because "they are infinitely flattering on virile forms just as they are on the supple female body."[8] As they explain in the introduction to Theocritus's Greek comedy, men and women can play the same roles interchangeably, for the *khiton*—a sort of toga that could be fashioned from any drapery or linens—was the clothing of both sexes.

Twelve photographs included in the volume (an assemblage that represents only a tiny fraction of the dozens more found in the Dieulafoy archives) confirm this fluidity: it is impossible to identify the sex of the actors or that of the roles they are playing without reference to the captions. They wear togas and loose-fitting bloomers, hats and scarves and other accessories in purposeful ambiguity. In fact, the images seem deliberately playful, in contrast to the seriousness of the Dieulafoys' preface. If they were performing in order to restore a sense of moral order, they were certainly having fun in the process.

In Jane and Marcel's private theater, gender difference was only present in the fictions being staged; it did not determine the casting. What's more, the costumes reveal the influence of the couple's travels in Persia (figure 32). The flowing feminine shapes depicted in the Greek comedy mimic the styles of the Persian men photographed near the tumulus; the costumes from the medieval farces are closer to the loose-fitting bloomers in which Jane and Marcel traveled. The couple's attention to the costume instructions underlines the centrality of costume to the whole enterprise: there are precise measurements and photographs of how to assemble the *khiton* on a woman, as well as an insistence in the preface of how crucial the costumes were, especially in a salon theater.

We are already deeply aware of the role of clothing in Jane's life, but Marcel left no parallel traces of his own sentiments; his works are purely academic, leaving little access to his imaginative world. In the home theater, on the other hand, Marcel the engineer was also the costume designer. We finally have a window onto his own perspective, which raises innumerable questions along the way: Did he too wish to abandon his gender of origin or move past it? Did he feel liberated in Persia by the flowing robes and less gender-determined sartorial demands? In Paris we see him only in his suits, but might he have shared or identified with Jane's rejection of gender norms, attracted as he was to a woman who easily passed as a man? These questions linger in the margins of their jointly authored *Private Theater* and in the gaiety depicted in the dozens of photographs of actors in costume in their archives. The photos are signed Dieulafoy, but it is unclear which Dieulafoy took them.

FIGURE 32. Costumed actors from a production of *La Sulamite* in the Dieulafoy home. Source: Jane and Marcel Dieulafoy, *Le théâtre dans l'intimité*, 1900.

> **FIGURE 33.** The Chevalier d'Eon as depicted in 1877. Source: British Cartoon Prints Collection, Library of Congress.

MADEMOISELLE de BEAUMONT, or the
CHEVALIER D'EON.
Female Minister Plenipo. Capt. of Dragoons &c. &c.

In addition to their book on home theater, Jane and Marcel collaborated on another project, though it never reached publication: a history of gender-crossing figures over time. Their archives contain Jane's notes as well as drafts of the work's future chapters, accompanied by dozens of sketches by Marcel. Their subjects included the Abbé de Choisy (1644–1724), the Chevalier de Fréminville (1787–1848), Leucippe (460–370 BCE), Mademoiselle Savalette de Lange (1786–1858), the Comte de Guiche (1637–1673), the Duc d'Aguillon (1720–1788), and the Chevalier d'Eon (1728–1810), all of whom were assigned male at birth and were known to have dressed as women. The Abbé de Choisy and the Chevalier d'Eon both lived as women for periods of time as well (figure 33).

In 1903, Jane and Marcel interviewed a more modern subject for their collection when Stuart, an American opera singer who presented as female, visited their home (figure 34). Stuart was an international celebrity, in large part because he was a man who performed in dresses and sounded like a woman. "Dear Mr. and Mrs. Dieulafoy, I must thank you again for the honor you have done to put me in your book," he wrote in a letter posted upon his departure; "I shall not forget to send you the photographs from America." "His throat examined by doctors is that of a woman," Jane wrote in her notes. "He is known as Stuart on his posters because being a man and singing in women's clothes, he can't do otherwise." This is the only trace, in all of her writing, of a medical explanation for gender variance.

With another unpublished work on cross-dressing in the theater also gathering dust in the archives, Dieulafoy's writings reveal someone who spent the better part of her adult life studying issues of gender identity. She wrote about it in multiple forms: in her travelogues, in her fictions, in her theatrical exploits, and in her nonfiction writings. Without ever addressing her own choices in the first person, she intellectualized her identity struggles and worked them out in safer territory, whether fictional or academic. But these later collaborations demonstrate that Dieulafoy's exploration of gender identity was neither private nor isolated. Rather, it was part of her relationship with Marcel. Their mutual emotional investment and their stalwart partnership—perhaps one that required no words but conveyed deep, unspoken understanding—was surely a stabilizing force and a determining factor in her confident gender expression.

> **FIGURE 34.** A postcard depicting Stuart, similar to one in the Dieulafoy archives.

„Stuart"

6 "MAY HE OR SHE REST IN PEACE!"

RATHER THAN BEING DENIGRATED as a hysteric or a pervert, the more likely labels for nineteenth-century women in pants, Dieulafoy maintained her title as the "intrepid explorer" long after her travels to the Middle East. Perhaps because she did not fit into any obvious category, Jane Dieulafoy seems—remarkably—to have been free to be herself. A fake epitaph written for the humor magazine *La Caricature* in 1896 captures the lighthearted way in which the improbability of it all was embraced by the Parisian public:

> He or she lies here, awaiting the resurrection,
> He or she was a good wife or husband
> a good male or female citizen
> knight, male or female, of the Legion of Honor
> May He or She rest in peace!

It also seems clear, from the many accounts and profiles of Dieulafoy (she was a popular, charming, inviting subject) that those who came into contact with her were under no illusions: her elegant men's suits had nothing to do with the clothes that she had worn out of necessity in Persia or during the Franco-Prussian War. Even in her own home, noted one writer, where she might have chosen an androgynous Persian robe, she wore the generic costume of masculinity—the black jacket, pants, and straight collar of French men.[1]

In these portraits, Jane comes across as her own person, strikingly comfortable in her own skin. There was something natural about her that set those around her at ease. To the surprise of many, she seemed to have no agenda other than living her life as she saw fit. Women's clothing, she often explained, was a form of coquetry that she simply had no need for. At a loss for words as to how to explain the phenomenon that was Jane Dieulafoy, numerous journalists resorted to describing her in great detail, leaving us a series of verbal portraits that match the photographic images that we have seen. A rather consistent profile emerges of the woman who dressed exactly like her husband. Where Marc de Montifaud—to whom she was regularly compared—wore bright colors and experimented with different fashions in her pants-wearing, Jane cut a figure that was Quaker-like, funereal and serious.[2] Her hair did not curl "in capricious waves" like other women; she looked rather like the fearless horseman. When she sat down, noted one visitor, legs crossed, holding a letter knife rather than a woman's fan, ready to chat, "I thought I might be in the presence of a young Cambridge student"—someone "trained in physical exercise, supple and fit in a form-fitting vest." But when Dieulafoy spoke, her "harmonious voice" and charming eloquence invited comparison to a university professor and distinguished actress all rolled up into one.[3] In another account, this time from the London *Daily Mail*, the writer described Dieulafoy's "well-cut dress suit" and "glazed linen shirt," which, he added, "she wears over a board."[4] This small yet telling detail aligns Dieulafoy's sartorial habits less with comfort than with an explicit denial of physical signs of femininity. Her goal seems to have been to look like a man, and she appears to have taken measures to secure the illusion, whether for others or simply for herself.

Journalist Mary Summer's 1898 portrait of Dieulafoy in *La Vie Quotidienne* reveals the ideological milieu in which Dieulafoy circulated and sheds light on how she fit in among other women who shared her conservative, upper-bourgeois lifestyle. In a piece on five best-selling women writers, Summer writes skeptically of women's professionalism. Remarking on a novel by Julia Daudet, the wife of naturalist novelist Alphonse Daudet, Summer notes enthusiastically that female students and doctors would never be educators in the way a mother could be. It's not that she was against *all* feminism, she writes, for surely some feminist claims were legitimate. "But you, see, ladies, it's in vain that we try to take women out of their role, that we put a bunch of ambitious goals in her head, that she aspires to plead cases, to name deputies, or to herself be elected to parliament; God has made her for better destinies." But, Summer quickly interjects, not all women should be sent to the kitchen: for some women, writing could be "a refuge and a solace," especially if they were deprived of the possibility of motherhood. She then recounts Dieulafoy's visit to her home, in which the author's bewildered maid announced her as "a small, decorated [she always wore her red ribbon for the Legion of Honor] man with a woman's voice."[5]

The figure that Summer seems to take pleasure in describing should be familiar by now: the famous traveler, with her short hair and form-fitting suit. Despite her gender-crossing, she was still recognized as an insider, as Summer muses over what it would be like to see this "Parisian socialite" on horseback in the Persian deserts with a revolver in hand. The tone is of familiarity—*she is one of us*—even as what is described is extraordinary and even strange. Once Dieulafoy returned to Paris, Summer explains, "the intrepid traveler" could hardly content herself with a life of leisure; she became a writer instead. Writing is thus presented as a complement to travel—an audacious, active role for a woman—and Dieulafoy takes it on with the same "indefatigable ardor" that she used to direct the excavation sites in Susa.

While Jane Dieulafoy chooses to wear men's clothing out of a desire to "save time" and a lack of interest in "the foolishness of feminine ablutions," Summer cautions her readers against doing the same. "There is too much to lose, ladies," she admonishes; "we truly do not advise it." Indeed. For Dieulafoy challenges an entire system of gender in which women are defined by their willingness to take these pains with their appearance. By suggesting that there were other ways to be a woman, Dieulafoy challenged gender difference itself. And yet, there are no harsh words for her: "Should we not pardon a 'bizarrerie'—motivated with good cause—for an eminent woman?" Summer concludes.

Perhaps because Jane's appearance was so far from what her female peers could ever contemplate and her achievements so exotic, she was not perceived as a threat to the unwritten rules of French femininity. With her closely cropped hair and her masculine attire—her ability to pass, aside from her voice, as male—there was no fear that she would start a trend among fellow socialites. This was not a gradual step toward some sort of sartorial shift—a loosening of a corset, a shortening of a skirt. Dieulafoy's gender expression was seen as simply too extreme, too different, to pose a real threat within her upper bourgeois milieu.

In 1896, Dieulafoy was invited to speak at the French National Theater at the Odéon, the first woman to have the honor. The topic was Aeschylus's *Persians*. It was a tremendous privilege, and the audience drew sizable crowds.[6] The obstacle was not that women were prohibited from speaking in this venue; technically, it was that skirts were not allowed. There was a dress code for speakers and listeners alike involving a black suit and white cravat. It was not a problem for Dieulafoy, who was referred to alternately as *conférencier* and *conférencière* in accounts of this academic triumph.

With her lecture at the National Theater, Dieulafoy somehow managed to sidestep gender categories in one of the most conservative institutions in France. And yet, the seeming precedent did not draw concern. After all, the French public seemed to acknowledge, with a wink and a nod, that Jane Dieulafoy was not really a woman. Later, even when Dieulafoy advocated for the deployment of women in combat, she was not perceived as a threat, even when she pointed toward precisely the kinds of modern questions that would eventually threaten the gender binary as we know it: implicitly asking whether we should make these choices about who is prepared for combat, who can be a fireman or a president, based on individual capabilities rather than gender categories.

In an 1896 profile that appeared in the literary journal *Revue bleue*, journalist Frédéric Loliée attempted to describe the complex and contradictory valences that defined this public figure at the heart of Parisian high society. He, too, recognized that Jane Dieulafoy did not make sense:

> Former great traveler and one of the most valiant among those women who, whether feverish for discovery or seduced by the unknown, threw themselves, like men, into the turmoil of far off and perilous adventures . . . ; a complex personality, and a twofold character; a woman having long ago rejected her sex without denying it; virile in personality, masculine in dress as well as in thought; singular in habits; as independent-minded as is possible to be, and nevertheless attached by her enduring faith to the pure and

> simple principles of eternal morality; very unique, certainly, to the point of seeming "eccentric" . . . dear to her friends; criticized, sought after; subject to the conflicting judgments of those who know her and those who do not; Madame Jane Dieulafoy, the explorer of Susa, author of *Parysatis* and *Brother Pelagius*, the emancipated socialite under the black suit, is such a complex and original figure that she would attract the eye of the painter.[7]

Introducing Dieulafoy at the start of a three-page essay through this seemingly endless list of adjectival phrases (abbreviated here), Loliée articulates the challenge of describing her accurately, for each attribute seems to throw into question the one that follows or the one that precedes. Part of the reason that Loliée struggles—albeit with great eloquence—to find the terms to describe Dieulafoy is that such terms did not exist. Despite the fact that she embraced her identity as a (married) woman, it seems to have been clear to many who knew her that Dieulafoy's gender could not be fully described (or circumscribed). Like Mary Summer, Loliée notes with relief that Dieulafoy's female peers had ignored her affront to the female wardrobe.Dieulafoy's gender expression was not one with which other women seemed to identify, to his relief ("What would happen, good Lord!"). Even among pants-wearing women, on the other hand, she stood apart as something different.[8] And yet, Loliée's portrait is surprisingly sensitive. He describes Dieulafoy as a woman who had long ago "rejected her sex without disavowing it."

Though widely acknowledged, Dieulafoy's difference was difficult to summarize or label, placing her beyond nineteenth-century categories. Perhaps she managed to live her unconventional lifestyle without social repercussions precisely because transgender identity had not yet been named as something to be feared or contained. This absence of vocabulary may have forced Loliée to see past her gender expression while rendering Jane Dieulafoy clearly nonetheless:

> Let's appreciate, then, her work and literary oeuvre as they merit it; let's give full credit to the qualities of energy, initiative and imagination that she has deployed as explorer and woman of letters in turn; as for the rest, let's simply imagine that if she were other, she would not be herself, distinct from every other woman. She would not be Jane Dieulafoy. (690)

FIGURE 35. Jane Dieulafoy by Paul Dornac, 1893.
Source: Bibliothèque Marguerite Durand.

FIGURE 36. Jane Dieulafoy by Paul Dornac, 1893.
Source: Bibliothèque Marguerite Durand.

With her insistent refusals of available paradigms and her determined embrace of a style all her own, Jane Dieulafoy carved out her own space in fin-de-siècle France, right in the middle of one of the most conservative and traditional milieus. She inhabited that space with pleasure. The sense of comfort, confidence, and ease described in the verbal portraits of her contemporaries is reflected in the many photographs that remain. A sparkle leaps from her eyes, and her lips curl upwards in these posed photos, long before smiling was what you did in front of the camera. There can be no doubt that she liked having her picture taken—perhaps because the photograph allowed welcome visual evidence of the alignment of outside with inside.

In images taken in the 1890s by Paul Marsan Dornac, an eminent portrait photographer who captured many nineteenth-century intellectuals with his camera, one is reminded of the pictures of Dieulafoy against the lean-to in Persia and the pleasant certainty that developed during those travels. In Dornac's photos Dieulafoy sits at her desk, her finely tailored suit, accessorized with waistcoat and cravat, on full display. A somber shot depicting her with her arm leaning on the desk, legs crossed, aligns her with the other intellectual men at work from Dornac's album.[9] This is Dieulafoy in her new element, and the photograph offers yet another contradiction to the feminist theories that she espoused (figure 35). Is this really a person, you might ask, who wanted to be known as female? Like so many others, this photograph offers evidence of a confident, comfortable embrace of masculinity and its accoutrements.

In another frame, though, her chair is placed further from the desk, and she leans on her elbow, her body stretched out to meet the tabletop in a more geometrical version of the odalisque with which this story began (figure 36). The wider lens gives us a sense of the body in movement, and one can almost imagine the melodic voice—so often described—that would have accompanied it. Neither a man at his desk nor a woman displaying her body, she is something in between, both and neither. With the camera panned out to take in the whole room—a luxurious chamber of nineteenth-century bric-a-brac—Dieulafoy relaxes in the aesthetic multiplicity of this decor. Amidst the excessive ornamentation, she is simple, understated, and fully herself.

PART 2

RACHILDE: "TO BE STRANGE OR NOTHING AT ALL"

7 BECOMING RACHILDE

AT THE AGE OF SIXTEEN, the brooding adolescent known as Marguerite Eymery gathered her family members around the dining-room table to hold a séance. She conducted the experiment just as her grandparents had taught her. They were Spiritists, and like a surprising number of intellectuals of their generation, they believed there was life in other dimensions.[1] On the night in question, Marguerite tapped the table with her index finger and asked, "Dear spirit, are you there?" Suddenly, someone else seemed to speak through her: a Swedish count from the seventeenth century. His name was Rachilde, and he was an able storyteller. The tales came out vividly and naturally. Marguerite's mother, Gabrielle, was enraptured. She kept her daughter in her own bed that night and asked that the nobleman's spirit return the following evening. Meanwhile, she recorded in her diary everything that had transpired.

The adolescent confessed not too long after that the séance had been orchestrated by her preceptors—the abbots Raoul and Granger from the local parish, who were charged with her religious education. They had hoped that the young person's ruse would shock the family back into Catholic submission and that witnessing their daughter's attempts to channel the dead would make them see the error of their ways. They had underestimated the adolescent, however. And it was not exactly a ruse. The voice that emerged, through which Marguerite would go on to speak and write for the rest of her life—assuming the name Rachilde like a second skin—was very much her own. The writer André David would describe his first visit with his future mentor in terms that echo the story of the séance: as a young journalist, he sat down with the older writer, and a mind unexpectedly opened before him, "unguarded, like the doors of a lock-box from which invaluable treasures came flowing out."[2]

The séance, then, was not a performance but rather Rachilde's way of revealing herself more fully; it was also a means of liberation. "This is the story," she noted to her friend Homem-Christo, "that I allowed myself at my parents' house, in order to acquire the literary freedom that they didn't want to give me, and to get my parents used to a way of speaking that they would never have permitted without a skillful introduction."[3] She wanted her parents to become accustomed to this different voice, which could speak more boldly than a proper young woman. She had "emancipated herself," she later wrote, "through the means of my imagination."[4]

But when Rachilde confessed to her family about a year later, no one believed her. Her grandparents declared her possessed against her will by a "bad spirit."[5] When she told a family friend, Camille Flammarion, the truth about her supposed psychic powers, the famed astronomer, a Spiritist himself, denied her claims. "How can you be sure," he asked, "that this *Rachilde*, whom you think you have invented, does not actually exist very much outside of you?"[6] Even more troubling, when Rachilde published her first novel, *Mr. Novelty*, four years later, her mother warned the editor that her daughter was not its author. She still believed it was the work of the departed soul who had a habit of speaking through her.[7]

The séance was one of many moments in Rachilde's life in which she tried to make her difference visible. She tried to normalize, in Michael Finn's words, "a gender inbetweenness that the writer and many of her heroines [would] henceforth claim," by invoking the language of spirits embraced by her family.[8] Like so many instances of self-revelation, however, it was never quite understood. For the rest of her life, Rachilde would make her case in fiction and in essays, letters, and other published works. But unlike Dieulafoy's stories, her work had no moral frame or historical context through which to ascribe greater meaning to this feeling of difference. If Dieulafoy was focused on the *why* rather than the *what* of her gender, Rachilde was the opposite. She recognized her difference as a fact. But she always worked to give shape to that difference in her writing, trying to translate the precise nature of her gender variance into words and invoking the various discourses of her time to do so. Spiritism was but one of them.

Of the three subjects of this book, contemporary scholars have spilled the most ink on Rachilde, as her works grapple explicitly with prescient questions surrounding gender and sexuality. In the past two decades, several comprehensive biographies and dozens of scholarly articles have traced her life and writing. In most accounts, the prevailing narrative is one of audaciousness and willful subversion—Rachilde as a savvy self-promoter who cultivated shocking behavior in the interest of publicity and fortune. In the most recent of these biographies, however, Finn identifies a "bitter personal conflict" at the heart of Rachilde's work.[9] It's that human side of Rachilde that I wish to recover here, in bringing together the threads of her gender story. What was the nature of that conflict, and what questions might she have been trying to answer through her subversive acts and bold literary ventures?

ORIGINS

Influenced by naturalists such as Emile Zola, who was himself influenced by the new Darwinian science, Rachilde believed in heredity: your parents' traits determined your own. Over her lifetime, she painted many different images of her parents, Joseph Eymery and Gabrielle Feytaud. In Rachilde's most frequent version of the story, her father was the illegitimate son of the Marquis d'Ormoy and a certain Mademoiselle de Lidonne; Joseph's lack of a title masked this true nobility and the romantic backstory.[10] In 1993, a diligent researcher from Rachilde's hometown uncovered the truth. Only the illegitimacy was accurate: Joseph was the son of a family servant, Jeanne Eymery, who worked for a Madame Lidonne. Jeanne had given him up at birth, reclaiming him at the age of seventeen.[11] For her part, Gabrielle Feytaud was a talented musician from an aristocratic family; she had been presented at the court of Napoléon III. But she had fallen for Joseph, a handsome military man and former captain of an African regiment, and given up her cosmopolitan dreams. Once married, Joseph and Gabrielle settled in the remote Périgord region in southern France, now known as the Dordogne, where they both had roots. In February 1860, Gabrielle gave birth to a baby girl who was born with one leg shorter than the other and whom they named Marguerite.

Rather than sending their daughter to a convent, where most girls would have been educated, as Jane Dieulafoy was, her parents hired a tutor and sent her to the local priests, the abbots who, she claimed, orchestrated her séance. Private instruction made Rachilde even more isolated than she was already, as an only child in a rural environment. When she was not studying, she spent most of her days roaming around her family's enormous property in the swampy countryside. When the weather was warm, Rachilde amused herself with the many creatures that populated her wooded estate: her family's pack of hounds, the rats who had made a nest in the walls of her room, mice, garter snakes, the neighborhood owl. With them, the animal-lover always claimed, she got along better than with her fellow humans. "I never liked children because I like animals with an almost religious fervor," Rachilde wrote to Homem-Christo, years later. "Not having a brother or sister, I peopled the glacial solitude of my early years . . . with an incalculable number of adoptions of little siblings who kept me warm, physically and spiritually."[12] All the same, she was lonely and friendless. By the time she was in her teens, she cast an awkward figure: "very pale with no flush on her cheeks, eyes too big for her still childish face and a head weighed down under a dark crown of hair."[13] Neighbors assumed that the eccentric, solitary child was touched with madness.

By the time Rachilde was an adolescent, Gabrielle had come to regret her decision to marry Joseph and renounce a promising future. She never quite recovered from Joseph's final military call-up during the Franco-Prussian War. Her relief at Joseph's return was accompanied by revulsion and regret. Joseph was psychologically scarred by the bruising defeat of the war, and the couple began to fight with increasing intensity, with Joseph prone to raging explosions of temper, of which their daughter was often an observer and sometimes a victim. Rachilde wrote much later of how, within this "tiger's den" of her family, she "was witness to nameless horrors, which I thought were normal. . . . I heard my mother's cries reverberate from one hill to the other, and there was nothing to do except accept the blows for her."[14]

FIGURE 37. Rachilde as a young child.

Source: Médiathèque Pierre Fanlac, Périgueux. Reprinted with permission.

Gabrielle's parents lived close by. Urbain Feytaud, a former journalist and sometime writer himself (a *plumitif*, or pen-pusher, as Joseph called him disparagingly), had shared with his granddaughter the key to his library, which she claimed held over two thousand volumes (three hundred is a more accurate estimate).[15] Unlike the history books or the catechisms that her tutors had tried to persuade her to study, these books provided Rachilde's imagination with a welcome playground. At the age of fifteen, she found Voltaire, and then the Marquis de Sade, whose deep influence would be perceived in her later writings. In 1897 she would publish *The Marquise de Sade*, one of several novels that drew upon her childhood memories and in which desire and anger intersect explosively.

Rachilde often mentioned her father's disappointment that she had not been born a boy and stated that he had raised her as a boy, nonetheless. "Having been born a girl by accident of nature—they built my character by having me face all the dangers that one generally seeks to avoid for weak beings," Rachilde wrote in her memoir. "I was raised as a boy," she explained, and she had tried her best to be the boy that her father had wanted. She trained her mind in order to give him the sense that she had "a man's head."[16] "Did I already say that I had been raised as a boy," she asks, a few chapters later, "since I was only a girl, a very weak one, physically, but with a certain strength of spirit?"[17] But while Rachilde's father introduced her to many skills that girls her age would never know, the notion that she was raised as a boy leaves out part of the story. For as much as she was allowed to explore, taught to fence, shoot, and ride horseback, Rachilde was also subject to the expectations of nineteenth-century femininity. "A proper young [woman] should not drink wine, or eat red meat," she learned from her mother and grandmother. "If she has a cold, she should learn to blow her nose without noise or sneezing in her handkerchief. She should always stand up straight and never choose an armchair or a sofa for sitting on. She should wait until she is asked a question before giving her opinion and abstain from asking questions." The list went on and on: "At the table, she should never ask for anything. She should avoid looking at men above their shoes. She should laugh with discretion, never loudly, and avoid raising her voice in situations where people are arguing in front of her, even if she thinks she should come to someone's defense."[18]

The women in Rachilde's early life did their best to remind her of the feminine role that she was meant to assume. They did not want her to write, which she described doing in secret, with only the light of the moon to illuminate her carefully hidden pages. "A young woman must go to bed at nine o'clock and sleep through the night," she had been told. "She should keep her dreams to herself."[19] What's more, writing was no way for a young woman to pass her time: "When a child of fifteen embroiders canvas or linens, there is nothing more natural," Rachilde was made to understand, "but . . . on paper, that's a lot less solid, even less useful, and practically inconvenient."[20]

With her mother teaching her to be a young lady and her father mourning his misfortune in not having a boy, Rachilde spent her childhood between genders. And while being raised this way allowed her to experiment with masculinity, she never seemed to want to be a boy permanently. Rather, she often suggested that neither gender was quite the right fit. Rachilde's mother would compare her to the *loup-garou*, the werewolf whose legend shadowed the region. "Do what you want, Marguerite," she would tell her, as she busied her own restless hands with embroidery or the piano. "You will never escape from the curse that weighs on us. You are the last of the werewolves and you will bring Bad Luck to all those who come near."[21] Rachilde came to see herself as resembling that creature: an abnormal being, neither one thing nor the other, perhaps a wild animal.[22] This was one way of not having to choose sides. This very doubleness would define her, both in person and in writing, because gender presented itself as a question for which it seemed impossible to formulate a definitive answer.

The answers would shift over time. But the young Rachilde did not seem too troubled by the indeterminacy. There were directives to dress one way or another, to be a boy for her father and a girl for her mother and grandmother; these she approached "always with the same quiet indifference."[23] Gender fluidity appears to have been a place of comfort; it was normal to her, even if it seemed to trouble others.

ONE IS NOT BORN A WOMAN

Moving between genders was also preferable to the only alternative: becoming a woman. Much to her shock and surprise, Rachilde's father had tried to steer her onto that path—a more stable one that would put an end to the family's domestic turmoil. When she was fifteen years old, Joseph arranged her marriage. With Rachilde out of the house, he believed that he and Gabrielle, who were increasingly in conflict, would finally go their separate ways in peace; Rachilde would be "emancipated" in the only way possible for a woman. That is the term he used, suggesting both a change in legal status and the chance for a new freedom.[24] Joseph chose an older officer with few prospects, Jacques de la Hullière, thirty-five years old, a "tall, fat, leggy fellow."[25]

As the story goes, on the eve of the betrothal, when Hullière had been invited to a dinner at which the engagement would become official, Gabrielle threw her daughter's beloved collection of pets into the pond outside their home.[26] Later, when Rachilde realized that her mother had been slowly slipping into mental illness—and that the rest of her family knew this already—the gesture made sense. But at the time, she felt betrayed by both of her parents. She jumped in after the animals, in what she would later describe as a suicide attempt. Jacques de la Hullière was not the last of her suitors: after him came others, whom she also summarily rejected.[27]

Like many girls, Rachilde had been free to enjoy the privileges of gender ambiguity until adolescence, not realizing that this freedom would have to end so that she might assume her place in the social order. Rachilde told the story of her betrothal repeatedly in novels, nonfiction, and personal correspondence—reminders each of the extent to which this episode redirected her life and identity.[28]

But it wasn't the only version of her life that she shared. In a letter to the poet Robert de Souza, Rachilde skipped over the failed betrothal. In this alternate telling, her childhood, which was marked by "sadism and brutality," culminated in an episode in which she was goaded by her despairing mother to grab her riding whip and lash her father in front of the stable hands. "From this day forward," wrote Rachilde, "my father found in me certain qualities . . . and an extraordinary beauty . . . and so on and so forth." The whipping marked a turning point of sorts, she tells de Souza, after which, in order to cope (with what, exactly?), Rachilde forced herself to "pray to God and study the great authors." This worked until around age nineteen. At that point, "fearing males," she fell in love with an effeminate peasant who wore gold bangles and was, she claimed, the inspiration for *Monsieur Vénus*, the gender-bending *succès de scandale* that would launch her literary career in 1884.

In this, the fullest account of the violence that defined Rachilde's upbringing—are we supposed to intuit sexual violence as well, or at least a crossing of paternal boundaries? How else to explain the allusive logic, from a changed relationship with her father to an explanation of her own erotic investments? In Rachilde's novels, rape would be a common theme, and male authority figures are especially prone to sexual aggression.[29] Was the betrothal, which was acknowledged to be a means of shielding the child from her brutal home life, protecting her instead from a more specific paternal threat that erupted at the moment she ran to her mother's defense and became a different kind of target? If this was true, would it be surprising that Rachilde rejected the notion of substituting for such a father a husband much older than she was?

Rachilde often told how, after her engagement, she was haunted by a recurring nightmare: a drowned man, emerging from the pond outside her window, told her not to speak.[30] In some ways, the symbolism of this nightmare was self-evident: marriage meant the silencing of her voice, perhaps just as it was coming into its own. Despite her father's apparent willingness to see her in a role other than as his daughter, the path toward her future was that of conventional femininity and domesticity, one in which she would not have a say—either to choose the suitor or to direct the timing.

But what if that figure of the drowning man was not a phantom male aggressor compelling her to silence, as most scholars have assumed? What if it was a projection of her own muffled voice, imagined as male?[31] What if the drowned man was Rachilde herself? The possibility of marriage in this scenario would have represented a threat not just to her future but to her very identity. She had jumped into the pond, after all.

It was not long after the failed betrothal that the sixteen-year-old held her séance. By renaming herself, she took the first step toward carving out a space for her difference from others, "through the means of imagination," as she put it. The new sobriquet allowed for more than a neat transition from female to male—it allowed for fluidity and indeterminacy: a way to escape the fixed nature of nineteenth-century gender but also a way to *not* entirely renounce her female identity. That the name stuck so definitively suggests that she was at ease outside of binary notions of gender and that becoming

Rachilde solved a fundamental problem of self-designation. The name placed its author in her own ambiguously gendered category: suggestive, mysterious, and indeterminate. It declared her difference and made it visible, without resolving or explaining it.

Other efforts at self-emancipation followed, as the adolescent made her way toward becoming Rachilde for good. Eventually, the answer to the question of gender was simply "Rachilde." Allowed to ride to the regional capital at Périgueux, she found her way to the newspaper *The Echo of the Dordogne* and began offering copy. When she would show up at the newspaper offices in person, the editor was kind and discreet, if a bit surprised by the stories and articles she delivered to him, "which revealed no age and no sex." He took her seriously. "I owe that man the best literary advice I ever received," she noted in *When I Was Young*. What's more, he seemed to acknowledge and perhaps even accept her double being. When she was dressed *en homme*, he passed along messages to bring back to "Mademoiselle." When she was dressed *en femme*, he offered messages for "her brother."[32]

Rachilde's first years as a writer were defined by this fluidity. She writes of participating in military training with her father at the age of nineteen, reporting on the exercise as a war correspondent for the *Echo*. "Is that your son?" asked the general. Upon hearing the question, remembers Rachilde, "my father was overcome with joy . . . and terrible pain," while Rachilde herself trembled, suddenly aware that she was no longer "at the agricultural fair, in white muslin and a blue belt." Rather, she wore the same clothes as her father. She could not fail to note the meagerness of her disguise: her cumbersome hair hidden behind a feathered Tyrolean fedora (the kind she often wore in her early days in Paris), and her beautiful eyes, soon to be famous and so often mentioned in later portraits, already "too much, too fringed with lashes."[33] Despite the awkwardness—indeed, the apparent anguish of this moment—it is a story of acceptance, much like the encounters with her editor. Rachilde's father pauses, then speaks: "Allow me to introduce you to my daughter, who is a war correspondent."[34] The exercise continues, and the episode concludes when the general invites Rachilde to dine with the regiment. Exhausted, Rachilde wants nothing more than to sneak into bed, but she could not disappoint her father. Her grandmother, on the other hand, is perturbed by the whole adventure and insists that she return to feminine clothing. "Marguerite, it's a shame for a proper young woman to go to dinner with soldiers in a carnival costume," she scolds.[35] Rachilde complies, because, as she explains, "I am, above all, an actress of private life, a double being who is used to leaving one role for another." Those roles were, of course, male and female.[36]

There is little angst in these revelations but rather a sense of distance, that same "quiet indifference" noted earlier.[37] It is not simply the distance of time, for there are other stories in these recollections that are emotionally resonant: the story of Rachilde's realization that her mother has gone mad—and that everyone seems to know it but her—is one of pain and dejection. But while Rachilde's family ties are complex and often painful to recount, her gendered past is described in a more matter-of-a-fact tone. She describes her childhood negotiation of gender as a set of categories that held little meaning for her, even while they sometimes blocked the way for life's decisions.

Rachilde learned this lesson the hard way with her idol, Victor Hugo—a source of both affirmation and disappointment. In the wake of her broken engagement, she wrote him a letter.It seems that she looked to the aging author as a paternal figure who would replace her own, deeply flawed father. Instead of busying herself with chores that were meant "to make her forget her personal dreams," Rachilde asked Hugo whether he thought she had a future as a writer.[38] Writing offered a path forward, despite (or perhaps because of) her family's resistance. In her letter to Hugo, Rachilde included a copy of an essay titled "First Love." "Master," she wrote, "I am seventeen years old, and you like children. I have read you and I have tried out my voice. Listen to one of my efforts; I would be so happy and proud if you were to tell me, like my mother, 'Continue.'"[39] In fact, this is not what her mother had said—at least, it is contradicted by Rachilde's later recollections. Both parents disapproved of her literary propensities, her father despising the *plumitifs*, her mother disapproving of writing as an inferior art form, unlike music, especially for girls: "You are the opposite of an artist," she reportedly admonished Rachilde, "and if you can read and write, that's really too bad . . . ; those are narcissistic distractions."[40]

Rachilde later recounted how for weeks she awaited Hugo's response, meeting the postman at the top of the hill and sorting through the pile of letters each day. At last, an envelope arrived, and the master seemed to heed

her call with three simple words: "Thanks, congratulations, courage."[41] She would keep this letter until the end of her life.[42]

During this period, Gabrielle started bringing her daughter to Paris a few times a year. Through her cousin Marie de Saverny, she was able to connect Rachilde with an emerging literary world. Saverny was a reminder of the elegant, sophisticated existence that Gabrielle had given up in marrying Joseph but to which she was now contemplating a return, even if merely on the coattails of her daughter. While Gabrielle was ambivalent about her daughter's chosen path, she was also ambitious, and she was tempted by the possibilities of celebrity for Marguerite and a different life for herself.

In 1878, Saverny arranged for Rachilde to meet with the writers Catulle Mendès and Villiers de l'Isle-Adam. Mendès was already known for his erotic poems, though he had not yet written his most sensational novels, full of drug-induced orgies, same-sex desire, and sadistic encounters; the popular Villiers de l'Isle Adam had not yet published his most famous novel, *The Future Eve*. In this model of late nineteenth-century science fiction and misogynistic creativity, a fictional Thomas Edison invents a female automaton to replace a woman too homely to satisfy him, only to subject his female prototype to humiliating scrutiny.

The two writers promised to introduce Rachilde to her idol, Victor Hugo himself. When you meet him, they warned, you must go down on your knees and kiss his hand. Rachilde, who was still very young, believed them. Unsure how to impress the man, she showed up in her finest dress of pink tarlatan tulle, overlaid with white lace and hidden under a travel coat. Retrospectively, it is challenging to conjure this image of a hyperfeminine Rachilde, even though early photographs show her in women's clothing (figure 38). Arriving in the presence of her idol, she opened her coat to reveal how she had dressed for him and fell prostrate on the floor as she had been instructed by Mendès and Villiers. A pregnant silence ensued; then Hugo scooped her up off the floor "as one would a doll," roaring with laughter alongside the co-conspirators.[43] Perhaps Rachilde was aware, as she retold this story, how much it resonated with Villiers's own narrative of women dressed up to fulfill men's ideals.

< **FIGURE 38.** Rachilde in her early twenties.
Source: Médiathèque Pierre Fanlac, Périgueux. Reprinted with permission.

This humiliation apparently represented another turning point for Rachilde, as the episode took on a central role in the narrative that she spun about her literary origins. The stories of her letter to Hugo and of their meeting make up the introduction to *When I Was Young*: intertwined with the details about her parents and her childhood, Rachilde tells of this formative relationship with the famous author. Following the humiliating encounter, she writes, "I was confused, disappointed, enchanted, and very frightened all at once."[44] As she had no handkerchief, she was forced to dry her tear-filled eyes with the expensive lace of her skirt. She may also have been forced to realize that she was truly on her own, and that she would be writing not for Hugo's approval but for her own survival in a world that had no interest in her feelings. There would be a lot more confusion, disappointment, enchantment, and fear. Lacy skirts would be of no help at all.

8 BORN OF SCANDAL

RACHILDE MOVED TO PARIS IN 1881, having reached the age of legal majority. By 1884, she had yet to produce a new novel. What's more, the publication of her first book, *Mr. Novelty*, had earned her just two hundred and fifty francs and made only the barest impression. She pieced together an income by placing stories and reviews and taking up various freelance writing assignments, including a regular gig at the fashion magazine *L'Ecole des Femmes*, which was edited by Marie de Saverny. The work was unreliable and unsatisfying, with no end to the frustration in sight. Rachilde felt increasingly desperate for success—eager to establish her career and her voice, as well as to be taken seriously as a writer. She was also hoping to free herself from her mother, who had accompanied her to Paris. Gabrielle's erratic presence was a source of constant anxiety; years later, she would be institutionalized in the infamous Charenton asylum. Finally, Rachilde turned to the Belgian publishing house Brancart, knowing that they were willing to release any material that verged on the pornographic. She offered them *Monsieur Vénus*, a work she would later claim to have written in a two-week-long trance.

Billed as a "materialist novel"—shorthand for having erotic content—the volume was banned just days after its release, and its author was fined and sentenced to prison.[1] Rachilde avoided serving time by remaining in Paris. Instead, she became a celebrity as the untamed young woman whose perversity of imagination knew no bounds. She would go on to publish dozens more novels, stories, and plays over the next many decades. Gone were the worries about finding a willing publisher. Each work was different, yet all shared the theme of an unnamed form of sexual deviance, whose precise nature was often tinged with mystery. Even so, *Monsieur Vénus* was the publication that endured.

The story of the novel *Monsieur Vénus* is not just a story of unexpected success, however. Rather, it is the story of a writer and her creation stumbling together onto the literary scene, mirroring and refracting each other in unintended ways. The *succès de scandale* is the most memorable aspect of the book's appearance: Rachilde as the wild child, the mysterious celebrity writer, the savvy self-promoter. The truth, however, was more complex. While *Monsieur Vénus* launched her career as a writer, it unexpectedly pushed Rachilde's deepest personal struggles into the spotlight.

"BIZARRE TO THE POINT OF MADNESS"

Monsieur Vénus offered a wild ride of a plot. No one had ever read anything quite like it before. The novel follows the rebellious orphan Raoule de Vénérande, who is raised by her pious aunt Ermengarde (renamed Elisabeth in the 1889 French edition) on a lavish estate in Paris. Raoule prefers to dress in men's clothes and is so blatant about her gender-crossing that even the devout Ermengarde refers to her as "my nephew." Like her author, she chooses fencing over the activities of her female peers and keeps a collection of weapons in her bedroom. She alternates between gender pronouns, identifying with masculinity while also sometimes speaking as a woman to denounce the behavior of men. "I represent the elite of the women of our time," she tells her puzzled friend and would-be suitor, the Baron de Raittolbe, "sent by my sisters to declare that we want the impossible, because you love us so poorly."[2]

"Marry her!" advises a doctor, warning her aunt that if she does not, Raoule will be hospitalized for hysteria. But Raoule does not marry, nor is she hospitalized. The novel picks up ten years later, when Raoule falls for an effete florist named Jacques Silvert, who enjoys painting landscapes in his spare time while lounging about in ladies' nightgowns. Raoule eventually cuts her hair short and marries the feminine Jacques, as the groom to his bride. All of this is much to the chagrin not only of Aunt Ermengarde but of

Raittolbe, who is enamored of Raoule and maddened by her choices, especially her alternation between genders. The baron also finds himself curiously attracted to the effeminate Jacques, at the same time as he throws himself into the arms of Jacques's sister Marie, a prostitute. Eventually, Raoule jealously orchestrates a duel in which Jacques is killed, though she preserves his body. The novel closes with Raoule dressed alternately in male and female attire, making love to a wax effigy embellished with the hair, teeth, and nails that she has meticulously plucked from Jacques's corpse.

To say the novel caused an uproar would be an understatement. "I've just read a book—bizarre to the point of madness," declared the Parisian journalist Henry Fouquier in September of 1884.[3] Writing under the name Colombine in the popular newspaper *Le Gil Blas*, the normally voluble columnist seemed to struggle to describe the plot: "The story is that of a woman who marries—and by a terrifying perversion of everything—makes of her husband a woman and of herself a man," he recounted incredulously. "That's what a young woman of twenty has invented, dreamed up." In this early review, Fouquier reacted just as many others would in the months and years to come, marveling at Rachilde's youth and assimilating the author of fiction with the fictions that she created. Either she had an imagination like no other, he reflected, or she must herself be depraved, if not mentally ill. It was time for literature to distance itself from such perverse writings, he urged. As a result, he made of the novel something at once unfathomable and tantalizing to the paper's considerable readership, which numbered around two hundred thousand in the 1880s. It's no small irony that Rachilde—the writer as *succès de scandale*—was launched at least in part thanks to Fouquier.

With her daring plot, Rachilde had taken up the subversive idiom of the Decadent literary movement. During the same year in which Joris-Karl Huysmans published the novel *Against Nature* (*A rebours*), Rachilde shared the spirit of Huysmans's title and the overriding Decadent desire to shock by describing new experiences, sensations, and feelings. But the interest of her novel wasn't just that it was a bold story written by a woman who was presumably too young to know of such things. Rather, *Monsieur Vénus* captured everyone's attention because, while it echoed the Decadent zeitgeist of the day, it also defied comprehension. If its heroine and author suffered from shared perversions or even the same disease, as so many agreed, what exactly was the nature of this particular neurosis? What was Raoule de Vénérande all about, and what, by extension, was Rachilde? In this era, the lines between science and fiction were often blurred concerning the topic of women's bodies, and doctors and writers frequently borrowed from one another. Rachilde's novel promised to make some sort of contribution to the field of literary medicine, but its precise contours were anything but clear.

In the novel, Rachilde's protagonist was diagnosed with hysteria, a disease that had captured the French imagination and with which Flaubert had—a bit more indirectly—diagnosed his own Emma Bovary decades earlier.[4] By the 1880s, hysteria was such a common diagnosis for French women that it was known as *la maladie du siècle*—the disease of the century. Jean-Martin Charcot, the most prominent hysteria doctor, would regularly conduct public lessons at the Salpêtrière Hospital before an audience of medical doctors, writers, sociologists, and politicians, demonstrating his techniques of hypnosis on female patients, who were prone to convulsions and uncontrolled utterances. For a time in nineteenth-century Paris, any symptom a woman presented that was not readily categorizable became the basis of a hysteria diagnosis. And hysteria was not just the disease of the century but the disease of femininity: the sign either of an excess of its attributes or a failure to perform its obligations. The simplest cure was marriage, not least because of the procreative sex that went along with it—ensuring that the female body would be righted upon its natural course.

Rachilde evoked these widely recognized associations in her novel, directly referencing the Salpêtrière as the place where Raoule was likely to end up and placing her protagonist in some of the very poses that Charcot catalogued in his lessons. When Raoule gives in to a nervous fit, "her head thrown back, her breasts heaving, her arms clasped," she is actually reproducing "the bowed back body position Charcot made famous when he standardized the hysterical attack," as Janet Beizer has noted.[5] Rachilde's references to hysteria may also have been strategic: once Raoule was diagnosed with hysteria, she was allowed to behave in any way she pleased, under cover of the broadly defined diagnosis.

Rachilde's *Monsieur Vénus* was perceived as a reversal of nineteenth-century gender hierarchies—and a frightening attack on masculinity. "She gropes and dissects the male," wrote the journalist known as Montapic, who also published under the name Jean-Louis Dubut de Laforest.[6] Dubut was a writer of pseudoscientific popular novels that often quoted directly from medical treatises in describing the traits of perverse female characters; it seems that he could hardly endure the proverbial taste of his own medicine that he found in Rachilde's harsh depictions. His comments, like those of Fouquier, reveal a fear that Rachilde had access to an aspect of femininity beyond his scientific reach. This anxiety was overtly present in the work of many male writers who sought to reveal the mysteries of female sexuality in their works. In a passage from *Nana*, Emile Zola's 1880 novel about a high-class courtesan, the author has his protagonist pick up a realist novel much like the one in which she is featured. Nana scoffs at the book, remarking, "As if one could tell all!" With these words, the character essentially doubts her own author, suggesting that women would always know things that the male novelist could not.

Dubut, like Zola, was a writer who fancied himself a kind of doctor-scientist—of literature. He went so far as to beg Rachilde to provide the remaining answers: "In order to really judge, in order to determine as well as possible the more than bizarre make-up of Mademoiselle Rachilde, it would be necessary for her to write her own portrait, mind and body."[7] She must not yet fully understand herself, Dubut reflected, or why her imagination had run so wild. Such a study would necessarily be "rich in curious discoveries." Rachilde must be some sort of medical mystery, he implied, the nature of which only *she* could fully illuminate.

Most readers conflated the author with her protagonist: "I don't know where she found the framework for her book," wrote Louis Villatte in his review for *Le Décadent*, "but the basis of this story cannot be pure imagination. There is something true in this kind of sexual aberration."[8] Fouquier, for his part, was more blunt: "The heroine can only be the author herself." This way of understanding Rachilde reassured readers that the writer was not some sort of nefarious genius seeking to dismantle social structures. Rather, she was victim of a disease that clearly afflicted the society that had produced her. Rachilde was both a cautionary tale and a force to be contained.

But even while she was compared to her fictional creation, Rachilde was considered a young innocent who could not possibly know of the things that she recounted. According to Dubut, the novel emerged from "her hallucinations, which were at once hysterical and passive." He did his best to theorize how she could be this way: "Today she is nothing more than a virgin, the impure virgin of the book, of the pornographic novel, playing frenetically with vice, just as an impatient child who was eager to know everything would play with a doll that seemed alive to her." The childlike author, according to this logic, had dreamed up these "very original fantasies" without meaning to, "without looking for them, as she was still in the age of short dresses."[9]

All of these interpretations posited that Rachilde was not a serious writer, thereby reflecting a certain anxiety about female intellect during the second half of the nineteenth century, a period in which France feared that social progress and women's increasing visibility in the public sphere would result in a shrinking population. A woman's role, the thinking went, was to produce healthy children, not books, and certainly not scandalous ones! Again, the intellectual *bas bleus* were depicted as a social scourge, wreaking havoc on husbands and families, though ironically, in this context, a female hysteric—subject to the control of a male doctor—seemed less threatening than a female author.

Even with these points of reference, the heart of the controversy around *Monsieur Vénus* was its depiction of something fundamentally unfamiliar. Rachilde had created a protagonist who did not fit into known categories of behavior. It was unclear, to many, what exactly she meant to describe. Others feared that she had "invented a new vice." This strangeness was what seemed to most horrify Gisèle d'Estoc, a fellow writer and artist rumored to have had an affair with Rachilde that had gone sour, and indeed the only woman believed to have had a romantic relationship with her.[10] In 1887, d'Estoc published a treatise titled *The Publicity-Virgin*, in which she tore Rachilde apart, designating her as "Mademoiselle Raclife" and her novel as "Homme-Vénus"—both obvious clues to her polemic *à clef*. D'Estoc believed that Rachilde had purposely sought to create in the novel "an absolutely original depravity that would be unlike anything else—not like Lesbos, nor the disciples of Virgil."[11] It was an absurd idea, admonished d'Estoc, and the resulting novel was "so insane, that you can read the work from beginning to end, without understanding anything."

Rachilde was initially dismayed by these personal attacks. But she soon discovered the benefits of her new notoriety. With her star status, she mingled with a who's-who of nineteenth-century literary culture, many of whom were also just getting started. The poet Paul Verlaine, whose heart was famously broken by the haunting symbolist Arthur Rimbaud, marveled over Rachilde's writing to the illustrator Frédéric Cazals, a mutual friend who then introduced them. "My dear child," Verlaine wrote to Rachilde, "if you had invented a new vice, you would be a benefactor to all humanity."[12] When they met, Verlaine had just been evicted from his apartment by a skeptical landlord and was suffering from a leg injury. Rachilde promptly offered him her own place and stayed with her mother while he recovered and found new lodgings.

In late 1884, Rachilde met Maurice Barrès in the office of publisher Réné Brissy.[13] Barrès would gain fame for his trilogy *The Cult of the Self* in 1888 before immersing himself in far-right politics. He did not recognize Rachilde at first and was privately dismissive of the strange young woman who was making chit-chat with him while they waited for the editor to arrive. Looking over at the title of her new manuscript—*Silly Stories to Amuse Thinking Children*—he assumed that he was sharing the office with a children's book author or a teacher. But when Barrès noticed her name on the manuscript, he suddenly understood with whom he was speaking. He begged her forgiveness. "Did you really write this terrifying book . . . terrifying and so . . . delicious?" he said, referring to *Monsieur Vénus*. "It haunts me, that novel."[14]

Rachilde met the Decadent writer Jean Lorrain at the offices of *Le Gil Blas*, where she had been dropping off copy. Lorrain had recognized her as the author of *Monsieur Vénus*, and Rachilde had taken to Lorrain because his long, feminine eyelashes reminded her of her mother's.[15] Fast friends, he became both big brother and partner in crime. Lorrain introduced Rachilde to one of her idols, Barbey d'Aurevilly, godfather of Decadence and the author of the troubling short story collection *Les diaboliques*. In addition to his lurid, decadent tales, Barbey was most famous for his disdain of women writers. He despised the *bas bleus*, to whom he had directed a polemical treatise in 1878 and whom he saw as overtaking the literary marketplace and abandoning traditional female roles. For Barbey, the woman writer was but a variant of the prostitute, yet far more vile because "courtesans are in nature and the *bas bleu* is not!"[16] Like Fouquier and others, Barbey criticized women's writing as a product of the era's moral depravity, in which women had lost their way. But for him and so many of Rachilde's writer-friends, including such authors as Lorrain, whose works were characterized by misogynistic portraits of devouring, heartless women, Rachilde was hardly a *bas bleu*. She was in a category of her own.

Before entering Barbey's strange apartment with Lorrain, Rachilde had to promise not to comment on his makeup or artificially dyed jet-black hair. Clad in a red velvet bathrobe and surrounded by cats, the eccentric Barbey offered Rachilde his highest compliments for the novel that had troubled so many. He applauded her "extraordinary work."[17] In recounting this story, biographer André David recognized in it the same young girl who had "gotten down on her knees before Victor Hugo." But Rachilde was no longer a supplicant to the powerful older male writers she had idolized; she had rapidly become their peer. When she was later excluded from the most elite salons because of her scandalous reputation, Barbey, who had faced pornography charges himself, famously came to her defense.[18] During one of these events, a certain countess dismissed Rachilde as a pornographer. Barbey is said to have retorted: "A pornographer, perhaps, but quite a distinguished one!"[19]

RACHILDE, MAN OF LETTERS

Around the time of the publication of her novel, Rachilde took steps to change her look. She procured a pants permit from the Parisian prefecture of police, explaining that she needed to wear them in order to circulate as a writer. "I am unfortunately a woman of letters [the most common term for woman writer] and find myself called to perform the active vocation of reporter," she wrote in her application. "This is to earn my daily bread." She also described her need to dress as a man so that "people address my pen and not my person."[20] While she was initially rejected for lacking a medical reason—she was told that helping her journalism career was an insufficient one—she persisted. The permit was later granted, but there's reason to believe that by this point she was already wearing pants.

It was not the only thing she changed about her appearance. Rachilde also cut her hair, the "long, cumbersome" braids that she had never quite known what to do with (see figure 38). She stopped powdering her face. She dispensed

FIGURE 39. Pastel self-portrait of Rachilde, given to Jean Lorrain in 1887.
Source: Bibliothèque littéraire Jacques Doucet. Reprinted with permission.

with the lacy undergarments that she found frivolous, and she found bigger shoes. She learned to shake hands like a man and asked her male friends to call her "mon camarade"—my comrade, in the masculine.[21] She printed new calling cards that read "Rachilde, Homme de Lettres."

During this period, Rachilde became part of a group of writers and artists who were identified by a series of ironic names: the Hydropathes, Hirsutes, Zutistes (from the French expression "Zut!," or "Damn it!"), or its variant, the Jemenfoutistes (loosely translated as the "Idontgiveadamns"). Known for rejecting staid social norms, these young rebels would drink absinthe and wine and share their music and poetry at various coffeehouses and dance halls. The most famous of these was the Chat Noir, where Rachilde was frequently sighted during those years. According to some, she read aloud chapters of *Monsieur Vénus*.

With Lorrain and others, Rachilde enjoyed attending the various *bals* held around Paris during this time—dance parties in which, depending on the venue, costumes were welcome. It was at one of these parties that Rachilde met her future husband, Alfred Vallette, in 1885. He was immediately intrigued by her appearance, wondering whether she meant to imitate George Sand. "I have a secret fear of women writers," he flirted in one of his first missives. "I'm less afraid of you, since you've taken the pains of mentioning on your calling cards that *Rachilde* is a *man of letters*—taken to the extreme, most decidedly!"[22] Vallette would pursue her, on and off, for the next several years.

Rachilde often went to these parties with Lorrain, who sometimes dressed as a woman, and another friend, Oscar Méténier, both of whom were gay. On at least one occasion, Rachilde dressed as a marquise to Lorrain's marquis, playing with gender roles in this instance in her own kind of cross-dressing. Lorrain and Méténier delighted in the masculine look that Rachilde was still working to cultivate. In a letter to Laurent Tailhade, who was a member of this cohort, Méténier described "that adorable little boy whose name is Rachilde" and who was "just delicious dressed up as a man."[23] In her own reflections, Rachilde wrote of how, once she had cultivated her schoolboy look successfully, Lorrain warned her that he might appear to be compromising himself by going out with her.[24] It seems no greater compliment could have been offered. It makes sense that one of the only images of Rachilde from this period is a self-portrait that she sketched for Lorrain in 1887: she is in profile, her hair cut short (figure 39). With this offering, she acknowledged that Lorrain saw her the way she wanted to be seen.

9 A SYMBOL OF HER MIND

RACHILDE'S CLOSE FRIEND LORRAIN believed that *Monsieur Vénus* was "the symbol of Rachilde's mind." It's not hard to see why. While the novel is a work of fiction, its gender-nonconforming protagonist, who dressed in pants, cut off her hair, wore men's shoes, and referred to herself in the masculine, undoubtedly displayed some of the traits of its author. Rachilde readily and often admitted that her fictions were peopled with avatars of herself; in a telling turn of phrase, she called them "transvestites of her mind."[1] Rachilde left more clues of her deep connection to the story as she got older, starting with the letter to Robert de Souza in which she claimed that the inspiration for the novel came from a teenage encounter with an effeminate young man working in her neighborhood.[2] There is no way to verify whether there was a young man in the village of Le Cros at around this time who would fit the description, and the origin stories around the novel would become legion.[3] But what is most significant about the letter is Rachilde's desire, as time went on, to identify a source for the novel in her own childhood. In other words, Rachilde wanted de Souza to know that *Monsieur Vénus* was about her. She provided further autobiographical evidence in the 1902 short story "The Wolf Catcher's Daughter," published in the *Mercure de France*, the journal she edited with her husband. Set in the countryside of Périgord, it recounts the failed betrothal of an eccentric fifteen-year-old with a thirty-five-year-old fiancé selected by her father, a retired general. The adolescent, "half-masculine, half-feminine" wears a "Tyrolian fedora" just as Rachilde did in the 1880s. She is named Raoule.

But if Rachilde offered a piece of her own gender story in *Monsieur Vénus*, it was one that could not be readily assimilated. The overwhelming response to the novel was bafflement. Some friends applauded it as a welcome form of provocation, but others were troubled, among them Georges de Peyrebrune, an older woman writer who had become a trusted confidante. Peyrebrune and the writer Camille Delaville had taken an interest in Rachilde and worried together over her emotional well-being. "Can you be angry at someone for being crazy?" Delaville asked Peyrebrune at one point, recounting Rachilde's latest antics.[4] But Peyrebrune was appalled by the novel, which seemed dangerously extreme. She called Rachilde in to see her. "I read it," Peyrebrune told her. "I did not understand it, but I sense that you are a monster. Don't come back here."[5]

In some ways, Peyrebrune's response only confirmed Rachilde's fears: that to be honest would be to disturb and scare away. It is no small irony that the plot of *Monsieur Vénus* played out a similar dynamic. The Baron de Raittolbe's initial response to Raoule anticipated that of the Parisian public. This moment in the novel is worth looking at more closely, as a window onto Rachilde's awareness of the obstacles she would face in working out her gender story in such a public way.

Rachilde depicts the remarkable conversation between the two friends in the fifth chapter. The scene is as follows: Raoule has tried to sneak back into her home after a passionate tryst with Jacques Silvert, her effeminate new lover, but Raittolbe confronts her. Raittolbe is angry because he had hoped to sleep with her. Faced with his exasperated fury, Raoule promises to "explain everything." She assures Raittolbe that her story would more than make up for what he had missed out on earlier in the day, when she failed to show up at their promised rendezvous. The conversation that follows is a kind of "coming out" *avant la lettre*: Raoule tries to explain her gender identity and how it is entangled with her sexual identity. It is a telling moment, rarely appreciated as such—one that points to a story of painful vulnerability couched in the rebellious antics of the protagonist.

Raoule's interlocutor is not terribly interested in listening, and she talks more to unburden herself than to satisfy his curiosity. Having poured herself a glass of ice water to help her stay calm, Raoule forces open the conversation by announcing: "Je suis *amoureux*!"[6] This is a sentence that proves difficult to translate into English, which does not gender adjectives in the same way as French. "I am *in love*" is what Raoule says, but she uses the masculine form of the phrase "in love," so that the implicit meaning is that she is a *man* in love. To this, Raittolbe uneasily exclaims, "Sapho! . . . I suspected as much." And this would be one of the prevailing readings of the novel: that Raoule's apparent mannishness and a certain evocation of a "third sex" signify same-sex desire, following nineteenth-century notions for understanding such behavior. Raittolbe assumes Raoule is confessing Sapphic desire, itself a product of hysteria according to nineteenth-century thinking. Similarly, many believed that Rachilde was a lesbian.

But Raoule is quick to correct Raittolbe. "I am *in love* (m.) with a man and not with a woman," she clarifies, emphasizing the adjectival phrase in the first instance—"I am *in love* / je suis *amoureux*"—because the object of the love is secondary to the gendered nature of the condition of being in love. Raoule loves *as a man*, and this is the first thing she tries to articulate. But the object of Raoule's affections is male, and this fact places her in another category entirely, or at least beyond the categories that existed at the time.

According to the inversion model in nineteenth-century sexology, a woman who is attracted to women is really a man in a woman's body; that theory preserved a heterosexual framework for understanding homosexual behavior.[7] But Raoule did not see herself as a man *because* of her love for another woman; rather, she saw herself—and wanted to be seen—as a man, independently of her sexual desire, which happened to be for another man. There was no way to confuse this with Sapphic desire. What's more, gender and sexual identity could not in this instance be separated; because they deviated from the presumed heterosexual paradigm, they both required explanation. But there was no existing framework, medical or otherwise, to process such a thing. "Have pity on me!" exclaims Raittolbe in response. "I think my brain is collapsing."[8]

The conversation stumbles forward, with Raoule trying to explain herself "painfully," accompanied by a mounting excitement at the possibility of comprehension. She is described as "overexcited by a heartrending emotion," but she is quickly frustrated, exclaiming: "I am certain of never being understood!"[9]

"Let's use *he* or *she*," Raittolbe cries as Raoule wavers between pronouns, "so that I don't lose the little bit of good sense that I have left." But Raoule cannot adopt one or the other. Nor is she being playful or trying to shake things up, as modern scholars have assumed. This conversation is not a demonstration that gender is simply a social construct, as arbitrary as the colors pink and blue that align with masculinity or femininity, depending on various cultural and historic contexts. Nor is it an example of "gender trouble," to borrow Judith Butler's now classic phrase, which is often cited by scholars analyzing this novel.[10] Raoule does not wish to disrupt in order to subvert, as Butler's theory would suggest. Rather, for all of Raoule's flamboyant and provocative costuming and seemingly rebellious passing as a man, her use of male pronouns and twisting of grammar must be understood in conjunction with her emotional attempts to explain herself. As she speaks, "a tear whose wet brightness seemed to have stolen its light from Eden long ago rolled down Raoule's cheek." In other words, there is vulnerability alongside the audacity—something almost never acknowledged in Rachilde scholarship. The emotion stems from Raoule's struggle to express a complex sense of self that defies the rules of grammar, from trying to speak through a body that has no apparent language.

In the end, Raittolbe listens to Raoule and agrees to help her in her affair with Jacques, but not before "pouring out curses dreadful enough to make the hair of all the hussars in France stand on end." He promises to pick Raoule up the next day, "if I haven't blown my brains out" by then.[11] Peyrebrune, too, came around eventually. Just as Rachilde would discover with her own friends, acceptance of her apparent "eccentricity" often stood on the painfully thin edge of disdain, if not of horror.

OUTSIDE OF LANGUAGE

While Raoule, like her author, identifies with masculinity, it is clear that switching to a male pronoun does not fully account for her sense of self. Sometimes, Raoule seems to identify with femininity, describing herself in this chapter as part of a female elite. At other times, she declares herself a man and clearly wants to be seen as such—even to become one. In the midst of her explanations to Raittolbe, she offers a framework for understanding this fluidity, asking that she not be limited to a male/female either/or structure. "I always thought I was one when I was really two," Raoule states. Rachilde thus situates the conversation in the context of a longer process of Raoule's attempt to understand herself: "I always thought" serves as compelling evidence of a lifetime of questioning. Finally, in the last scene of the novel, Raoule alternates between masculine and feminine attire. A new pronoun is deployed to designate this last image: "they." With this switch, Rachilde presciently anticipates contemporary shifts in vocabulary to accommodate nonbinary gender.

Raoule's alternation between pronouns was seen as a kind of provocation—a form of behavior meant to shock. But in all likelihood, Rachilde was giving voice to something real and troubling: a sense of being outside of language itself. The linguistic challenges that Raoule faces—sometimes playfully, sometimes in frustration—resonate with many contemporary trans memoirs that take up the initial problem of the nonbinary—especially in their youth—as one of ineffability: the gap between their sense of self, on the one hand, and the pronouns and labels in which they are meant to fit seamlessly, on the other. In a recent essay in the *New York Times*, Giancarlo Valentine discusses how, as a nonbinary teen, he "couldn't assert my truth in language, because I didn't know how." The language simply did not exist. He sees the emerging vocabulary for expressing nonbinary identifications—"they/them, zi/zer and so many others," that is, ways to be neither male nor female, or both—as a new kind of lifeline.[12] But without such a language, Rachilde was on her own.

It is not wrong to recognize, as early readers did, that Rachilde likely "put something true of herself" in *Monsieur Vénus*. Also, we need not look for this truth in a single protagonist. Raittolbe falls for Jacques too, in the end, and he may have served as a stand-in for the kind of man that Rachilde may have imagined herself to be. When Raittolbe flees at the novel's close, Raoule subsumes his role in their love triangle, playing both his and her parts in the necrophilic relationship with Jacques. Sharing the first two letters of Rachilde's own assumed name, Raoule and Raittolbe together offer a glimpse, multiply refracted, of the author's fictionalized self-image.

A sense of gender plurality and fluidity is present throughout Rachilde's writing. In her youth, she saw herself as a double being, slipping between genders at will. In a curious chapter in *When I Was Young*, she describes an encounter with the "human beast" Césarien, a young man who claimed to be her brother, with long lashes and eyes resembling her own. In his haunting look, she recognized "a very strange *woman's* gaze, in the eyes of a man."[13] While recounting this anecdote, Rachilde notes that she had long put the figure of Césarien to use in her fiction. Throughout her oeuvre, one finds a fascination with siblings and pairs: Marcel and Marcelle in *Madame Adonis*, who turn out to be the same person; the "princess of darkness" in the novel of the same name and her animal counterpart, Hunter; and in the 1921 novel *Japanese Mouse*, whose male protagonist suffers from "a cerebral duality, the sinister and cynical question of the eternal masculine predominating over the eternal feminine."[14] In the 1932 *Playing with Fireworks*, Rachilde presents Catherine and Amelia as "two sisters. More specifically, two soul sisters. With the slight difference between them that they did not have the same sex if you admit that the soul has a sex."[15] The siblings share the same sex, then, but not the same gender, which seems to be the distinction that Rachilde was trying to work out all along. Taken together, these works show a lifelong effort to theorize gender through her fictions, in all likelihood to determine her own sense of duality, long before there was a language in which to do so.

THE QUESTION OF SEX

Behind the public spectacle that *Monsieur Vénus* created about Rachilde's identity, she described a deep, often overwhelming terror. At around the same time that she was gallivanting about with her fellow Zutistes, she was sharing more serious feelings with Peyrebrune. In a letter of 1885, she describes a conversation with her editor. "Your novel is too literary," she reports him as saying. "Why don't you have your heroine raped a little?"[16] (For once, she does not.) She shared with Peyrebrune her horror at this request, while in an earlier letter she complained about a different editor (Simonin) who had come to her apartment in search of sexual favors. Peyrebrune, in her own story about a woman writer in Paris, *The Novel of a Bas Bleu*, confirmed that this was par for the course. Describing herself as "nauseated" by the incident, Rachilde wrote to her older friend: "I am convinced that certain lives are worse than certain deaths."[17] Rachilde was deeply invested in the novel she was writing at the time and was just as deeply worried about how she would survive the process of writing it. "I will have gone mad in ten years' time," she wrote, "if I have the patience to wait until then."[18]

What was widely perceived as shameless self-promotion was probably the reverse side of a basic fight for survival. Rachilde shared the vulnerability that any single woman would have experienced, supporting herself in Paris among predatory editors and men who spotted an easy target. Perhaps this is what she meant when she told police she needed to wear pants, so that men would address her pen rather than her person. It sounded facetious, but it was deadly serious: not appearing to be a woman could indeed be a form of self-defense. Rachilde's challenge, however, was also more specific. She may have wondered whether she really was a woman in the first place. As she fended off gossip about her life—with whom she may or may not have slept—perhaps the most daunting rumor was the suggestion that she hadn't slept with anyone at all.

Sex is everywhere in Rachilde's fictions, while it is also a curiously elusive topic and rarely associated with easeful pleasure. As Michael Finn has pointed out, in at least four of her novels the heroine's first sexual experience is rape; other, more seasoned characters are also sexually assaulted.[19] In addition to rejecting the inherent violence of the sex act, Rachilde rejected the procreative role assigned to women, which she saw as another form of violence. The heroine of *The Marquise de Sade*, Mary Barbe, informs her husband on their wedding night that there will be no sex—ever—for this reason. When pleasure does come for Rachilde's heroines, it is through other, nonpenetrative means: a neck bite, a rubbing of the skin, a kind of cerebral vibration or brain seizure, and various forms of self-pleasuring. The most memorable of these takes place in the 1900 novel *The Juggler*, in which Eliante Donalger brings herself to orgasm, fully clothed, by running her hands along the curves of an alabaster vase.

Monsieur Vénus offers a window into some of the issues that may have troubled Rachilde regarding the physical act of sex, offering evidence of a difficult relationship with her own body that may have presented a psychological barrier to intimacy. There are many erotic scenes in *Monsieur Vénus*, but it is never clear what sort of physical contact Raoule and Jacques are enjoying, beyond "a strange and sexless love that produced every kind of pleasure."[20] At several moments in the novel, desire seems to be at its height but consummation is impossible. In one such moment, Jacques is overcome with desire and accuses Raoule of not knowing *how* to love, despite being "vice-ridden"—a criticism that echoes Lorrain's own puzzled commentary about his friend, whom he labeled the "chaste pervert." After Raoule jettisons her dress and corset, sneaking out to Jacques's place in a man's suit, the two are depicted as "united in a common thought: the destruction of their sex."[21] And yet, Jacques sighs to her that night: "You will always be lacking in one thing"—a hint of the bodily barriers that may be keeping them physically apart. Finally, they marry, but on their wedding night, in the midst of their lovemaking, "a heartrending cry was heard." It is Jacques, who feels "as if he had just been crucified in a spasm of pleasure." The precipitating incident is that Raoule had released her breast from her white silk waistcoat, in order to feel her flesh against his own. In response, Jacques exclaims in frustration: "Raoule, you just aren't a man! You just can't be a man!"[22] Sexual fulfillment is impossible between them, and it is Raoule's body that is in the way.

The details of these scenes suggest quite a complex set of identifications. After her confession to Raittolbe, Raoule stares at her devout aunt, who is saying her prayers, and wonders to herself whether anyone had ever asked the Virgin Mary for a change of sex.[23] (This is another sentimental moment in the novel rarely acknowledged in scholarship.) But while Raoule seems to dream of being a man in body as well as mind, she also does not reject her own body entirely, willingly introducing her breasts into the sexual encounter. In fact, Finn has noted that "the baring of breasts is one of the key indicators of passion in Rachilde-related texts" and also that breasts played a key role in her intimacy with both Barrès and d'Estoc.[24] Raoule's alienation from her body is partial and limited, it seems, to genital sexuality. It is worth noting that this discomfort is not uncommon among those who are gender nonconforming and who may feel particularly disconnected from certain parts of the body associated with the biological sex with which they do not identify.[25]

The question of Rachilde's sexuality was one of the issues that captured the imagination of Rachilde's contemporaries, animating the many attempts to portray her in writing. In 1886, in an essay titled "Mademoiselle Salamander," even Rachilde's friend Lorrain offered a portrait of her. He opened his piece with the playful question "Couche-t-elle?" ("Does she have sex?"), thereby addressing the perceived conflict between Rachilde's erotic fiction and the absolute lack of evidence that she had ever actually slept with anyone. Oscar Méténier referred to this preoccupation in his own novel that same year: "What they forgave her least of all, was her restraint," he wrote of Mary Staub, the character he based on Rachilde. Everyone would watch her at the balls and in restaurants and cafés, "and never had anyone heard of anyone who had been out with her boast of having slept with her. It was indecent."[26]

Rachilde was undoubtedly as confused by her sexuality as everyone else. During her first years in Paris, she had been involved in an obsessive—and somewhat one-sided—relationship with Catulle Mendès, despite his humiliation of her years earlier. In her importunate letters to Mendès in 1882–1883, she shared the traumas of her childhood and details of her personal struggles, describing in one letter "the monster born of my heart and mind" who lurked within. She also wrote of her betrothal at fifteen to an older man. In this telling, however, Mendès replaced Hugo as her idol: Rachilde wrote that she refused to wed the chubby suitor out of protest, responding to the unwanted marriage with the dream of making real literature. "Thereafter I only lived," she declared, in the youthful, symmetrical cursive she would soon abandon, "in order to write one day like Catulle Mendès so that he would know that I existed."[27] Despite the forthright confidence of these declarations, the same desperation that Rachilde would describe about waiting for Hugo's letter appears here too. Her desire for approval is palpable, as she chastises Mendès for not responding more quickly. "It's the eighth time that I've been to the post office. They sort the letters in front of me and respond: Nothing," she wrote in exasperation. "Did you receive my letter?"

Despite Rachilde's clear attraction to the older man, their sexual encounter appears to have ended in her refusal. She tells the story in detail in the autobiographical preface to her 1886 novel *To the Death*: "Rachilde . . . suffered a brain seizure under the specious pretext that Catulle Mendès was an attractive man. . . . She saw Catulle Mendès, listened to him, did not love him, but also loved him." These words notably echo the ambivalence of her feelings for her father, and there was surely a pattern of infatuation with older men who did not treat her well but upon whom her sense of herself as a writer seemed to depend. Rachilde concludes: "She was thus not Catulle

Mendès's mistress [and] Doctor Lasègue had to come . . . to examine the surprising problem of hysteria occurring during a paroxysm of chastity in a depraved milieu."[28]

What Rachilde seems to describe is a mental breakdown in the middle of a sexual encounter—interrupted by her "paroxysm of chastity"—the opposite of the desired sexual paroxysm. For whatever reason, she could not go through with the sex act, although she acknowledges having experienced a "brain seizure," a term she would use to describe a certain kind of sexual fulfillment in later fictions. The result was a bout of hysteria, during which she lost control of her legs for approximately two months. She had to be treated by Charles Lasègue, a well-known hysteria doctor who specialized in the paralysis that often accompanied the disease.

In some ways, Rachilde's experience with Mendès also describes an experience with d'Estoc: Rachilde was said to have chased d'Estoc away. Rachilde seemed to have taken herself to the brink with both male and female partners, and then, in both instances, fled or refused them. There is other evidence of her resistance to genital sexuality. Though she was intimate with Maurice Barrès, they never physically consummated their affair, and Barrès went on to marvel over their shared ability to "remain chaste in the worst ecstasies."[29] Another writer, Paul Devaux, described her as a fellatrix of the gay men with whom she surrounded herself. For all of the eroticism of her writing, Lorrain noted, Rachilde did not seem to understand the least bit about actual sex.

With Mendès, the moment of crisis arose at the possibility of sexual consummation, and hysteria was the diagnosis. While paralysis offered a textbook symptom of the disease as it presented in nineteenth-century France, the diagnosis acted as a helpful placeholder for something more specific but harder to describe. Hysteria was a way of designating that something was "wrong" in the realm of female behavior without needing to identify exactly what that something was. For Rachilde, it was linked to her refusal to assume not just the traditional female social role but the traditional female sexual role. Mendès's response to Rachilde's discussion of their relationship, which was said to have angered him, was to publish his own essay about her, entitled "Virgin."[30]

Rachilde adored Mendès and never quite got over him. They stayed in touch throughout the years. In a lengthy letter from 1908, she implored his wife, Jane, whom she did not know very well, not to divorce him, as she feared it would destroy Mendès's ability to produce art.[31] It's quite possible that in the 1880s, Rachilde feared that her refusal of Mendès meant that something *was* wrong with her—that her own gender nonconformity was a form of mental illness, which, after all, ran in the family. Though she seemed, in *Monsieur Vénus*, to mock the catchall, protean nature of hysteria and the summary way in which Raoule was diagnosed, this did not mean that Raoule was emotionally well. The problem, perhaps, was that there *was* a problem with both Rachilde and Raoule, something that provoked a psychological crisis and made them feel separate from others. But, as Rachilde also makes clear in the novel, the doctor who was brought in to treat the young woman had absolutely no idea what that problem was or how to properly care for her under the circumstances. The same might be said for her author.

Nonetheless, hysteria offered a useful shorthand, both for Raoule in *Monsieur Vénus* and for Rachilde in the preface. It made the departure from feminine norms appear normal in their abnormality: recognizable, familiar. It may well have been the reason the novel was not censored in France, where hysteria was so commonplace. In 1889, the French publisher Félix Brossier agreed to publish a new edition of *Monsieur Vénus*. Barrès, with whom Rachilde still maintained a friendship, offered to write a preface. "My dearest Rachilde," he wrote her. "Do you know that I have a mad desire: I want to offer you twenty lovely pages in which I would explain how and why this work is a masterpiece."[32] In an essay that he titled "The Complications of Love," Barrès assumed a scientific tone and confirmed the naïve, autobiographical readings: Rachilde had written the novel at the age of twenty, "without thinking." This part was a narrative to which she would hold fast: that her writing was automatic, channeling her subconscious rather than her rational mind. In Barrès's terms, it was pathological. The novel was born of the *maladie du siècle*, he declared, and it would interest doctors and literary types alike. Rachilde's book, he wrote, "is simply an extension of her life." Barrès sent Rachilde a draft of his essay. She declared it a work of art and suggested edits of her own.[33] By this point, then, she was willing to allow her work to be considered a symptom of a disease, perhaps even a case study. Some part of her may have believed it, as well.

SECOND SKINS

For much of *Monsieur Vénus*, the object of focus is not Raoule de Vénérande's body but rather Jacques's, and in particular, his skin, linking this story to Dieulafoy's *Brother Pelagius*, in which Marguerite had wrestled with her "envelope." In one of Raoule's earliest sexual encounters with Jacques, she uses drugs to ply him out of his sense of being in his own skin and then wants him to feel through her own body, part by part, as if it were his own. But in the second half of the novel, *his* body is the object of her jealous rage, as she digs her nails into his skin in response to Raittolbe's beatings of Jacques. While Jacques and Raoule had shared the mutual fantasy of the "destruction of their sex," it is his body alone that is destroyed—jointly by Raoule and Raittolbe, the shared authors of this violence.

As the attacks upon Jacques's body reach their peak, Raoule announces to Raittolbe that "Jacques is no more than a wound; he is our work of art."[34] These words notably echo Rachilde's description of herself in an 1885 letter sent to Peyrebrune, not long after the initial publication of *Monsieur Vénus* in Belgium. "It seems that I am no more than a wound," she wrote, "and that all the impressions of the air dig into me and mistreat me."[35] If Rachilde identified with Raoule and Raittolbe, she seems to have seen herself in Jacques as well, as the wounds in his skin express her sense of having no barrier from her surroundings. Literally embodying her words to Peyrebrune, perhaps Jacques symbolized Rachilde's vulnerable, feminine side—the side of herself that she shared only with her female friends and that felt so beaten down by the world.

The violence of this part of *Monsieur Vénus* has been read as a transgressive aspect of its erotics. It has been assumed to be a form of sadism—quite literally, as Rachilde had read her grandfather's copies of Sade's works and would publish her own *Marquise de Sade* in 1887.[36] But little sexual pleasure is depicted in the violent scenes; rather, their drama is of a different sort. Raoule's aggression is described as a way to express her own fury (*colères*), the result of the "incomplete metamorphosis" she has undergone.[37] In other words, Raoule rips up Jacques's skin in anguish over the contours of her own. In this, Rachilde's novel anticipates the more recent literature around transsexuality, which recognizes the skin not simply as a covering for the self but also as a site of identity.[38] There is no single way in which those who are cross-gendered or gender variant experience their bodies, and theories of transgender embodiment have elicited much debate. Even so, there are shared themes. As Jay Prosser has documented, many trans writers describe having acted out against their skin, through cutting or other self-destructive acts, as a way to create a sense of being in their own bodies. Indeed, argues Prosser, many transgender autobiographies ask the question, How does the trans subject "survive without a skin of their own?"[39]

Rachilde's novel asks and answers this very question in its own dramatic way. (It's not the only Rachilde novel describing laceration and scratching of the skin: *Minette* and *The Animal*, both of which feature relationships with animals, also depict such attacks.) The shocking theme may have its roots in the vulnerability she mentioned to Peyrebrune when she described herself as an open wound. She might very well have identified with Jan Morris, who wrote that, as a child, she wanted to "throw off the hide of my own skin."[40] Raymond Thompson describes the way he would puncture his own skin to confirm his sense of self. "It felt as if I came into this world with no physical form to protect me. I was not a solid, tangible human being, like everyone else seemed to be. I felt vulnerable and alone."[41] Thompson points to the rage he felt along with this sadness; Rachilde had reasons to rage, as well, if sexual and other kinds of brutality had been part of her childhood. In her letter to de Souza, she makes her father's aggression a part of the story, the factor that tilts her toward the young man whose feminine form had caught her attention in the first place.

The twentieth-century fictionalized notion of a woman "trapped in a man's body" or vice versa, and the implicit gore connected to the possibility of a surgical remedy, have long excited Hollywood and the public imagination. This interest is a product of early media fascination with some of the first individuals to undergo gender confirmation surgery. Christine Jorgensen, who underwent the procedure in 1951, became a celebrity through her frequent television appearances, inspiring early Hollywood interest in the subject. Decades later, transphobic films such as Jonathan Demme's *The Silence of the Lambs*, in which a transsexual named Buffalo Bill is found to be murdering women in order to create a body out of their skins, and Pedro Almodóvar's *The Skin I Live In*, in which a plastic surgeon murders a man and transforms him into a replica of his own late wife, harnessed the voyeuristic interest once again. These films exploited some of the very real preoccupations of the trans subject: how one might have, in Halberstam's helpful articulation, "the desire for forms of embodiment that are necessarily impossible and yet deeply desired."[42] Cinema has co-opted those real feelings, decontextualized them, and served them up disparagingly in the most lurid forms of entertainment.[43]

Long before Hollywood, Rachilde used Decadent tropes with a similar purpose. French Decadent writers heartily embraced a combination of sex and violence in order to entertain. In telling the story of Raoule and Jacques, Rachilde drew on Barbey d'Aurevilly's 1878 *Les diaboliques*, or "Devil Women" stories. In one of these, "A Dinner of Atheists," a jilted lover seals a woman's sex with wax. Rachilde also wrote in the vein of Villiers de l'Isle Adam's 1883 "Cruel Tales"—perhaps her own form of revenge on one of the men who had made her seem like a ridiculous little girl in front of her idol. In one of Villiers's stories, a woman dies but comes back to life each night when her lover arrives to make love to her. In defending herself to the prefect of police against the charge of immorality, Rachilde also explicitly named René Maizeroy's *Two Friends*—a tale of two lesbians—and Paul Bonnetain's *Charlot Has Fun*—about masochism—as inspirations.

By exploiting the shock value of her subject, Rachilde steered attention away from the troubles of her protagonist and the human impulses that motivated her. For a study in contrast, we might compare the gender stories told by both Rachilde and Jane Dieulafoy, each using the narrative frames that they found most resonant. Dieulafoy wrote herself into the tale of Joan of Arc in a story that celebrated gender fluidity as heroism; Rachilde, on the other hand, cast herself as the perverse antiheroine, the quintessential femme fatale of the most virulently misogynistic Decadent tradition. A difference of background and personality may have contributed to these choices, in addition to the fact that they were working out different kinds of gender identification. But the evolution of their imaginative paths may also have been determined by the story lines available to them. Imagine if, instead of reading Maizeroy's misogynistic, homophobic *Two Friends*, Rachilde had been able to read Radclyffe Hall's 1928 *The Well of Loneliness*. In this novel, the heroine, Stephen, like Rachilde, is born to parents expecting a son. Her parents give her the name they had already selected, sure as they were of the sex of their progeny. Stephen's kind governess, an "invert" like herself, tells her: "You're neither unnatural, nor abominable, nor mad; you're as much a part of what people call nature as anyone else; only you're unexplained as yet—you've not got your niche in creation."[44]

The violent, disturbing ending of *Monsieur Vénus*, in which Jacques is killed in a duel with Raittolbe that was orchestrated by Raoule, is a testament to the sensationalism that Rachilde took up instead. Jacques is transformed—with his own hair, teeth, and nails—into an elaborate sex toy wrapped in transparent rubber skin. But look past the gore and you can see a kind of bodily resolution, at least for Raoule, with Jacques serving again as a palimpsest for her own fantasies. His new form allows the couple, finally, to consummate their marriage, as Raoule's husband to Jacques's wife. In the original Belgian version of the novel, the wax effigy was equipped with a spring that made Jacques's legs spread apart. This allowed Raoule to penetrate him and to play both male and female roles not just in mind but in body as well. When the prefect of the Parisian police confessed to Rachilde that he had understood nothing about her controversial novel, Rachilde "defended" herself by explaining that in her quest for something new, she wanted to write about a woman who could "bugger" men, noting that anything was possible with the help of technology.[45]

Monsieur Vénus was not, then, unlike *The Silence of the Lambs*. Both works translate the "trouble of the transsexual into the transsexual as trouble," to use Prosser's formulation.[46] In nineteenth-century France, this was an easy slippage: to be gender nonconforming was necessarily to threaten social structures. The novel, in its irreverence and daring, seemed to confirm this fact, and Rachilde was eventually willing for her work to be packaged as a cautionary tale—a symptom of nineteenth-century neurosis. Her willingness was perhaps another aspect of Rachilde's doubleness of mind: at some moments, the determined, indomitable writer—buoyed by friends like Lorrain and Barrès, Verlaine and Méténier—seemed to take pride in her affinity with the defiant Raoule. At other moments, however, looking into the eyes of Peyrebrune or Delaville, or perhaps Mendès, whom she so wanted to love, Rachilde may have been filled with terror and self-loathing. She may have been convinced that some part of her truly was the raging, unlovable Raoule. Perhaps she was concerned that gender nonconformity *was* a social scourge and that she was in fact some form of hysteric, the "Buffalo Bill" of her day.

Prosser has described transgender writing, and memoir in particular, as a kind of second skin, to compensate for the "damaged or flawed body image, the subject who imagines him or herself skinless or with a broken skin."[47] The solution is to render the transgender experience in words, to create a language for it, a substitute vessel, its own "second skin." During her conversation with Raittolbe, Raoule had exclaimed in frustration that, though she had read entire libraries and studied lovers as if they were books upon her shelf, "I have not yet written my book!" Jacques, "whose body was like a poem," becomes in this sense "Monsieur Vénus," Raoule's original creation. Through his own new transparent lining, he offered a "second skin" for Raoule—a way for her to live out her own truth. For Rachilde, writing itself was connected to clothing, offering an extra barrier between her self and her world. As she had told the police, she wanted her pants so that people would look at her pen rather than at her person. Perhaps she needed that protection over a body that sometimes felt like an open wound. Just as Jacques became Raoule's work of art, then, *Monsieur Vénus* may also have been an unconscious effort to create new membranes between Rachilde and the world—the urgency of its production a way to stay alive and its swirling rage a testament to the anger and frustration of needing to do so. If the wax effigy is Raoule's "book," *Monsieur Vénus* is Rachilde's, a story of nonbinary gender that might one day find its way onto the shelves that lined Raoule's living room, alongside volumes by "Parny, Piron, Voltaire, Boccaccio, Brantôme."[48] At the end of this long tradition of erudite, scandalous libertines, Rachilde seems to have imagined herself.

10 FREEDOM THROUGH IMAGINATION

AS MUCH AS RACHILDE WROTE FICTION as a way of translating a complex self to the world, she was herself also a topic of voluminous commentary, both in fiction and nonfiction. To encounter Rachilde, whether in person or on the page, invited efforts to render her in writing. In some ways, *Monsieur Vénus* was a story that launched a thousand stories, the catalyst for an explosion of words about Rachilde. The phenomenon was no doubt fueled by the challenge of describing a way of being in the world that seemed to defy nineteenth-century language. Most people seemed to agree that there was something inarticulable about Rachilde that nonetheless invited repeated efforts at articulation.

For many, Rachilde was guilty of just one thing: boldly promoting herself. According to this rendering, if Rachilde was a product of contemporary culture, it was not the culture of rampant vice and decaying morality. Rachilde was not a sex monger but rather a publicity monger, cultivating a certain image of herself in order to sell more books. Rachilde's reputation was in this sense a gendered one: it was nearly always women who were seen as publicity hounds, apparently tricking people into buying their wares. "Publicity! Publicity! Publicity!" scowled Jean Ernest-Charles, one of the most vocal critics of women writers. Women authors, he argued, put men at an unfair disadvantage and contributed to the denigration of the literary field.[1] Unlike the *bas bleu*, who was depicted as sexually unappealing, this image of the woman writer was associated with promiscuity. The woman writer who was too eager to sell was simply another iteration of the prostitute—a symbol of social ills and the declining republic.

Gisèle d'Estoc was one of those who scoffed at the widely circulating idea of Rachilde as a hapless virgin, remarking that others in her cohort were irked at the notion, which to them defied belief: "When people . . . wanted to persuade us that a young, virtuous virgin had given birth to this monster: *l'Homme Vénus* . . . Oh! Seriously! We were stunned."[2] D'Estoc also played upon the public skepticism about women writers as publicity hungry (witness her own title, *The Publicity-Virgin*). In d'Estoc's view, once Rachilde had published her dangerous book, it was no accident that she saw numerous elite "salons open their doors to her" and "princes throw themselves at her feet."[3] It was Rachilde's plan all along, she wrote: do whatever it takes to shock, and make yourself a commodity in the process.

Ironically, in their efforts to render her in writing, Rachilde's many acquaintances, both friends and adversaries, shared in her struggle to find the words and the appropriate frame of reference for a kind of identity that had yet to be theorized or categorized. For her detractors, the terms hysteric, hermaphrodite (connoting physiological difference then as now), lesbian, and even third sex, were bandied about, sometimes in the same paragraph. There was no distinction between sexuality (whom you love) and gender (who you are) to help clarify the matter, nor were there meaningful distinctions between mental illness, sexual perversion, or some sort of physiological condition, all of which would place her outside of social bounds. Rachilde's friends, on the other hand, conveyed a sense of playful eccentricity in their portraits of her, depicting a person whose gender was always shifting, depending on the point of view.

Many of those who knew her commented that she did not so much look like a masculine woman but rather both male and female at once. In his essay "Mademoiselle Salamander"—its title an allusion to her shape-shifting, ambiguous quality—Lorrain described Rachilde as looking like an innocent, "pale schoolgirl with a simple, reserved look," but at the same time having the profile of "a Greek ephebe or a young French romantic, who wouldn't have been at school." Her striking and most recognizable feature were her famous eyes: "Oh! The eyes! Long, long eyes, weighed down with unbelievable lashes and clear as water, eyes that are oblivious."[4]

A shared gender fluidity may have been what inspired her romance with Barrès. "You have the soul of an honest woman in the body of a depraved man," she wrote to him. She sometimes addressed him in their correspondence as "my girl."[5] After Rachilde modeled the protagonist of *To the Death*, Maxime de Byron, on Barrès, he returned the favor; in his 1888 novel *Under the Eyes of Barbarians*, part of the *Cult of Self* trilogy, he described the character based on Rachilde: "At the first layer you see a young woman wrapped around a young man. Isn't it the story of a soul with its two elements, female and male?"[6] So many of Rachilde's friends described her in a similar way, as seeming to be a thing and its opposite. "Devilish angel and angelic devil," wrote Verlaine, "feminine man and masculine woman, all at once."[7]

In his novel *Décadence*, Oscar Méténier was inspired by Rachilde in his depiction of the fictional actress Mary Staub, who is described as having "the look of a precocious and depraved kid." He used a name that referenced Mary Barbe, the autobiographical protagonist of Rachilde's forthcoming novel, *The Marquise de Sade*. When Staub was around, wrote Méténier, everyone seemed to forget a simple truth: that "she was and only wanted to be a man." Later, one of Méténier's characters demands of another, "My dear, you owe us an explanation, a speech about the sex of Mary Staub," echoing Dubut de Laforest's vaguely clinical request and the general reaction around Rachilde.[8]

Even the conservative Peyrebrune, who was aghast at *Monsieur Vénus*, was not averse to capitalizing on her friend's unique self-presentation. In her 1886 novel *A Female Decadent*, one recognizes the protagonist Hélione d'Orval, a female poet who, like both Rachilde and her most famous character, wore pants and liked to fence and hunt. Hélione is chastened later in the novel when she is brought to the countryside, a region not unlike Rachilde's native Périgord (which was Peyrebrune's home as well) to spend time with her sister and her new baby. In this novel, then, Peyrebrune imagined Rachilde returning to a more innocent, traditional lifestyle. The sister shares Rachilde's own given name, Marguerite.

A few weeks after Rachilde sent a copy of *To the Death* to Barrès, describing it as her "newborn," he dubbed her "Mademoiselle Baudelaire" (a sobriquet credited to Mendès) in an essay in *Le Voltaire*, where he had just begun a regular column. Commenting on her newly published autobiographical preface, he wrote that the charm of Rachilde was that she was "a monster: she tells us this directly, she invites us to say it ourselves."[9] Lorrain, too, would call his friend—fondly—"this young literary monster," and also "a kind of third sex, as enigmatic as she is seductive."[10] But by the end of his essay, Lorrain seemed to criticize his own criticism, noting how Rachilde managed to be different things to everyone: "A woman for the schoolkids, a pretty boy for old men, revenue for her publisher, a man of wit for the journalists, a monster for the imbeciles," he wrote, before referring to her as "Mademoiselle Salamander, my only friend."[11] In this poignant conclusion, Lorrain describes Rachilde as an ephemeral reflection of whoever happened to be looking at her.

In addition to the practical struggles for survival, Rachilde's sense that she was losing her mind—even as she delighted in her new existence—may well have been connected to this sense of being sui generis. She was aware of being unstable, and as a result, being sometimes unmoored from language itself. Telling stories about herself was one way in which Rachilde created her own context while affirming her existence. In recounting the story of her pseudonym, she had described it as a way in which to "emancipate myself through the means of my imagination."[12] As it turned out, she would continue to do just that—self-emancipating with words—throughout her long life. With the reverberations from *Monsieur Vénus*, she may have realized that she, too, could have a say in how she was seen. She could tell her story better than anyone else.

"TO BE STRANGE OR NOTHING AT ALL"

The thirty pages that introduced the 1886 novel *To the Death* offered a tantalizing self-portrait: just enough to draw readers in without fully satisfying their curiosity. In this preface, Rachilde told her life story, culminating in an account of her first five years in Paris. This version of events—naming names, as it were—seemed as if it were intended to indulge the public's appetite for intimate detail. Flying through her childhood, the broken engagement and the mental breakdowns, Rachilde described the whirlwind of unexpected celebrity on the heels of *Monsieur Vénus* as well as her embrace of its opportunities. She condemned some of those who had persecuted her in its wake: she mocked Fouquier, who had accused her of being a mother-hating, pleasure-seeking hermaphrodite, and for doing so behind his silly feminine pseudonym, Colombine. Of the novel in question, Rachilde wrote that "in the hour of poverty," her choice lay between writing it and throwing herself in the gutter. Much to her surprise, she claimed, the novel turned out to be a triumph, and a "new era opened up" for her.

This overtly autobiographical piece marked a turning point in Rachilde's approach: if readers were to conflate author and protagonist, why shouldn't she? She describes herself as "a crazy woman, a monster, a neurotic"—but one with nothing to lose: "The neurotic who doesn't care about weighing down her reputation, who would hazard even a spot of blood on her white dress, is capable of all kinds of things that can't be confessed, isn't she?" Now that they had accused her of having loved "men, women, dogs, cats, and horse-drawn carriages," what did it really matter? "She wanted to have fun; she was twenty-four years old!" she wrote of herself. "Rachilde was becoming entertaining, and when you entertain a certain Paris, they forgive you for everything else!"[13]

Rachilde notes that it was her editor who came up with the idea of the preface, "in order to fill thirty pages."[14] Perhaps. She boasted of this introduction to Barrès, with whom she was in an on-again, off-again relationship at the time, describing it as "a preface–self-portrait that you'll find entertaining. Very audacious."[15] To Peyrebrune, she apologized that she could not convey her gratitude fully in writing and assured her that her acknowledgment would not tarnish the older woman's reputation. She also noted that she had followed Peyrebrune's advice to just describe herself in "a couple of words"; however, those words were "strong," because Rachilde "only knows how to tell the truth."[16]

Rachilde was likely being honest, as her stories always contained some kind of truth: the inclusion of an oft-repeated autobiographical tale gestured toward a more complex meaning, whose nature she might still be trying to work out. So it was with the tales of the pseudonym and the betrothal, both of which reappear with slight variations throughout Rachilde's writings, and so it was with the origin stories of *Monsieur Vénus*. Even in the preface she gives more than one explanation: the novel was both a conscious choice to write something salacious that would pay the rent and the product of a feverish two weeks of writing over which she had little control. In fact, the very matter of her authorship was somewhat ambiguous. In the original edition, the name Francis Talman appeared on the title page alongside hers. As she told it, she had met a man named Talman while fencing, and he agreed to fight for her if she were to be challenged to a duel on the heels of publication. If he played any role in the creation of the novel, then, it was as a protector rather than as an author. But there is no record of such a person, and subsequent editions eliminated his name. It is more likely that he never existed at all, being yet another "transvestite" of Rachilde's mind: a male figure that acted as a stand-in for the parts of her own imagination she could not readily acknowledge. Rachilde's stories, after all, were never to be taken at face value. Their repetition told you that an event was important or that a particular fact was rife with meaning, but it couldn't always tell you why, or what that meaning was.

The "legend" of Rachilde's hair offers another case in point. When she cut it off, she told many of her friends that she had sold it to a Russian prince for a price that she could not refuse. Closer to the truth was that she found her heavy tresses "encumbering." They went the way of the lacy female undergarments and face powder that she discarded at the same time. No one necessarily knew about the lingerie or the powder, but the hair would have been obvious. How to explain to others a move so clearly connected to gender difference and so much more permanent than a pair of pants one can take on and off, under the guise of work or costuming? Like her pseudonym, and like her rejection of marriage at age fifteen, the thing being rejected was a symbol of femininity itself.

In explaining her decision to dress like a man, Rachilde had noted that a single men's suit cost far less than a closet full of women's clothing. The starving-artist narrative also offered a certain explanation for Rachilde's male haircut: she needed short hair so as not to have to waste time on a frivolous feminine toilette and in order to be taken seriously. The story of the Russian prince, on the other hand, was too outrageous to be anything but a fabrication and thus offered a wink to anyone who was paying closer attention. Something's not quite right here, Rachilde lets you know, but she won't tell you what. Some, like d'Estoc, *were* paying attention. D'Estoc was maddened by this particular fiction, describing the "legend that shows the beautiful and supposedly young woman, having cut her magnificent hair, to sell it (500 francs) to a prince (if it wasn't a barber, it was therefore a prince!) who has it locked up in a chest (golden, right?) for which he keeps hold of the key (on his heart, that much is certain)."[17] *Doesn't everyone understand that she is lying?* she raged. But the fabrication was also the point. The strategy was not altogether different from Dieulafoy's method of deflection: whether marveling or cursing at the silliness of Rachilde's fiction, now you've forgotten to be concerned with the question behind it all, that of Rachilde's gender.

BEING RACHILDE

In the preface to the 1888 novel *Madame Adonis*, Rachilde wrote that "If I wear men's hats, it's because I have short hair, and if I have short hair, it's because I wear men's hats" (see figure 2). By that time, such a statement could be recognized as fully Rachildian—playful, enigmatic, and frustrating—but not inaccurate. She had developed a certain kind of voice, and it was one that seemed to revel in its own indecipherability. But Rachilde's confusing public statements were also commentaries on her being, and in her seeming doublespeak there was another kind of truth: the logic of Rachilde was necessarily self-referential, because—as far as she could tell—there was simply no other referent available.

From this vantage point, *Monsieur Vénus* offered its author an unexpected salve: like her pseudonym, it created a space for that indecipherability and a way to sidestep questions of both gender and sexuality. The preface of *To the Death* was the culmination of this process. It allowed Rachilde to ride out the wave of fascination with the novel and embrace it for her own purposes. These purposes were not, as d'Estoc and other cynics might have it, the "shameless self-promotion" with which we have become so familiar in celebrity culture. Rather, and despite the fact that it had troubled her initially, Rachilde seized upon her reputation as upon a life raft.

In her words, the choice was "to be strange or nothing at all," and with that qualification she presciently embraced her own queerness, as it were. Following her protagonist, she would not be a "he" or a "she," and "they" was not yet a possibility. Instead, she would be simply "Rachilde." Like the hysteria diagnosis and the pseudonym, being strange solved a certain problem.

While Rachilde had carefully steered clear of sex and scandal in *To the Death*, by the time of its publication the pendulum had swung back the other way. She was on the verge of publishing *The Marquise de Sade*, a novel based in part on her childhood. In this piece of fiction, she didn't shy away from the sexual precipice, depicting rape and other forms of violence. In the wake of *Monsieur Vénus*, protagonist Mary Barbe's pronouncements on her wedding night are especially resonant. When she refuses to sleep with her new husband, explicitly rejecting her procreative obligations, her words feel like some sort of alternative manifesto: *Je suis assez, en ETANT*, she roils. "I am enough, by BEING."[18]

Modern scholars and contemporary biographers are right to recognize, like the frustrated d'Estoc, the extent to which Rachilde fashioned her own identity, putting it unabashedly on display. But to call it a striptease or a crafty manipulation belies the fact that these choices were made out of necessity. In describing her clothing choices in the 1880s, Rachilde wrote later: "One shouldn't imagine that I wanted to cross-dress (*se travestir*)."[19] It's worth pausing on that verb, *se travestir*, which means to disguise oneself with clothing. This was never Rachilde's intention. The look that she cultivated was meant to be her own—a reflection of her self rather than a distortion of self, as the French verb suggests. Her clothing was a means of self-expression, just as Raoule de Vénérande's gender-crossing language, which has often been described as a form of linguistic *travestissement*, was more about the revelation of an alternative self than about denial or disguise.

Rachilde was caught outside existing gender categories and had no choice but to find a way to express herself. She was fiercely brave and outspoken, and deeply curious about sexuality; this was not an act, it was simply the reality that she faced. Since most others in her situation seemed inclined to hide who they were, being herself in public could look like a stunt. But being Rachilde was the only way for this complex person to continue to exist. Indeed, it's fair to say that Rachilde did not so much invent *Monsieur Vénus* as that the opposite was true. The public storytelling made room for the person who had motivated it. In this sense, *Monsieur Vénus*—the best-selling, rule-breaking, attention-grabbing *succès de scandale*—was ultimately—and unexpectedly—what created the writer Rachilde.

"TO WRITE SO AS NOT TO THINK"

In the preface of *To the Death*, Rachilde described *Monsieur Vénus* as a form of literary suicide. To be understood, she may have feared, would entail her banishment from literature, but to be misunderstood would be its own way of dying; either way, there would be pain. The gleeful romp through her life ends with a call to her publisher: "Monsieur Monnier . . . I have finished." "Why in the world are you crying, my little Rachilde?" he responds. Indirectly relayed through Monnier, Rachilde's tears are playful and poignant at once, a nod to the veracity of what she has just written and its betrayal of self, while refusing sentimentality all the same. Monnier's question is enough to suggest that while Rachilde may not have been truly dying of hunger, she may still have felt that her life was very much on the line. She made this clear in *The Bitten One*, the novel that retold the story of the genesis of *Monsieur Vénus*, in which she cast herself as the aspiring male writer Maurice de Saulérian. Maurice tries to kill himself at the outset by throwing himself into the Seine. Instead, he ends up writing a novel.

By constructing herself as Maurice, Rachilde confirmed the fact that the drowned man who had haunted her years before was a version of herself: the male authorial voice who struggled so hard to be heard. Once rescued, Maurice is paralyzed for several months, just as Rachilde would be after her thwarted affair with Mendès. The drowned man and the hysteric have merged in this telling, alternately gendered versions of the fear of insanity that plagued Rachilde. Death and insanity haunt them, and the only cure is writing.

Monsieur Vénus was a death of sorts but also a kind of rebirth, as gender transitions so often are. (Some people, posttransition, refer to the name their parents had given them as their "dead name.") As for so many who have faced the challenges of gender variance, the possibility of doing so in writing likely saved Rachilde's life, even if it terrified her. Liberation was available chiefly, as always, through imagination. Allowing her imagination to lead her may have also offered a kind of reprieve: "to write, so as not to think," as Maurice described it in *The Bitten One*. The same thought is picked up again by Laure in *The Animal*, as she embraces her nocturnal, animal self for the same reason: "One doesn't think anymore."[20]

The first story that Rachilde published after *Monsieur Vénus* was titled

"The Joy of Loving," an ironic title, as the tale contained very little joy. She published it under the masculine pseudonym Jean Yvan—a pseudonym of a pseudonym, by that point. It tells the story of a man named Jean, to whom she has given the same name she had assigned herself as his author. Jean falls in love with Danielle, an extraordinary woman, Rachilde writes, who had "the mind of a being who didn't have a sex" and who "wasn't a woman except in her body. Intellectually, she would have been a man, if she hadn't hated women so much."[21] Jean finds himself going mad through his love for Danielle, but it's not the madness that leads to his demise. Rather, it is the articulation of his feelings in writing that sends him over the edge. But Jean has no choice: the writing is compulsive, dictated by "an unknown voice within," in striking parallel to the internal voice that pushed Dieulafoy's Marguerite to become Brother Pelagius. Only when the voice is stilled can Jean stop writing, and at that point he finds himself wordless again, "unable to express any of the thoughts that he had just transcribed."[22]

Jean is immediately terrified: he finds the letter that he has unwittingly written "vile" (*immonde*) but also "beautiful."[23] Danielle reads his words and barely survives. Rachilde never tells us what the letter says, only relaying its strange, incomprehensible nature—a bracing combination of urgency, necessity, and danger. The story ends with Jean shooting himself while hovering over Danielle's sickly body.

Perhaps *Monsieur Vénus* represented a kind of automatic writing that Rachilde didn't quite control, a story that she felt compelled to write. Something similar happens in *The Bitten One*, when Maurice writes his controversial novel in three weeks, not leaving his room, writing on blank walls instead of paper. Like Jean's letter, the novel he produces is described as "vile" (*immonde*) but also as a triumph.

In her ninety-three years, Rachilde wrote over fifty novels and dozens of short stories and plays. Nonetheless, *Monsieur Vénus* always held a special meaning for her. To some colleagues and friends, she dismissed it as puerile, while to others she presented the volume as a way of becoming better acquainted. In 1903, she sent a copy to the lesbian poet Lucie Delarue-Mardrus (still married to Egyptian doctor Joseph-Charles Mardrus at the time), for whom it piqued a flirtatious interest.[24] Later, she discussed its significance in a letter to the gay sexologist Marc-André Raffolovich, whose work challenged established views of homosexuality.[25] In her courtship with Alfred Vallette, it served as both an intellectual touchstone and a tool of seduction; in his letters to Rachilde, her future husband admired its success, probed the novel's meaning, and used its gender play in his efforts to win her over.

By telling a story that could not be fully understood, Rachilde carved out a place for herself in the vernacular. In the process, she cracked the gender binary open so wide that she had enough room to explore for decades. The hysteric was just the beginning; this would be her life's work. But while *Monsieur Vénus* was a kind of coming out, Rachilde must have known that most of her readers could not truly understand what exactly she was confessing. This fact was both the blessing and the curse of gender variance in the nineteenth century: the curse of existing outside of epistemological categories and thus being subject to the trauma of seemingly inarticulable difference, and the blessing of escaping certain kinds of hatred because your critics simply did not understand you. They could not hit the mark simply because they could not see it.

All the same, in telling this particular story, Rachilde had found her voice.

11 DEATH BY MARRIAGE

IN 1889, RACHILDE MARRIED Alfred Vallette and gave up pants-wearing for good. "I buried my life as a boy," she later wrote of this transition.[1] That verb should give us pause. Rachilde had already died a few times already: when she jumped into the pond to avoid marriage, when she assumed a pseudonym, and when she wrote *Monsieur Vénus*. Dying had become a metaphor for the transition to a new way of being in the world.

Vallette and Rachilde's courtship is recorded in the letters that he sent to her between 1885 and 1889; her half of the correspondence has not survived. She published his letters several years after his death, under the title *The Novel of a Serious Man*. "Un homme sérieux" was the nickname Vallette had chosen for himself early on, in response to Rachilde's cajoling. It became a term of endearment, of sorts. That the sum of his earnest letters to her equaled a "novel" suggests how far he always was from truly understanding the person whom he convinced to spend her life with him.

Vallette, an aspiring writer himself, was immediately smitten with Rachilde when he met her at the Bal Bullier in March of 1885. Intrigued by her fierceness of spirit and her daring self-presentation, he was also troubled by her choices: "Aren't you afraid of breaking the law?" he asked.[2]

In one of their first exchanges, Rachilde asked her possible suitor his opinion of *Monsieur Vénus*. Vallette's response was a rambling meditation that revealed a general bewilderment. Rachilde seems to have asked him whether he believed she was its author—evoking the Francis Talman rumors—or whether she merely signed her name to it. He responded that either way it was a mistake for her to associate herself with the work. The story, he wrote, was simply not credible: "That a working class florist could lose himself to this extent because he has a woman's job, I don't believe it."[3] This comment proved more than anything that Vallette was among those who did not understand the novel or the way of being that it meant to depict. As for the style, he found it fairly well written but of a "virile" nature that made him also doubt whether it was her voice at all.

It's unclear whether Rachilde wrote back to Vallette at this point. Perhaps his incomprehension caused her to immediately lose interest; the correspondence breaks off abruptly. When the two come back into contact six months later, Vallette has a greater understanding about the person he is addressing, writing to Rachilde as "that strange double flower, neither man nor woman, perhaps."[4] By the end of the next letter, he has taken to calling her Mademoiselle-Monsieur. Various terms of gendered endearment flow throughout the letters: little brother, my dear marquise and my dear little king, dear little Enigma (f).[5]

Vallette seems attracted most of all by the comradery of their relationship: "You are the only woman, or woman writer, or ordinary woman, whom I can talk to while thinking as well," he observed.[6] He was a serious man, after all. In some ways, so was Rachilde.

In 1886, Rachilde was involved in a tumultuous relationship with the writer Léo d'Orfer, which she seems to have broken off definitively that summer. The following year, she refused Vallette as well, and they did not speak for well over a year. In July of 1888, Rachilde invited him to go boating. Vallette was surprised to find her in the floral dress of a working-class girl, with a man's overcoat and men's open-toed sandals. He was baffled by her new look, asking, "Why this new costume?"[7] He remained no less enamored, however. Over the next several letters, Vallette became increasingly adamant in his romantic pursuit, begging her to let him come to her apartment. Rachilde seems to have offered the excuse that her mother was in town, but Vallette rejected this reason. He never seemed to fully grasp what it meant to be entangled in a difficult familial relationship: "But why in the world are you so troubled by the intrusion of Madame your mother in your life?"[8]

Stubborn in his pursuit, Vallette had fallen in love with Rachilde, and this time he had no intention of giving up: "I don't consent to not seeing you anymore and not receiving any more of your letters," he wrote. "Come on, let's admit that I am in love with the author of *Monsieur Vénus*." Rachilde, he noted, seemed afraid, and he was not sure why. She was not telling him everything, he suspected. He pushed her on this point: "You have already told me so much that one more confession or one less is not going to upset you, I would think."[9] In the end, Vallette offered a deal: "You know that I am madly in love with you. Allow me to place my madness in the face of the other madness." In other words, trade my madness (of being madly in love) for the madness of your mother.[10]

In making his appeal to Rachilde, Vallette acknowledged their shared disdain for marriage. He proposed instead *une union libre de raison*—a play on words suggesting a combination between a *mariage de raison*, or arranged marriage, and a free union.[11] A *mariage de raison* differed from the love marriages—the *mariages d'amour*—that had slowly become the norm in nineteenth-century bourgeois French society. The free union was the more libertine idea, popularized by utopian socialists who did not believe the church or the government should be involved in sanctioning adult relationships. Divorce had become legal in France only a few years earlier, in 1884. Marriage and the laws associated with it were much debated in the 1880s, and these terms would have been used in common parlance.

Vallette offered the brazen suggestion of a reasoned free union in all seriousness. But it was not the free union espoused by certain European and American feminists, that is, the new companionate marriage that sought to make the relationship more equitable. Rather, Vallette wished to take care of Rachilde. "I beg you to allow me to become your guardian," he wrote. He also made clear that he was proposing an alternative model of marriage, in that there would be no expectation of having children. "I'm not going to ask you," he insisted, "that which you don't want to give to anyone, even the one that you would love, since you claim that . . . the reproductive instinct should be left only to animals."[12] At this point, Rachilde and Vallette seem to have had an understanding: there would be no sexual intercourse in this relationship, if there was to be sexual contact at all. The extent of their physical relationship remains unclear. Unlike her letters to Barrès, which spoke of "chaste ecstasies," her letters from Vallette contain no hint of passion. This was to be a marriage of minds, not bodies.

Rachilde did not accept right away, but within a few months they must have come to an agreement. In March, she wrote to Georges de Peyrebrune that she was getting married, seemingly out of exhaustion. "I am in the situation of a person who is tired of being told to rest," she explained. The exhaustion came in part because of her mother. Though she was living in another part of Paris at this point, Gabrielle's presence still loomed large. Vallette looked toward the practical: Gabrielle lived far from her and shouldn't be a nuisance. But for Rachilde the toll was emotional above all: the psychological drain of a complex relationship with the woman whose mental instability was a constant reminder of her own perceived troubles. It was a fault line within the family. Five years later, in 1894, she would write to Peyrebrune of Gabrielle's need to be institutionalized as soon as possible.[13]

In her teens, Rachilde had rejected marriage precisely because it was a denial of her freedom, specifically her freedom to become a writer. But while she joked to Peyrebrune that her marriage to Vallette would be the end of her freewheeling days ("Come April, I'll be finished with freedom"), accepting Vallette's *union libre de raison* did not require the erasure of her writerly identity. Vallette had offered himself as "a guardian who will fasten me to my author's desk."[14] For Rachilde, this marriage would provide a way of remaining a writer, then, and of not having to work so hard at staying alive in the process; she would have "a regular position"—with the aid of an intellectual partner and protector.

During this time in Rachilde's life, she may have felt overwhelmed by her many obligations; she was finishing *The Bitten One*, which she described as her first serious work, as well as the novel *Minette* and the French reissue of *Monsieur Vénus*. Her friend and mentor Camille Delaville had just died, and her mother was unwell. These pressures likely made her more receptive to the marriage offer.[15] She would not have to worry about where to live—Vallette had originally proposed separate residences—or how to put food on the table. To be Madame Vallette offered a way to be "Rachilde, homme de lettres" in the way she had always longed to be.

But there would be no love. "I know that I will never love my husband with passion," she wrote to Peyrebrune in conveying the news of their nuptials in March.[16] In late April, she turned to her for more advice on how to be "a proper woman." "I try so hard to be intimate with him and to listen, but I never understand and *even so*, he has the effect on me of a stranger."[17] Rachilde had never been attracted to Vallette, but apparently she was also still wounded from the loss of someone she did love, someone "vile and miserable" who was forever lost to her but who had filled her "cold bed" with torturous memories for the past three years.[18] In all likelihood, she was mourning d'Orfer. Rachilde writes of how hard she had been working "to hide my distress" and of how adept she was at wearing masks. In these deeply revelatory letters, she made it clear that she was marrying because she could not figure out a reason not to.

"I'm twenty-nine years old, and I'm so dead to everything and everyone that I am accepting a marriage like I would accept a suicide," she wrote.[19] By marrying Vallette, a man who, even if he didn't understand her, at least allowed her to write, Rachilde made the devil's bargain of accepting to die once more in order to live a bit longer and with less pain. In that sense, it was helpful to have love out of the picture.

Vallette felt a sense of intimacy, while Rachilde did not. In the last, undated letter of their correspondence from before their marriage, he told her that "your secret will be my secret. . . . You will have nothing else to worry about from anyone."[20] But if she had revealed some sort of secret, it did not seem to bring them any closer.

Rachilde married Vallette on June 12, 1889, in a small civil ceremony in the presence of four witnesses. She gave birth to their daughter Gabrielle four months later. The baby had not been part of the original arrangement. There is no mention of the pregnancy in the correspondence nor in the letters to Peyrebrune, although it was likely they spoke about it in person. Rachilde was used to talking to her "with an open heart."[21]

"THE NIGHTMARE OF MARRIAGE"

When Rachilde discussed having put to rest her "life as a boy" in the 1928 volume *Why I Am Not a Feminist*, she noted matter-of-factly that "when I got married, I simply dressed like everyone else and let my hair grow back out."[22] She neglected to mention her pregnancy or her daughter, but it is hard to imagine they did not play a role. On a practical level, the physical experience necessitated the sartorial shift. It must also have wreaked havoc on Rachilde's sense of self. This part of her life remains entirely undocumented, a glaring absence, considering her wide-ranging testimony to bodily rages of various sorts. In all that Rachilde wrote about marriage and procreation, in her correspondence and fictions, there is next to nothing about childbirth or motherhood; most often there are aunts and guardians in the role that a mother should play. Her novels provide some clues as to why this might be.

In the original Belgian edition of *Monsieur Vénus*, Rachilde had included a chapter in which she railed against sexual power hierarchies. "The man seated on her right in the clouds of some imaginary heaven has relegated his female companion to the second rung in the scale of beings," she wrote. Male superiority was a direct result of "the inferior role that her form imposes on women in the generative act." Procreation, claimed the narrator, enslaves women. It is a product of modern civilization, which has ignored the pleasures of "extinct generations—Rome, Athens, Lesbos." The reader is advised to "forget natural law, tear up the procreative pact" and look instead for the "secrets of passion without procreation."[23]

The "procreative obligation" was a major part of Rachilde's resistance to marriage. In many of her stories, the consummation of marriage is the tipping point. In *The Marquise de Sade*, Mary Barbe tells her husband Louis on their wedding night that there will be no intercourse, because she does not want to become pregnant. Her mother had died bringing her brother into the world, she explains. "I don't want to die the same way, and, supposing that I don't die, I don't want to go through the torture of childbirth." In *In the Well*, Rachilde referred to husbands as the "executioners" of their pregnant wives, asking if these women would ever be able to forgive them.[24]

In Rachilde's later novels, the focus on conjugal relations shifts from the refusal of procreation to the brutality and humiliation that engenders it. In *Madame Adonis*, a doctor is brought in when Louise fails to conceive. As a result, "the young woman suffered more," because "she had no recourse against the violence with which she was being threatened." The physical situation of marriage is described as one of hopeless doom: "She wondered how she would escape from this prison."[25] In *The Juggler*, Eliante Donalger remembers her own wedding night with her now deceased husband: she had wished for a quick death, unable to believe that "*this* was what happiness was."[26] And in *Princess of Darkness*, Rachilde depicts "the nightmare of marriage."The young heroine, Madeleine, whose aunt is a Spiritist, is presented with the choice between marrying a doctor, Edmond Sellier, and marrying the devil, the satanic Hunter. But Madeleine does not want to marry at all.

Edmond Sellier bears a striking resemblance to Vallette. Described as a "reasonable man"—evoking Vallette's own "serious man"—Sellier offers a similar bargain to Madeleine: "If I don't have you . . . I think I will kill myself," he tells her. "I don't want any more of my role as a reasonable man! . . . Don't love me, so be it; I accept your indifference, and I will try to make myself loved after the marriage as I am able to; but repeat to yourself that my only unhappiness would be to not see you anymore."[27] Like Rachilde, Madeleine tells her future husband that there were to be no children. But Sellier has sex with her while she is unconscious, leading to her pregnancy.

Had Vallette betrayed Rachilde's trust in a similar way? His missives during their courtship are alternately pleading and aggressive. In the undated letter in which he offers her a *union libre de raison*, she can't have been pregnant, as he had assured her there would be no sex. But Gabrielle Vallette was born in October, meaning that by the time Rachilde wrote to Peyrebrune in March, she had conceived. Was there some sort of betrayal, as between Sellier and Madeleine, that had put her in this compromising position, forcing her into this marriage in a way to which she could not readily admit?[28]

There would be no further children for Rachilde, and for the most part Gabrielle was raised away from their home until she was older. Rachilde's own mother took care of her granddaughter for at least a part of the time. In a letter to Peyrebrune, Rachilde wrote that her mother was increasingly unwell and would likely need to be hospitalized; but her mother was caring for her daughter and was enraged at the possibility that the child would be taken away. "I don't know if you have an idea of this horrible situation?" writes Rachilde. "My daughter held hostage by a madwoman!"[29]

Later, around 1907, Rachilde would write to Aurel—a female friend with whom she shared the kind of intimacy she had with Peyrebrune—about being preoccupied with preparing Gabrielle for marriage and thus being unable to work. In her archives, there are a few letters from Rachilde to her daughter in which she discusses the most mundane preparations of their country house.

But aside from a mention or two in passing in the biographical accounts of close male friends like André David and Auriant, Gabrielle is absent. Neither Rachilde's feelings about giving birth to her own daughter, both physical and emotional, nor any feelings about caring for a baby or young child and the complex impulses they might create, are to be found in Rachilde's colorful and varied depictions of women. Nor does Gabrielle herself make it into Rachilde's texts in any real way. Unlike so much of Rachilde's life, their relationship does not come alive on the page.

MADAME ALFRED VALLETTE

Once married, Rachilde traded in her *homme de lettres* calling card for one that read "Madame Alfred Vallette." But before long, she was signing in her own hand over these printed letters, writing over and around them as if to emphasize their superficiality. She was never really known by Madame Vallette, in the end; she insisted that she should be called Rachilde. She continued to answer to both "Monsieur" and "Madame."

Vallette and Rachilde formed a productive union in other ways. Their lives together were bonded through the creation of *Le Mercure de France*, the other "newborn" they brought into the world together in 1890. Vallette would serve as director until his death in 1935. The journal, he often told people, was a gift for his wife; he had chosen her favorite color, mauve, for its cover.[30]

The *Mercure* placed the couple at the heart of Parisian literary culture for several decades. For twenty-five years, their Tuesday salon was among the most famous in Paris, attracting distinguished literati alongside celebrities like Liane de Pougy, the courtesan turned princess, and the actress Sarah Bernhardt. One frequent guest was Auriant, originally Alexandre Hadjivassiliou, an Egyptian writer who became a close friend. He noted that with their office and salon arranged side by side, Vallette's and Rachilde's separate spaces gave a first impression of the gendered setup of a Muslim country, with men on one side and the harem on the other. But unlike in Egypt, on the Rue Condé these compartments were not separate: men and women would wander back and forth between the chambers.[31] Surrounded by the men at the helm of the *Mercure*, Rachilde was in her element. These were young writers who were far more interesting than the "young crazies whom she had tried to seduce in olden days" according to Auriant. Rachilde was entirely comfortable conversing with them as peers.[32]

Rachilde continued to write with barely a pause during this period, beginning a new stage of her career as a playwright. One of the goals of Vallette and *Le Mercure* was to launch a symbolist theater, in order to inject new life into an art form seen as stale.[33] Rachilde's plays were part of this symbolist initiative, "a theater of the soul, where the corporeal would be less important than a mystical inner life."[34] Inspired by Rachilde and Vallette, the young playwright and poet Paul Fort founded the Théâtre d'Art in 1890, and Rachilde's first play, "The Call of Blood," was one of the first to be produced in this venue, to warm reviews. Several more would follow.

Rachilde's most important role was as book review editor for *Le Mercure*, a post she held from 1897 to 1922. In her archives, one finds letters from young writers hoping to catch her attention. During that time, she reviewed friends and enemies with equal incisiveness—Colette, her husband Willy, Gyp, Pierre Lôti. Every important literary name hoped for her approval.

Over the years, Rachilde came to respect Vallette immensely. They were business partners more than anything else. Auriant described how secure Rachilde felt at Vallette's side, far from "the treacheries of literary life."[35] Vallette offered her "that freedom that seemed as necessary to her as space is to a wild horse," while also pushing her as a writer and an intellectual.[36] But no amount of respect could overcome the fact that Vallette bored Rachilde. In letters to Aurel, Rachilde explained why she likely would not come to a soirée to which they were invited. Too often, she explained, she felt that she was expected to come with the one thing that she could not manage to bring: her husband, who did not, as a rule, leave the house after dark.[37]

Next to his "wild horse" of a wife, Vallette was buttoned up—quite literally. He wore a dolman jacket buttoned to the collar, which allowed him to avoid any sort of tie, since he was "horrified by ribbons and any sort of useless male accessories."[38] In Rachilde's writing, we see echoes of Vallette not only in the "reasonable man" that was Sellier but also in the boring fiancé Henri of *The Animal*, described as "a simple man"—another variation on Vallette's nickname. There's nothing particularly terrible about Henri, but he is "that murderer of love that we call: an orderly man."[39]

In another autobiographical novel from later in her life, *Duvet-d'ange: Confessions of a Young Man of Letters*, Rachilde offered a description of her husband at work. The novel centers around the young writer known as "Duvet-d'ange" (a play on his noble-sounding name, Ange Ernest Le Duvet), who comes to see Edmond Dormoy, the editor of the *Mauve Review*. Duvet-d'ange encounters a man "whom you can only see at his place, for it seems he never goes out." In giving Vallette the name Dormoy in this novel, Rachilde tied him to another imaginary figure: the Marquis d'Ormoy, who she claimed spawned her own father out of wedlock. Linking her husband to her father, Rachilde suggests that her marriage replaced one kind of brutality with another. He is "always calm, very polite," writes Rachilde of Dormoy. "One feels that he has the habit of making himself understood in few words, and to be promptly obeyed."[40]

Duvet-d'ange was the second to last novel that Rachilde would ever write. She was eighty-three when it was published in 1943, and her husband had been gone for nearly a decade. In it, she gives us a glimpse of her life holding court in what was the shared home of both her marriage and the *Mercure*. Indeed, these two things were hardly separate. This was the bargain she had made: to choose writing over love. In this, Vallette kept his promise. She did not have to become someone else in order to marry.

QUEEN BATHILDE

In the playful self-portrait offered in *Duvet-d'ange*, Rachilde is "the queen Bathilde," Dormoy's wife. Duvet-d'ange is enamored of the "strange creature in a black satin sheath covered in black lace," her hair hidden underneath a black velvet headband. Bathilde's face is unpowdered, and her hands are like those of a man. Despite her different self-presentation, little had changed. "No one can seem to agree upon the kind of talent that she possesses," notes the young man. Everyone wonders "did she or did she not have lovers?"[41] Even though Bathilde was not wearing pants or a man's haircut, she was styled according to her own singular taste, which did nothing to resolve the gender ambiguity: "Is it a man or a woman?" the young writer finds himself asking, even with the sartorial clues.[42]

Duvet-d'ange might have stood for any number of the younger men that Rachilde had cast her spell upon. In the novel, he is described as "stupefied"

FIGURE 40. Portrait of Rachilde by the artist François Guiguet.

by her (*médusé* is the French word, with its own gendered context in reference to the Greek myth), just as André David, Homem-Christo, and the writer Alfred Jarry were enthralled by the older Rachilde, whom they came to consider a dear friend and mentor. More famous than any of them, "she derived no pride, no vanity" from their adulatory presence, according to

FIGURE 41. Portrait of Rachilde by the artist Lita Besnard.
Source: Bibliothèque littéraire Jacques Doucet. Reprinted with permission.

Auriant—himself a younger man mesmerized by the eccentric Rachilde.[43] In his 1924 biography, *Rachilde, Man of Letters*, David describes the sense of awe he felt on visiting the office of the *Mercure*, aware of the many famous men who had preceded him on those very steps. More than anything, though, he was enamored of Rachilde's generosity to young writers like himself. "Allow me to thank you, Rachilde," he writes, addressing her directly in his biography, thus changing registers in the midst of his otherwise neutral writing, "for adding my more modest name to all of those young poets and novelists that you showcased and publicly designated as talented."[44]

Several years after Vallette died, Rachilde moved upstairs from the apartment they had shared with the *Mercure*. She spent the rest of her life in that smaller space, surrounded by memories: a photo of Victor Hugo, as well as a bit of fabric that had belonged to him, given to her by Catulle Mendès; a photo of Charles Baudelaire, to whom she'd been compared as "Mademoiselle Baudelaire" by Lorrain and Mendès; a portrait of Alfred Jarry, a writer and friend whom she had admired deeply; and two portraits of herself: a pastel by François Guiguet from around 1890 and another by Lita Besnard from 1919 (figures 40 and 41).[45] In this way, she kept track of the many lives she had lived. Her home was a museum for her plural existence, allowing the parts to add up to a kind of whole, which was in turn much more than the sum of its parts.

12 WHY SHE WAS NOT A FEMINIST

AT FIRST, RACHILDE'S DECLARATIONS in *Why I Am Not a Feminist* make it clear why the matter of her politics was not settled. She describes writing and wearing masculine clothing as a means of freedom from patriarchal constructs. "Unlike other well-brought-up young women, I didn't come out of my parents' home in order to follow Prince Charming on the great Paths," she writes of her youth. Rather, "I had gone to the Rue des Ecoles [her first address in Paris] in order to seize the freedom of writing that my parents had refused to give me."[1] Dressing like a man, in this telling, was a way of choosing writing, and thus another rejection of the traditional path of marriage. The language here echoes the story of convening the séance in order to acquire "literary freedom."[2] More specifically, both the séance and the pants-wearing are described as a way of releasing herself from nineteenth-century expectations of femininity. "Above all I love freedom," she declares, "most of all my own!"

As different forms of feminist expression came into view in the 1920s, the tendency to see Rachilde as a pioneer on this political front apparently frustrated her, giving rise to her lengthy meditation on the subject. She recounts how a young American feminist had recently asked her at a literary salon, "Why, my dear master, do you insist on not cutting your hair when it would be so useful to our cause? Short hair is a sign of unity and independence."

Profoundly irritated, Rachilde responded in a perfectly Rachildian way: "If I disguise myself as a woman," she told her naïve interlocutor, "that's because, in my biographies, they call me the *Chevalière d'Eon*." The young woman was shocked—stunned into silence by Rachilde's cagey reference to the seventeenth-century knight, born male, who lived the second half of his life as a woman. Had she understood the confession? Rachilde was linking herself to one of the people to whom Jane Dieulafoy had devoted a biographical study, along with the Abbé de Choisy and the opera singer Stuart. In naming d'Eon, Rachilde questioned the young feminist's assumptions about her "true" identity: like the Chevalier/ière, she could not be defined by a single sex. If the young woman caught the reference—as she may have, for the knight was a well-known figure in popular culture—she might have known that d'Eon's sex had long been in question and that some assumed he had been assigned female at birth. In making the comparison, Rachilde was affirming the fluidity of her own gender. She wasn't being facetious; she was being direct.

Indeed, it was precisely in such defiant statements that Rachilde tended to reveal the truth, knowing, perhaps, that she would not be taken seriously or deeply aware that she simply could not be understood. If Jane Dieulafoy's strategy was strategic deflection, always pointing her interlocutors elsewhere, for Rachilde it was more straightforward: she would be truthful to the extent that truth was possible. Those around her would invariably see her as being playful and droll.

Rachilde's point—certainly lost on the young American—is the answer to the titular question as well, which, in its simplicity, need not require an eighty-four-page pamphlet. Even as Rachilde put on pants to reject her presumed place as a woman in a patriarchal culture, her clothing choices were not an emancipatory way of expressing femininity. They were a way of declaring her *difference* from women. The freedom she sought was not merely from patriarchal structures but from womanhood itself. In other words, the answer to the question "Why I am not a feminist" was simply "because I am not a woman."

This was a sentiment that Rachilde expressed repeatedly to her closest friends. In Peyrebrune's *A Female Decadent*, the character based on Rachilde, Hélione, declares outright: "I am not a woman."[3] It's not hard to imagine the young Rachilde saying something similar to her confidante. Of course, these days one does not have to be a woman to be a feminist. But while there were men at the turn of the century who supported feminism, it was nearly always the women who assumed the term "feminist" as a form of political identification; this was certainly the case in the public imagination. The feminist label may have maddened Rachilde for this reason. In a letter from 1891, shortly after she gave up wearing pants, she responded to a request for comment on the then-burgeoning feminist movement in a tone of polite exasperation: "The funny thing is that you are the twentieth person in the past year who has asked me about this," she wrote, wondering why that would be the case, given that she had always "distanced myself from the emancipators."[4]

The feminist label was often affixed to Rachilde both because of her presumed gender and because of her resistance to it. She chafed at the notion that her achievements had a special status because they had been accomplished by a woman. Even while she recognized certain aspects of herself as female, her desire to distance herself from the exclusive category of woman was insistent. And yet, just as when she told her parents that she had faked the séance, no one seemed to believe her. The novelist Maryse Choisy, with whom she became close in the 1920s, cites at least four occasions when Rachilde interrupted her to say, "But as for me, I'm a man."[5]

In 1846, social theorist Pierre-Joseph Proudhon famously declared that there were only two kinds of women: housewives or harlots. Rachilde seemed to agree with this assessment. At the end of *Why I Am Not a Feminist*, she describes herself as follows: "Not being of the species of females"—here the more clinically oriented *femelles* rather than *femme* is suggestive of the female biological role—"nor of the species of courtesans, I am content to remain a reporter, that is to say, to remain neutral by taking notes without taking sides."[6] Unable to see herself as either kind of woman, wife or mistress, Rachilde chose neutrality.

Rachilde's remarks in this essay help clarify some of the changes that followed her marriage, which are often misunderstood. The fact that she had given up her pants and "buried" her "life as a boy" by 1890 has made it easier for critics to view her earlier behavior and self-presentation as a calculated performance. It's hard not to dwell on the pants, linked as they are to the mythology of Rachilde. "The man's suit was a statement of intent," argues Jennifer Birkett. They were a way to "parlay her own image to make a splash in the male-dominated literary pond of fin de siècle Paris," according to Frazer Lively.[7] The fact that she stopped wearing them has been used as implicit evidence that they were but a ruse to affirm Rachilde's true motives of self-promotion and literary success. But it is more likely that it was never the pants that truly mattered for Rachilde. She was the anti-Baudelairian when it came to fashion, which she loathed as "a hysterical gesture imposed on women" and as "a collective hallucination" all the more dubious because of its fleeting nature. While the pants may have felt right in the 1880s, it seems that later, especially as feminists jettisoned the corset, wearing them felt more like a *travestissement*.

The images that we have of Rachilde serve to unsettle any preconceptions of her and confirm the inadvisability of designating her gender according to her clothing choices. The most famous image of Rachilde from the 1890s is a photograph that shows her in a long, coat-like dress with puffy gigot sleeves (figure 42). She sits sideways on a lyre-backed chair, facing the camera. Her chin leans demurely on her right arm, which is propped upon the chair's back. The copy of this image housed in the collection at the Jacques Doucet library in Paris is inscribed to her husband. It's a strangely feminine pose—at odds with how we might imagine the author of *Monsieur Vénus* or *The Marquise de Sade.*

But, as Melanie Hawthorne has astutely observed, there's another image from that same sitting. In it, Rachilde wears the same long cloak, with the same decorative brooch at her throat (figure 43). This time we see Rachilde in profile. She wears a fedora, just as she often described both herself and her female fictional characters as doing. This pose is different in other ways too, starting with the shift to that same side view that she had offered Jean Lorrain in her self-portrait. (This copy is offered to her friend Cazals, the Decadent artist.) The gentle smile is gone, and she looks beyond the frame with an allure of mystery. Tyrolean hat atop her head, a piece of paper in her hand, she is in motion, headed somewhere. Our gaze is drawn to her telltale sideburn—a traditional marker of masculinity but with a distinctly feminine upward curl—and we note the smooth lines of her coat, a reminder that she is not wearing a corset. We see the other photograph differently through this lens: the loose bun atop her head becomes a way to wear a man's hat with ease rather than part of a prim, feminine style. Taken together, we are no longer as far from the shape-shifter of the 1880s as it may have seemed.

FIGURE 42. Photograph of Rachilde, around 1895, inscribed "To Monsieur Alfred Vallette, my husband."

Source: Bibliothèque littéraire Jacques Doucet. Reprinted with permission.

A Cazals, une
grande dame russe qui
à Rachilde!

The focus on Rachilde's pants-wearing as a ruse to gain professional success—and as the only sartorial mark of her rebellion—steers us away from the complexity of her relationship to gender and its expression. When Rachilde gave up her pants, she did not embrace her femininity any more than she abandoned the feminism that she never espoused. Without pants, Rachilde could still gesture toward masculinity or temper her feminine appearance with a touch of rebellion, be it with a masculine fedora or the velvet bands that she wore later. In the days when she wore pants, on the other hand, she did so with other feminine accessories, attaching to her hat the kind of veil popular in women's fashion at the time. It was an unusual look, to say the least (figure 44).[8] Rachilde's style was all her own.

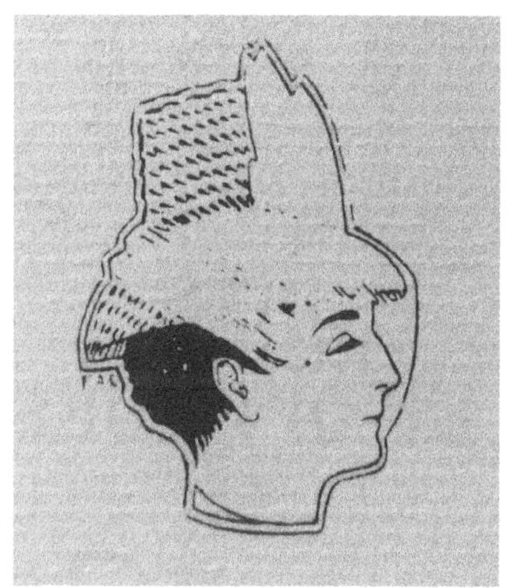

FIGURE 44. Sketch of Rachilde, with the veil attached to her hat, by Cazals.

What's more, when Rachilde retired her pants, she in no way retired her resistance to the gender binary. She claimed to have chosen neutrality: staying on the sidelines of gender. But it looked more as if she was choosing difference. Perhaps this choice was made in order not to be easily misunderstood as something else, in the absence of a context in which to ground herself, or a form of clothing that would allow her to declare her gender identity in a satisfactory way. "Having exited humanity," she wrote to Homem-Christo, "I have no desire to go back in."[9]

For a time, Rachilde seemed to accept a softened image; or perhaps she enjoyed hiding behind it. Ernest Gaubert's 1907 biography featured a "portrait of Rachilde" by Marguerite van Bever from 1898 that was no more than an engraved reproduction of the earlier studio photograph (figure 45).[10] Van Bever had simply embellished the image with various decorative touches: a lavishly upholstered chair instead of the spare lyre-back, an embroidered bolero around Rachilde's shoulders, and a loose knot beneath the brooch. In the background, a leafy vine imprinted upon a Japanese screen stretches behind her head, as if to emphasize the verdant motif of the chair and necktie. Who was this floral, effeminate Rachilde?

< FIGURE 43. Photograph of Rachilde, inscribed for the artist Frédéric-Auguste Cazals. Source: Bibliothèque littéraire Jacques Doucet. Reprinted with permission.

FIGURE 45. Portrait of Rachilde by Marguerite van Bever.

Source: Ernest Gaubert, *Rachilde*. Paris: Sansot, 1907.

Renderings by Ouvré and Nel Harroun published in successive editions of Rachilde's *Portraits of Men* seem to be more consonant with her fluid sense of self. In the portrait by Ouvré that accompanied the original 1929 edition, Rachilde appears almost clownlike: her eyebrows are furry, black arcs that contrast with her slicked-back white hair (figure 46). We know from photographs that there is more hair tucked behind her head, but in the drawing she might as well have a man's haircut. Just as one's eyes settle on the pronounced contours of her face, the delicate lashes come into relief, the lips darkened with rouge, the textures of the feminine clothing. A gender-ambiguous Rachilde comes into view. In a later edition of the volume—there were at least half a dozen—the Ouvré portrait was replaced with a sketch by the flamboyant music hall dancer Nel Harroun, who embodied, some say, a real-life "Monsieur Vénus" and who was the subject of Rachilde's 1934 novel *My Strange Pleasure*.[11] Harroun softened the contrast between the hair and eyebrows, allowing Rachilde to fade into the feminine swirls of her clothing and coiffed hair for a different look entirely. In this sketch, she might well be a music hall dancer herself (figure 47).

THE LEGEND OF THE WEREWOLF

Rachilde credited her long life with her faithfulness to herself. "If I'm alive at an age when, undoubtedly . . . I should be dead, it's because I have always had, despite all the exaggerations of my life, a respect for logic: I don't do what is contrary to my animal instinct." This instinct is what sometimes made her uncomfortable with social norms. "I don't imitate human gestures when I feel far from that aspect of humanity," she added.[12] The reference to animals was not mere rhetoric, for Rachilde often described her affinity with them. The most recent ways of thinking about transgender offer a framework for reconsidering this identification. In an issue of *Transgender Studies Quarterly* devoted to "Trans* Animalities," Eva Hayward and Jami Weinstein describe ways in which trans identities can be seen as expressing the limits of the human. The nascent field of trans animal studies considers how a more elastic relationship between male and female might lead to a different way of thinking about the degree to which humans are separate—or not—from the rest of the animal world. By collapsing traditional lines between male and female, the relationship between human and animal is also thrown into

FIGURE 46. Portrait of Rachilde by the artist Ouvré, 1929.
Source: Bibliothèque littéraire Jacques Doucet. Reprinted with permission.

question. Human/nonhuman becomes a binary that is just as arbitrarily rigid as male/female.

In this light, Rachilde's lifelong interest in animals and her willingness to see herself on a continuum with the creatures she adored can be understood as one of the ways in which she worked out her gender story. As she grew older, Rachilde frequently alluded to her sense that she had long felt

FIGURE 47. Portrait of Rachilde by Nel Harroun, 1929.
Source: Rachilde, *Portraits d'hommes*, 1930.

detached from the human species.[13] She described herself as a "strange creature"—a kind of *other.* Most often, she declared herself to be a werewolf—a *loup-garou*. She made this statement repeatedly: in *The Garden of Mystery*, her correspondence with Homem-Christo, her letters to Auriant, and to many other friends. While it sounded facetious, like so many of her assertions, it contained a kind of truth.

According to Périgordian legend, the children of a defrocked priest would be cursed for five generations. Rachilde, the great-granddaughter of such a man, claimed that she had inherited the curse, which therefore made her a werewolf—a cult figure of the region in which she was raised. Her mother had introduced the notion, worrying that her daughter was afflicted. But over the years, Rachilde had come to embrace the metaphor. Rachilde's most famous protagonist bore the name of the priest, the abbot Raoul, who had educated her, the one who had encouraged her to conduct the séance that led to her own rechristening. The priest, defrocked or not, had reentered her own genealogy in this way. In "The Wolf Catcher's Daughter," Rachilde had named her gender-crossing protagonist Raoule, just as in *Monsieur Vénus*. This other Raoule ran off with a wolf instead of the man she was supposed to marry. The fates of the priest, werewolf, and gender-crosser were thus united in Rachilde's imagination, all three connected, perhaps, through her sense of how she came to exist just beyond the edges of humanity.

The plot of Rachilde's late novel *Duvet-d'ange* also centers around the identification of woman and wolf: Bathilde befriends the young writer because he has written a poem about a werewolf. "Admit that you wanted to make fun of me," she tells the young man, who is bewildered by her insistence that she is in fact a werewolf, just as he had described in his fable. "Look at me," she commands, with a glint in her eye, "and tremble."[14]

The figure of the werewolf may have served as a way for Rachilde to conceive of her difference from the humans that surrounded her, a way of reaching beyond gender, through her affinity with the wildlife with which she grew up. In a letter to Auriant, she wrote of how she used to go around on all fours as a child, and how she experienced a pleasure in nature "completely unknown to humanity."[15] The pleasures that she sought throughout her life might similarly have seemed absent from the human world in which she lived.

Werewolves and other creatures haunt Rachilde's fictions: wolves who run off with adolescent girls, cats who fall in love with women. In several of Rachilde's later fictions, *Minette*, *The Animal*, and *The Shewolf Leader*, she flirts aggressively with the relationship between human and animal. In *The Animal*, the angry tomcat Lion scratches off Laure's face and transforms her into a cat, a striking replay of Raoule's attack on Jacques in *Monsieur*

Vénus. The transformed Laure is then described in terms often assigned to Rachilde: "a devilish feline, an unknown monster, frightening."[16] The animal fictions offered Rachilde another way through which she explored her sense of being double, a "strange creature" who was alternately special and terrifying (figure 48).

These fictions have stood apart in Rachilde's oeuvre, but they are consonant with her other writings. In fact, they reveal that many of the questions explored first in *Monsieur Vénus* are present in other fictions, even if in less recognizable forms. The wax effigy-as-transgender-sex-toy in *Monsieur Vénus* has been recognized as an early manifestation of Donna Haraway's postmodern feminist notion of the cyborg, which Haraway imagined in 1984 as a way to break free of binaries such as human/animal and human/machine, which were subject to rigid, encompassing patriarchal structures. The fantasy of the animal merging with the human is another realization of the cyborg and aligns with Rachilde's exploration of gender plurality. Indeed, the animal fictions offered another way in which Rachilde explored her sense of being double, alternately special and terrifying in her strangeness.

FIGURE 48. Sketch of Rachilde as a cat woman, by A.-F. Cazals. Rachilde included this image on her personal stationery, signed here.

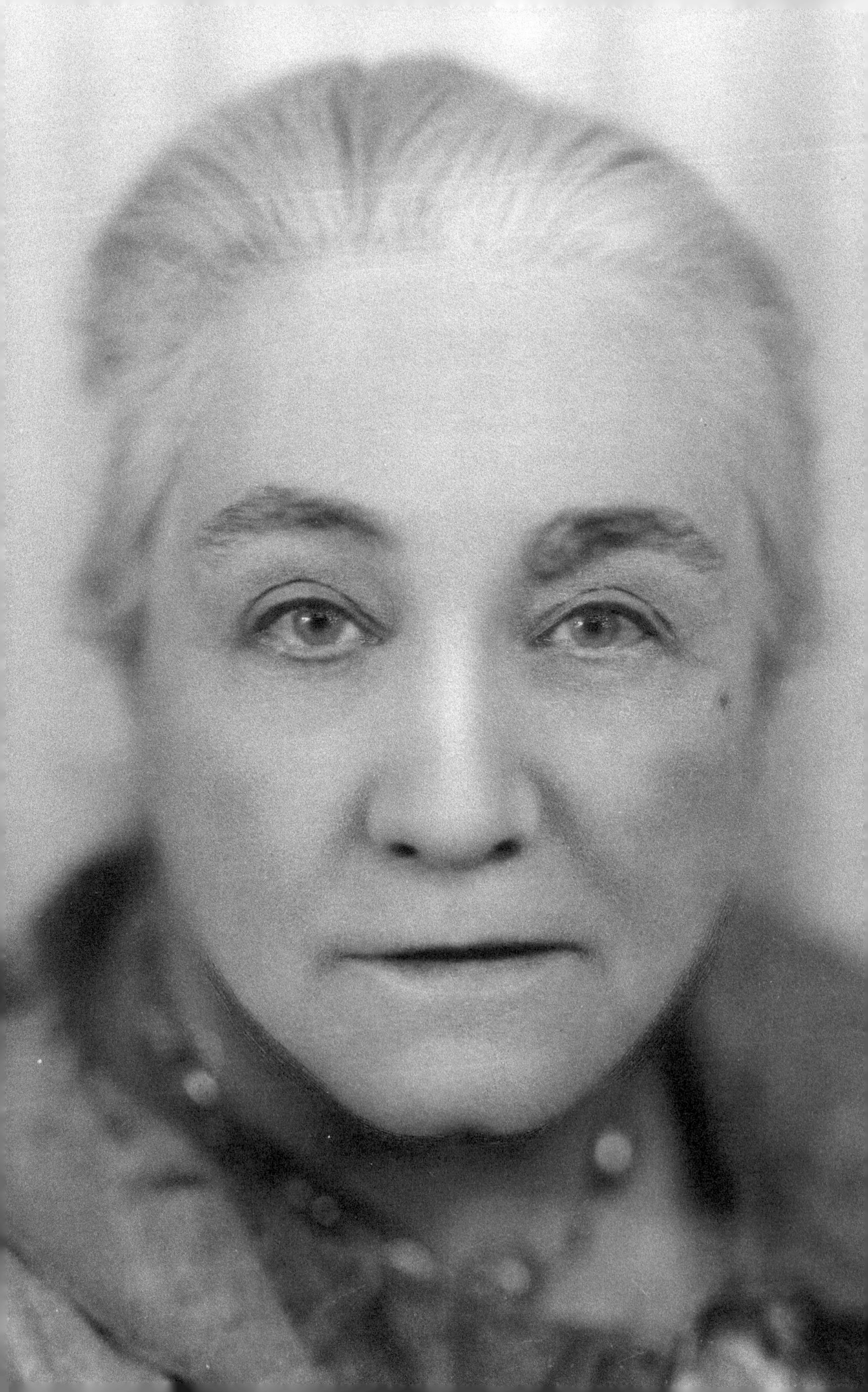

FIGURE 50. Rachilde with Homem-Christo.
Source: Bibliothèque littéraire Jacques Doucet. Reprinted with permission.

Human and animal, male and female, Rachilde's self-image, like certain modern iterations of trans identity, continually challenged the "the boundaries between, and existence of, differentiated, essential kinds," to follow Hayward and Weinstein.[17] In place of the gender differentiated in Rachilde, we find "and . . . and . . . and . . . ."[18]

As a final avatar of Rachilde, then, the matronly Bathilde is significant. She is a self-identified werewolf who presents as both male and female at once, neither one thing nor the other. Traditionally, the werewolf is a figure of horror—and there is a good deal of violence in Rachilde's animal fictions.

< **FIGURE 49.** Photograph of Rachilde in 1928.
Source: Roger-Viollet.

FIGURE 51. Portrait of Rachilde by the woman writer and artist Noêl Santon. Source: Bibliothèque littéraire Jacques Doucet. Reprinted with permission.

But the werewolf created by the octogenarian Rachilde is a benevolent figure. When Duvet-d'ange gets over his anxiety with Bathilde, he finds himself dazed by his new "queen," the "funereal tale of the werewolf far off."[19] With this last story, Rachilde offers herself up as a less threatening figure. The werewolf no longer terrifies, once you get used to her.

Rachilde's transition into her complete self was not a crossing over, as it was to a great degree for Jane Dieulafoy. Rather, it appears to have been a state of constant flux, a life of werewolf-like changes that had to fit not just the circumstances around her but the circumstances within her. Perhaps this is why, unlike Dieulafoy and Montifaud, Rachilde largely stayed away from cameras, with their pretense of scientific accuracy. "Dreams can't be set down," wrote Rachilde to Homem-Christo, speaking of the limits of photography as failing to capture the fleeting or the unstable.[20]

A few photographic portraits of Rachilde survive from the twilight of her life, however. In these, her pronounced, masculine jawline and bold eyebrows seem perfectly compatible with feminine accessories: shapeless dresses adorned with necklaces and scarves (figures 49 and 50). More compelling than the photos, perhaps, are the many artistic efforts to render Rachilde visually, several of which can be found in her archives, as they were offered to her as gifts (figures 40, 41, 46–48, and 51). Just as in the 1880s, when so many of Rachilde's literary friends took to their pens in order to capture her difference in writing, these visual renderings seek something ineffable, dynamic, fleeting. And just as no two photographs, even from the same sitting, present her consistently, no two of these renderings seem to capture the same person. And yet, one recognizes Rachilde in them all.

PART 3

MARC DE MONTIFAUD: "I AM ME"

13 BECOMING MARC

THE EARLIEST SURVIVING PHOTOGRAPH of Marc de Montifaud was taken by the renowned photographer Nadar (figure 52). Montifaud sits sideways on a chair, her arms crossed over its back, with a dark screen behind her. Her angular face is framed by an oversized collar of thick cotton triangles edged with hatch-stitched lace that overhangs her shoulders. But there is something wrong with this effort at adornment: it is the stiff lace more suitable for table coverings and doilies than apparel. The dress fills the image with folds of fabric where a lap should be. Nor is Montifaud constrained by a corset, as was the custom for women of her time and class. Nothing seems to be holding her body into its desired feminine contours in this tent-like garment, with its heavy and unwieldy looking fabric. It is hard to imagine how she was able to move around from within it.

It is Montifaud's expression, however, that most unnerves. Even with one eyebrow slightly raised, her eyes are heavy as she looks past the camera's lens. She appears not just sullen but dissociated, psychologically disconnected from her body, from the moment. Indeed, she is expressionless, as if her self had been overpowered by the dress. Go ahead and take my photo, she seems to say, but you won't be able to see me.

A few years afterwards, Montifaud would abandon women's clothing for a dapper bowtie and waistcoat. In photos from the decades that followed,

she cut a more confident, comfortable figure, easily passing for a man with her closely cropped hair now framing her broad, square jaw. In one striking image (figure 53), she gazes toward the camera, the slight upward curve of the lips suggesting pleasure. Her eyes are much more alert. She is equal parts elegant and handsome—even dandyish. Now she looks directly at the camera. Locked with the camera's lens, her eyes convey an unspoken pact or perhaps an invitation. This time, she seems to show trust: a belief that the camera will capture her in the way she wants to be seen.

It's difficult to say exactly what had changed for Montifaud in the time between these photographs—what allowed her to realize this fuller expression of self. Despite the voluminousness of her writing, she did not reflect explicitly on gender. She never revealed why she chose the name Marc or why she signed her name "Paul Erasme" years later. Aside from a few sentences, she did not reflect outright on her decision to wear men's clothes, as she began to do for good in the 1880s. Nor did she offer, like Dieulafoy, a series of parables revealing the logic that might have driven such a decision.

If Dieulafoy was consumed with the *why* of her difference, and Rachilde with the *what*, Montifaud left little evidence she was preoccupied with either. What clearly troubled her was that the world she inhabited did not want to make room for her as she was. But Montifaud managed to carve out a place for herself in spite of these limits. Rather than writing on the topic of gender-crossing, she wrote in order to assume her gender more fully, taking on a man's name and explicitly assuming a man's vantage point. Montifaud would be a man through her writing—and force others to make their case against her right to do so. In this way, she worked tirelessly to be seen the way she wanted to be seen, even if she could not quite be understood.

BEGINNINGS

Little is known about the early life of Marie-Amélie Chartroule de Montifaud. Her mother was Catholic; her father, a doctor, was a *libre penseur*, or freethinker. Indebted to the rationalist philosophy of the French Enlightenment, freethinkers rejected the conventions of religion, politics, and social mores in favor of rationally developed beliefs based on their own life experiences. Montifaud clearly followed her father's path: question everything and believe only what you determine for yourself to be true.

< **FIGURE 52.** Marc de Montifaud by Nadar, around 1880. This portrait was included in *La Galerie contemporaine*, 1st ser., vol. 3. Paris: L. Baschet, 1878.

FIGURE 53. Marc de Montifaud, around 1900.

Source: Bibliothèque Marguerite Durand / Roger-Viollet. Reprinted with permission.

Montifaud showed signs of artistic promise at an early age. Like other young women of the time, she was sent to a private studio to study, as admission to the Ecole des Beaux-Arts was closed to them until 1897. She trained in the atelier of the Romantic painter Jean-Baptiste Tissier, an official state artist of the Second Empire who served as mentor to many young women in their pursuit of art. Under his direction, Montifaud became a talented painter on wood and ceramics.

In July of 1864, Montifaud married the Spanish count Juan Francis Léon de Quivogne, Comte de Luna. According to public records she was nineteen, but most accounts in the contemporary press described her as having married at fifteen or sixteen, and she never corrected the record. "Child prodigy" may have been one of the myths that she was constructing for herself—or perhaps, child bride.[1]

Léon de Quivogne was more than a decade older than Montifaud and had been married before. He shared her family's aristocratic background and her interest in art. At the time of their marriage he had been working in Paris for several years as personal secretary to the esteemed writer and critic Arsène Houssaye. Houssaye was editor of *L'Artiste*, a publication he had acquired in 1843, soon transforming it into the most prestigious art journal in France.

It is unclear how Montifaud met her husband. By May of 1865, she was also writing for *L'Artiste*, signing her pieces "Marc de Montifaud." It seems likely that Montifaud's parents had organized the marriage. Were they worried that their cerebral, free-spirited daughter would have difficulty finding a match? Or was it rather her lack of a fortune that posed the greatest obstacle to betrothal? Montifaud's younger sister, Marthe, would never marry. Perhaps Montifaud's parents were acquainted with Houssaye, who was closer to their own age, and had asked him to find an older man who would both tolerate their daughter's passions and rein her in. If this was so, it didn't work. Years later, when Montifaud was repeatedly indicted for writing pornography, her mother "begged all the writers she knew to do whatever it took to turn her daughter away from this dangerous and deplorable genre of writing."[2]

By all accounts, Léon de Quivogne was enamored of the brilliant and passionate young art student. He surely knew that he was marrying an intellectual: as an adolescent, Montifaud had already published a few minor pieces in the magazine *Plaisir et Travail* and had written a novel, as yet unpublished. Léon gave Montifaud permission to continue to publish her writings, for a husband's permission was, in fact, required.

Under an unusual agreement, Montifaud's father—with no sons to whom he could pass on his pedigree—had asked Léon to add the family name to his own. So both Marc and Léon had the surname "Quivogne de Montifaud"—a curiously egalitarian arrangement. Even the name "Madame de Montifaud" was quietly subversive for the time. It acknowledged her married state while attaching the title of matrimony to her own family name. She did not lose part of herself through marriage by assuming the name of another; she was no Madame Bovary. If anything, Léon would be a corollary of Marc and not the other way around. He even took to signing his name professionally as "Léon de Montifaud," dropping the Quivogne entirely,[3] a striking gesture for a man to make. As a result, when Marc was addressed professionally as "Monsieur de Montifaud," as frequently happened, it was a name that referred to her husband as well.

Like Rachilde, Montifaud had taken a pen name that gradually became assimilated with her private identity. It was not quite a pseudonym, then. Rather, the name allowed her to carve out a distinct public space for herself that could yield the privileges of male authority without directly undermining those of the proper married woman. From the beginning, "Marc de Montifaud" was a means of having it both ways. This was evident in the most ordinary affairs of daily existence. She received mail sent to "Monsieur de Montifaud" and letters addressed to "Marc" throughout her life. Some were written by readers who assumed her to be a man, while others came from friends and colleagues. Often the gender on the outside did not match the gender within: sometimes the envelope would read "Monsieur Marc de Montifaud," while the letter inside would be addressed to "chère Madame." But just as often, the reverse was the case. To her intimates, she alternated between signing "Marc" and "Marie." Even her mother seemed resigned to this fluidity. In a letter dated around 1880, she wrote on the first page to her "cher trèsor" (dear treasure [masculine]), whom she addressed as "mon cher enfant" (my dear child [masculine]) before offering kisses in closing to "ma chère enfant" (feminine)—a casual, unacknowledged slip between gender pronouns.[4]

Montifaud's early critical writing, which began to appear with frequency in the pages of *L'Artiste* in the mid-1860s, was nothing short of stunning. It would have been difficult to imagine that behind the male signature was the hand of an inexperienced young person fresh from private tutoring. Her work was erudite, opinionated, incisive, and serious, allowing the reader to assume that "Marc de Montifaud" was the man his signature suggested. Montifaud's first two essays for *L'Artiste* were book reviews—shorter pieces written in a formulaic style—but by May of 1865 she was given the important assignment of reviewing the Salon, the central event of the Parisian art scene. In every year since 1667, hundreds of artists had submitted their paintings and sculptures for display. In the nineteenth century, the walls of the exhibition galleries were packed with hundreds of tableaux without an inch to spare, and the halls were full of crowds eager to see the latest submissions, the best of which would be selected by the French government for the permanent collection of the Louvre.

Montifaud's first Salon review was written in a four-part series, the copy length required to cover the extensive collection in the galleries. She began her critique with a bold theory of art and its role in French society, declaring her reverence for artists in search of Truth and demonstrating a subtle understanding of their role in a changing society. She then commented on works by Cabanel, Corot, Meissonier, Gérôme, and Moreau—although she dismissed out of hand Manet's *Olympia*, the portrait of a prostitute that had been unveiled that year to historic controversy, requiring at times a police presence to fend off the violence threatened by its detractors. Montifaud announced that Manet's *Olympia* and his *Jesus Mocked by Soldiers* were both immature "eccentricities." If only the painter had "a healthier mind," she noted, he might produce some real works of art.[5]

The second installment of Montifaud's first Salon review ends with Montifaud's pronouncement that "one must not look at too many paintings in one day." Her eyes were in need of a break after all the stimulation, she wrote, and more essays on this Salon would follow in subsequent issues. Attributing her choice of words to her mentor, Houssaye, Montifaud noted that, after making one's way through the Salon, one no longer has "the visual virginity that is the true guiding light of the painter and the critic."[6]

With this casual mention of virginity, Montifaud gave one of the first signs that her writing would make no pretense of observing the constraints of femininity, thereby enabling the reader to believe that the author was a man. She did not feel the need to distinguish between what Houssaye was inclined to say and what might be appropriate for her to repeat. In addition to referencing virginity—the sort of topic that was the purview of men alone in 1865 and long afterwards—Montifaud felt perfectly confident in aligning herself throughout the essay with the painter and the critic, both of them masculine roles. Linguistic gestures of this kind implicitly guided readers to do the same. The insistent signposting of masculinity distinguished her from other women writers who used pseudonyms, a rather common practice at the time. Montifaud's authorial persona kept her identity a secret. It's no wonder that certain readers were amazed to discover, years later, that "Marc" was also known as Marie.

Montifaud would review the Salons for *L'Artiste* in serial installments for many years to come. She has recently been recognized by art historians as an important and influential voice at this pivotal moment in French visual culture, when the nascent Impressionist movement was transforming both the market and its tastes.[7] Some scholars still cite her early observations on Cézanne and Manet without being aware of Marc de Montifaud's assigned gender. There is ample reason to believe that she would not have objected one bit.

UNDRESSING MARC

In 1870 Montifaud published her first book, *The History of Mary Magdalene*. She was trying her hand at something new: a bold historical work that was a far cry from her art reviews, in which she had focused on style and aesthetic theories. Instead, the biography of Mary Magdalene unapologetically depicted this central figure of Christian gospel as one of many "courtesans of antiquity"—and as Jesus's lover. This book would be one of many efforts by Montifaud to recover the history of sexuality, in order to demonstrate two seemingly opposing facts: that *eros* had long been a part of the French Catholic tradition, and that sexual mores were arbitrary products of culture, determined by time and place.

In other ways, *The History of Mary Magdalene* was a continuation of Montifaud's efforts to explore and define herself under the guise of a male signature. With this work, Montifaud sought to make the transition from the realm of art criticism to the even more masculine domain of history. History, more than art, was the work of men. The Paris Salons were filled with women—circulating, admiring, and socializing. But in the scholarly chambers of the Bibliothèque nationale, where Montifaud would spend so many of her days, it was a different story entirely.

When *The History of Mary Magdalene* was released, Houssaye printed excerpts in the January 1870 issue of *L'Artiste*. The unattributed introductory remarks were written in the third person, but it is likely Montifaud had a hand in writing them. For one thing, they described the work in the terms she would use to defend it for years to come: "What Mr. [Ernest] Renan did for the life of Jesus, Mr. Marc de Montifaud has attempted to do for the life of Mary Magdalene."[8] In 1882 she would call it "a work of contemporary criticism meant to be the pendant to Renan's *Life of Jesus*."[9]

"It's a bold and curious work, this *History of Mary Magdalene* by Mr. Marc de Montifaud," the introduction begins. "Readers of *L'Artiste* are very familiar with this writer who made his start here with studies of art, in which he proved that he knew how to see with his eyes." Throughout the paragraphs that follow, the author is referred to as "Mr. Marc de Montifaud"—rather than "Mr. Montifaud," or simply "Montifaud"—both of whom could be taken for her husband. The full name appears four times in these brief introductory paragraphs.

Noting that readers had sometimes chafed at the forced eloquence of "Mr. Marc de Montifaud" in his art criticism, *The History of Mary Magdalene* is presented as a departure in style. "Critics have pointed to a rhetoric that leans a bit too much toward eloquence," the author explains. But now "Mr. Marc de Montifaud has stripped off that fancy dress; he has understood that Truth is all the more beautiful when it marches fully nude."[10] For a writer who was supposedly celebrating a newfound simplicity, this allusion to women's clothing—the fancy dress—was a rather clumsy illustration of the evolution of her style. But with a little hindsight, these few words convey much more.

For readers in the know, the comment about the dress offered an inside joke: Montifaud had already discarded a female accessory by writing under a male signature rather than the female name by which she was also known to her close friends and family. This bit of tongue-in-cheek is another piece of evidence that Montifaud, a budding humorist, played a role in writing these paragraphs. Eventually she would join the editorial board for *Le Tintamarre*, a popular satirical newspaper; within a few years' time she would publish hundreds of *nouvelles drolatiques* (droll stories) that relied on puns and double entendres for their scabrous humor. In many of these tales, Montifaud's wordplay served as a means for naïve young women to enjoy sexual pleasure without realizing that they were transgressing. Innuendo and linguistic slippages enabled the reader to recognize the subtext of the conversation of these ingénues, while the young women themselves remained sexually innocent. Meanwhile, the author was (theoretically) a young woman herself. Carefully chosen language, for Montifaud, would become a clever tool for gender play.

We might go one step further, though, and take this particular sentence literally: that with this metaphor the writer was actually describing another practice in more concrete terms. In 1882, when Montifaud made a brief mention of her transition to men's clothing—the only time she wrote of it—she stated that she had already dressed as a man "in many circumstances where I had ventured in certain outlying neighborhoods."[11] In these suburbs, she discovered that she could "pass" without anyone being the wiser. It's not entirely clear what those "circumstances" were, although she suggests they involved footwork for her novels. But might she also have experimented with this habit to help her work as an art critic, perhaps when visiting art exhibitions, in order not to call attention to herself?

In Montifaud's archives at the Bibliothèque Marguerite Durand in Paris, there are a few indications that she had conducted the work of art criticism *en homme*: a rectangular red ticket to the Palais des Champs-Elysées, granting entrance to the Salon of 1867 (figure 54); an undated invitation to Edouard Manet's opening; and another from Gustave Courbet. All three invitations are addressed to "Monsieur de Montifaud," the art critic.

If Montifaud had presented herself as a woman when she showed up on the Champs-Elysées for the Salon in 1867 or when she attended Manet's and Courbet's openings on the Place de l'Alma in the years following, she would have been forced to expose the masculine image she had been cultivating in her art criticism. What's more, if she had presented herself *en femme* as the rightful addressee, she'd have had to first convince the guard that the card was not meant for her husband. It would have been simpler—and perhaps even safer—to assume a man's appearance. It's not hard to imagine the defiant Montifaud doing just that. She likely slipped in along with the massive crowds, flashing her entrance card at the unknowing guard without further discussion. Indeed, whereas, for Rachilde, men's clothing made the

FIGURE 54. Entry ticket for "Monsieur de Montifaud" to the Salon of 1867. Source: Bibliothèque Marguerite Durand.

rebellious young writer *more* visible, for Montifaud, it may have allowed her to "pass unnoticed," to borrow the phrase used by Dieulafoy to justify her own choice of dress in Persia. What's more, a masculine appearance may have helped Montifaud to examine certain works of art without calling too much attention to herself: specifically, it may have given her better access to the female nude.

In principle, there were no restrictions on women's attendance at exhibitions during this time. But there was a problem with women viewing nudity. Representations of nudity were often displayed inaccessibly in the exhibition halls: paintings were hung as high as possible to make them more difficult to see, not just for women but for everyone. Women were not allowed to train in the Ecole des Beaux-Arts alongside men for the very reason that the centrality of the nude to formal artistic training would have exposed them to indelicate circumstances. Even in private tutorial settings, life drawing was seen as inappropriate for women. But Montifaud was fascinated by the nude, which she too regarded as the most important subject of art and which would take center stage in her writing. In her review of the Salon of 1872, Montifaud criticized the lack of representations of the human form; in 1874, she complained that the new Impressionist exhibition, which was seen at the time as the work of young "rebels" seeking attention for themselves, featured more landscapes than bodies.[12] "If there is anything we regret," she wrote, "it's seeing studies of the nude abandoned for landscapes."[13] Refused the privileges of masculinity by the rules that limited her art education, perhaps she had found other ways to gain access to her favorite subject.

In truth, there would have been no deceit involved in attending as a man. It was *this* Marc de Montifaud who was invited to the Salons, after all. If there was trickery, it was in the wiliness of the language games that guaranteed her (or him) this invitation, the subtle gender play that forced her readers to unquestioningly view her as a man. By alluding to the author's clothing, Arsène Houssaye appears to have been in on the joke. He would remain close to Montifaud and her son throughout his life.[14] With the mention of the "fancy dress," Montifaud and Houssaye surely both knew that the allusion to women's clothing would be taken for a simple, albeit awkward, metaphor. In reality, it was something closer to a revelation.

In the introduction to *The History of Mary Magdalene* excerpted in *L'Artiste*, the work is described as "a danger, an audacious act, practically a sacrilege." In fact, it was an outright act of machismo. This assessment of the book was affirmed in the first reviews, which were included in later editions. "Take it as an insolent poem or a historical study," Emile Zola wrote in *Le Gaulois*.[15] In *Le Figaro*, Alphonse Duchesne confirmed that the daring subject matter was treated with "all the seriousness of history, without all the erudite resources, all the stylistic innovations."[16] Commenting on the importance of this "historical study," neither critic had any inkling he was reviewing the work of a woman. Montifaud had thus successfully begun the public task of "taking off her fancy dress," in order to get closer to Truth. In a sense, this would be her life's work.

Writing as a man would be a way for Montifaud to express her gender difference throughout her life. Her male signature was not quite a pseudonym, and it was certainly not a disguise. It was integral to Montifaud's identity, intimately connected to her self-expression, and she seemed to delight in the fact that readers did not doubt her masculinity. Under this name, Montifaud's writings were daring but not entirely shocking; they were extensions of a libertine tradition with a long history in France. But eventually, Montifaud's irreverence caught up with her. The writer's games, a source of private pleasure, turned into an all-out battle between Montifaud and those determined to shut her down. The relentlessness on both sides suggested that this was not simply a fight over the boundaries of literary propriety. There was more to the story.

14 MONTIFAUD ON TRIAL

AS SOON AS SHE PUBLISHED *The History of Mary Magdalene*, Montifaud came under scrutiny by the authorities. It started with being forced to change the title, which had originally been *The Courtesans of Antiquity*. The work was wildly successful nonetheless and went through four printings before the Franco-Prussian War broke out. The real trouble came a few years later, during the repressive regime of Patrice de MacMahon. This was a period in which the Catholic Church was attempting to reassert its power in France, and writers and journalists were a frequent target. With her audacious history and erotic themes, Montifaud seemed to have sparked the ire of the religious right, perhaps unnerved by discovering that there appeared to be a woman behind the man's signature. Even after the MacMahon regime collapsed in 1877, Montifaud remained in the crosshairs of a judiciary stacked with right-leaning sympathizers. They were urged on, she later claimed, by her personal enemies, who seemed determined to put an end to her literary career. In a few years, erotic literature would flood the market with more regularity, after new freedoms of the press took hold in 1881. With religious transgression then exempted from *outrage à la morale publique*—the generic censorship charge of "offense to public decency"—Montifaud's erotic tales and riffs on Catholic history would be less legally controversial. But she had the disadvantage of being ahead of her time.

The first serious legal difficulties arose in 1876, when Montifaud published a reedition of Pierre-Corneille Blessebois's *Alosie, or The Loves of Madame de M.T.P.*, a libertine text from the late seventeenth century judged by some to be pornographic. Having already ruffled feathers on account of *The History of Mary Magdalene*, Montifaud was charged for the first time with offense to public decency. To be sure, this fate had been shared by many more famous colleagues, including Charles Baudelaire for his *Flowers of Evil* and Gustave Flaubert for *Madame Bovary*.[1] But Montifaud was treated as a woman, and the stakes proved different as a result. Male transgressors were sent to Sainte-Pélagie prison, a relatively lenient facility for admonished writers and artists; previous inmates included Honoré Daumier, the celebrated caricaturist, and the painter Gustave Courbet. But Montifaud was fined and sentenced to eight days at Saint-Lazare prison, a forced labor camp that was the fate of prostitutes and violent female criminals. In her 1879 novel *The Perverts*, she would describe the horrors of this place: "To be sent there is in some ways to descend into a living grave."[2]

Montifaud was shocked by her sentence to Saint-Lazare and would rail against it for years to come. In a letter written to *Le Figaro* shortly after her trial, she recounted the surprising turn of events that culminated in the sentence. Throughout the proceedings, she noted, the judge charged with reviewing her case had not hesitated to signal to her that he found the whole trial rather silly. He seemed to agree that it was all a tempest in a teapot: Montifaud had written about sex like so many others before her. The book in question wasn't even her own but rather the reproduction of a forgotten work by a seventeenth-century writer. How could the reimpression of a "two-hundred-year-old pamphlet" constitute an act of provocation, she asked. Hers was a work of history, not morality. The judge concurred, noting: "Let the record show that Montifaud has said, 'Blessebois, as a man, does not interest me; he is a fool; but I thought that if we were going to eliminate him from memory, we could put him in the library instead.'" (This statement did not actually reflect Montifaud's point of view, as she would go on to defend Blessebois in further writings.) In Montifaud's account, the judge rolled his eyes along with her at the irony of having to read the offending passages aloud and laughed at Montifaud's dry reference to the age of her accusers, as she mocked those "narrow-minded men whose hair—for good reason—could hardly stand on end in horror." But this magistrate was not in charge of sentencing, and the presiding judge felt otherwise.[3]

Montifaud—a member of the nobility, it's worth remembering—then told of the shock she felt when "they dared carry out such infamy on my person." Not believing the verdict could be true, she ran to the prefect's office to confirm the order and was horrified when this official, who received her "with perfect politeness," asked if she wanted to request a pardon. Montifaud rejected that possibility outright, as she would have debased herself by admitting wrongdoing. Terrified, she fled to Brussels in the dark of night, the first of many exiles to escape the French legal system.[4]

Montifaud was able to avoid imprisonment at Saint-Lazare: from Brussels, she negotiated for a sentence in the Maison Dubois, a mental institution. She returned to France and served her time there, but she was hardly chastened, and her legal troubles continued. The following year, she published another historical study, *The Vestal Virgins of the Church*, featuring bold depictions of the sexual pleasures of beloved Christian figures. Once again, she was found guilty of affronting public decency, and she was sentenced to three months in prison—with extra time for recidivism. In addition, she was retroactively billed for the costs of her time in the Maison Dubois. The remaining copies of *The Vestal Virgins* were destroyed and further production halted. Again, Montifaud negotiated a stay in the Maison Dubois instead of the dreaded Saint-Lazare.

"MY MIND CANNOT ACCEPT THIS LOGIC"

In protesting her sentencing to Saint-Lazare, Montifaud demanded to know how a simple "publishing infraction" could earn her the fate of a prostitute. But to law enforcement, it was a matter of sex. "It wasn't at all to inflict personal injury upon you," the police prefect told the countess, "but because the administration would not put a woman in Sainte-Pélagie."[5] Montifaud appeared to be oblivious to the fact that her sex might consign her to a different fate from that of her male peers. But, so often, feigned ignorance was a way for her to perform her defiance. She believed that logic was on her side, even if culture wasn't.

Montifaud lamented the injustice of her detractors' relentless pursuit of her and called them out for treating her differently than Balzac or Zola simply because she was a woman. She castigated her critics for wondering, when reading her works, "how a supposedly honest woman could treat the depiction of certain passions without blushing." She objected that she had been criticized "like a woman who had blatantly acted against all social structures." She fumed that she was prevented from being the "archaeologist, bibliographer, and critic" she knew herself to be simply because she was a woman.[6]

But this was precisely the point—and not one that any of her detractors meant to keep secret. The irony of Montifaud's self-defense was that the Jesuits attacking her would likely be the first to agree: her sex *was* the problem. A proper married woman, with a child, no less, should not be writing about the subjects she chose to address and in such explicit detail. Surely Montifaud understood this.

Montifaud cited the Decadent writer Barbey d'Aurevilly in her self-defense, for he too had been condemned for "offense to public decency." She looked to his description of the relationship between truth and morality for proof of the injustice at hand and cited his words from the preface to the novel *An Old Mistress*: "Truth cannot be sin or crime; if one overindulges in truth, too bad for those who overindulge."[7] But Barbey's defense was irrelevant to Montifaud's case precisely because of her perceived femininity. In fact, his statements stemmed from his trial for *Les diaboliques*, a collection of stories (admired by Rachilde) in which sex and Catholicism are provocatively mixed. Barbey was an avowed Catholic, a legitimist of the monarchy, and—most crucially—a man. His trial actually hinged on whether women readers would be harmed by his work. When he agreed to halt the sales of the novel in question, the case was dismissed. Montifaud, on the other hand, could not be so easily separated from her work and its dangers. At stake, in the view of her critics, was her own "feminine purity," not that of her readers.

Montifaud's insistence on the injustice of being sent to Saint-Lazare did not abate with time. In her 1884 preface to the memoirs of the gender-bending Abbé de Choisy (an appropriate place, it must be said, for such remarks), she professed her confusion: "What I found unnatural and perhaps unfair is the fact that offense to decency can be purged for all writers at Sainte-Pélagie, and for me alone, IN JAIL."[8] Montifaud's rage is palpable on these pages. It wasn't just that she was ordered to Saint-Lazare; it was that she was "excluded" (as she put it) from the treatment given to all the other writers. Zola, she noted furiously, was sent to Sainte-Pélagie for the very same infraction.[9]

Sainte-Pélagie seems to have represented a badge of honor, an implicit affirmation of her masculinity: a way of showing that she and Zola were engaged in the same enterprise. Montifaud's continued publication of works that she knew would be condemned was perhaps a way of proving that she could transgress just as well as any man.

Montifaud denounced the rationale for her sentencing: "I admit that despite my enormous efforts, my mind can simply not accept the logic of this sentence, and I doubt that the reader can either," she insisted.[10] To her, the logic of being sent to Sainte-Pélagie was irrefutable: she was a writer, sentenced for a written infraction. But did she truly think that readers would agree that prison housing should be determined by the nature of the crime rather than the sex of the offender? That, in 1876, a woman would be sent to an all-male prison simply because she was a writer? Her explanation was telling: that her "mind could not accept the logic." She could not accept the fact that it was her (presumed) femininity that would define her, rather than her acts. She seemed to operate by a different logic, and her best defense was to act as if everyone else did as well.

Eventually Montifaud left off writing her provocative histories, but not because it was dangerous to her freedom; rather, it had become nearly impossible. In preparing these studies, Montifaud conducted her painstaking research at the Bibliothèque nationale, together with the renowned book collector Paul Lacroix—known to Parisians as "Jacob the bibliophile"—who helped her track down forgotten manuscripts from earlier times in history. While Dieulafoy would travel halfway around the world to Persia, facing off against famine and bandits, Montifaud took a more direct route to the heroes of the past, in whom she may have hoped to find a glimpse of her own difference.

But more recently, when she ordered her books and documents from the library's holdings, they rarely appeared, though she spent long hours waiting for them. "I won't describe for you these demoralizing mornings," she later wrote, "when my waiting was in vain, when I devoted myself to fruitless efforts, waiting for a document for a work in progress, and was forced to give up."[11] Her detractors had convinced the librarians to ignore Montifaud's requests.

She did not relent; she could not let her enemies win. When her attempts at historical research were stonewalled, she turned to the novel instead. She was inspired by giants like Balzac, Hugo, and of course Zola to believe that the genre would be able to stimulate both her intellect and her imagination, to provide her with what she was seeking: recognition, self-knowledge, and at this point, more than a little vengeance. Just as importantly, the novel offered a new way to live outside the restrictive conventions of nineteenth-century femininity. Fictional characters enabled her to speak through her own voice or to assume new ones.

Montifaud's first fictional effort was *Madame Ducroisy*, the first of a trilogy modeled after Balzac's *Human Comedy*. She called hers *The Contemporary Comedy*. "My goal was to devote myself to the analysis of the human heart, like our master Balzac," she wrote, and references to him occur throughout the work. Like Balzac, Montifaud imagined that each novel in her series "should form a whole and provide a sincere and brutal depiction of our Parisian society."[12]

While Montifaud claimed that her work was no different in substance from that of Balzac and Zola, she loaded her first novel with barbs directed at the very authorities who had been coming after her, along with a large dose of eroticism. *Madame Ducroisy* was almost immediately condemned for offense to public decency; eleven of its passages were deemed obscene. Montifaud and the printer were fined five hundred francs, and Montifaud was sentenced to four months in prison, which she served once again in the Maison Dubois. While it was not Saint-Lazare—and thus not quite as humiliating—the Maison, which was run by Jesuits, proved just as inhospitable. At one point, a worker warned her that the doctors had put arsenic in the medication she had ordered for her acne. She pretended to swallow it and then dumped it in the garden, narrowly avoiding, it seems, an untimely death.[13]

During Montifaud's time at the Maison, she planned the next two novels in her series, which she described as having been "birthed in the horror of confinement, under the surveillance of the Jesuits."[14] These too were a kind of revenge fiction, in which she took aim even more directly at the corrupt underworld connections between the courts, the newspapers, the politicians, and the church, all of whom she blamed for her fate.[15] In *The Perverts*, she depicted a secret society of these men (and a few women), working together to target their enemies. By focusing on these activities, Montifaud calculated that the implicated parties would not want to call attention to their own wrongdoings through a public prosecution; the trial of *Madame Ducroisy* had sent her book sales rocketing. In this, she seems to have temporarily outsmarted her enemies: the next two novels, *The Perverts* and *Sabine*, escaped the scrutiny she had experienced before.

But the reprieve did not last long. Another spy was sent to scope out Montifaud's net worth and family fortune, and the retroactive legal indemnities for *Madame Ducroisy* and her stay at the Maison were demanded accordingly. Montifaud could not readily pay these fees. She fled to Belgium once again.

In 1880, Montifaud returned to Paris, but she was still far from chastened. Before long she had published her *Droll Stories*—erotic Rabelaisian tales in which young damsels stumble accidentally onto the pleasures of the flesh. The entire printing was seized, and Montifaud was sentenced to six months in prison, in addition to another fine of five hundred francs. By the time the verdict was issued, however, she had already fled to Brussels with her husband and young son.

GENDER IN THE PUBLIC EYE

Montifaud recounted details of this period—"one of the most painful of my life"—for the first time in an open letter to the left-leaning Belgian lawyer Félix Delhasse in 1882.[16] In this revealing text, Montifaud detailed the sequence of the plot against her, as powerful forces sought evidence that her life mirrored her writings. She watched helplessly as a vicar from the local parish whispered that she and Léon were not married but rather living in sin, and as her friends fled her company, fearful of ruining their own reputations by association. Friends disappeared, she wrote, because her Monday soirées had been infiltrated by visitors "of all social classes," including a certain marquise whose goal was to seduce Montifaud, in a fruitless effort to expose the illicit "hidden passions" for other women they were convinced she must have been entertaining.[17] A mysterious doctor was brought in to surveil her most intimate correspondence.[18] Rumors about her lifestyle abounded, destroying what had been an otherwise impeccable personal reputation.

Montifaud never revealed what caught the attention of those who came after her; she claimed only total bewilderment at the cause of their animus.

But it's hard to imagine that her gender didn't have something to do with it. In the letter to Delhasse, she protested the implicit suggestion that women weren't allowed to write about certain topics. A fair amount of misogyny had been unleashed in response: press accounts reviled her as a *bas bleu* or a hysteric. But the worst feeling against Montifaud—feeding the conspiracy that required her to flee her home repeatedly—was not outrage at the revelation that these books were written by a woman. Rather, it was outrage at the revelation that these books were written by a woman who had convinced so many that she was a man.

This reaction, in its disproportion, may have been driven by the sense of having been "tricked."[19] Once they were aware of her identity, Montifaud's critics believed that she was still hiding something, that she could not simply be a wife and mother who spent some of her days writing about sex and others researching religious figures. But while they searched her home frantically for the secret with which to confront and prosecute her, the real secret had already been revealed: that this writer known as Marc de Montifaud, with his seemingly masculine writing, was not who they thought he was. In a society still dependent on the stability of gender roles, and in a society in which those gender roles were increasingly called into question, this would have been extremely unsettling to some.

To a certain degree the court scenes recount this sense of betrayal: the jarring disconnect between the person on the witness stand and the image of the author many had conjured from the page. Reporting on the trial, Octave Uzanne wrote that no one would have suspected that this "book lover" had been "hiding a young blond woman, tall and frail, with listless blue eyes and a charmingly bold attitude, behind the male wrapping of this cheerful-sounding name."[20] Journalist Léon Chapron, who returned to the topic of Montifaud repeatedly and with escalating misogyny, seemed to relish the moment of Montifaud's sentencing. "With this mention of Saint-Lazare, Madame de Montifaud felt a cloud obscure her angelic blue eyes," he wrote. "Her soul—her immortal soul—received a horribly painful shock," he noted, slipping in the word "frisson" with its erotic undertones.[21] In a separate account, he recorded the "sharp groans" that issued from her mouth.[22]

Chapron tried to fit Montifaud's story into the usual narrative about the *bas bleus* being mentally unstable. In 1877, he denounced her as part of a disturbing trend. "Isn't it high time that public modesty return, that it cuts short the grotesque ravings of these women?" he asked. "Could they be wives and mothers, these madwomen, these crazies, these hysterics?" he continued, before suggesting that "we shut these *bas bleus* in a mental institution where they would subject them to special showers."[23] But Chapron's account of Montifaud's "hysteria" doesn't quite agree with those of others. At the trial in which Chapron reported her distress, a reporter from *Le Figaro* described Montifaud as seeming "hardly troubled by the sentencing." Other news accounts confirmed Montifaud's equanimity in appearance even as she admitted her shock.

The truth is that Montifaud's trial never quite made the headlines. Press accounts were limited to updates of the "court gazette" columns rather than front-page news. Her story did not rise to the level of an "affair" and never quite captured the voracious Parisian imagination, with its appetite for scandal, in the way one might expect, perhaps because Montifaud didn't quite fit the expected mold for scandal. She may have been perceived as the woman who didn't quite resemble a woman ("she always has that same look of a woman dressed as a man," noted one reporter[24]). But she didn't tantalize or provoke, or even frighten. She was always accompanied by her husband, and their only concern seemed to be publishing more books. As a result, Montifaud's story was not a true scandal but rather a whimsical *fait divers*, a tantalizing bit of news with an efficient and reliable shock value, quickly digested and just as quickly forgotten.

As Montifaud continued to publish controversial works and her detractors continued to pursue her in court, the public's initial sympathy for her—for she had been seen by many as having been disproportionately targeted—gave way to incredulity. Some became more and more baffled as she continued to produce the kind of work that had landed her in court in the first place. In May of 1878, *Le Figaro* reported dryly of her latest indictment: "Today, Madame de Montifaud will protest; tomorrow, she will put on airs of a victim, and the next day, she will go to prison. Honestly, does she have the right to complain?"[25] In 1880, in *Le Figaro*'s "Courtroom Gazette," where the latest legal news was usually reported without much commentary, Albert Bataille wrote that "Montifaud was sentenced to six months in prison, for having published a new pornographic novel, whose name I've forgotten."[26]

In other words, after a while Montifaud was hardly news at all.

MADAME DE SADE

Montifaud did make the headlines on one occasion, however. On September 10, 1882, a story appeared in *Le Figaro* titled "Madame de Sade," taking up the first two columns of the front page. In this piece of fiction, the frail, pitiable young protagonist, Valérie Milotte, is sentenced to three months in prison and a fine of two thousand francs because of her pornographic publications, which she had signed using "the venerated name of the Marquis de Sade as if it were a brand." The hitch? Valérie's husband had put her up to it, knowing that the judicial rebuke would send sales skyrocketing; then he enjoyed the profits while she served her time. But Valérie didn't mind prison: it was a refuge from the abusive husband who forced her to churn out the work of her troubled mind.

When Montifaud read "Madame de Sade" in the daily paper, she was livid. It was not hard to recognize herself in the married female character relentlessly pursued by the court system for erotic writing. Montifaud had only just returned from exile in Italy (where the climate was better for her son's health), after being sentenced for her *Droll Stories* and initially fleeing to Belgium. She and Léon had come home quietly, and she had waited months before appearing in public so that the dust of scandal might settle once and for all. She had hoped that her enemies had lost interest in her. The short piece on the front page of *Le Figaro* proved painfully otherwise.

It is possible that the newspaper's editor, Francis Magnard, had recognized himself in *The Perverts* and *Sabine*, which had escaped punishment even though they skewered the relationship between politicians and the press. *Le Figaro* had favored MacMahon's government, and Montifaud had long suspected that Magnard and others were working closely with the Catholic conservatives who wanted to put her away. But if their motivation was the provocative nature of her writing, Montifaud was quick to point out that by Magnard's own standards publishing the story about "Madame de Sade" should also be considered an affront. "*This* offense to morality is committed *through* the press!" she declared, as she tried to persuade a magistrate to take action against the paper.[27] Besides, it was one thing for the newspaper to ridicule Montifaud—she had come to expect it—but it was another to drag her husband into the mix. Montifaud was enraged by the suggestion that Léon—her steadfast partner through it all, to be sure—was somehow responsible for her creative process.

In her letter to Delhasse, Montifaud denounced the author of the piece, René Maizeroy: he was a "small earthworm and a miserable runt" who had "ejaculated his garbage" upon one of the most popular broadsheets in town.[28] Rachilde had cheekily responded to similar accusations of pornographic influence by titling one of her novels *The Marquise de Sade*. But Montifaud took a different tack. She and Léon went to their friend Fernand Xau, editor of the rival newspaper *Le Voltaire*. "I have a child," she reminded him. "My dear little Marc"—indeed, she had named him after herself—"whom you know, and I owe him an honorable name. Yet, they pass off my husband, the most loyal of men, as the most wretched of them all."[29] Xau reluctantly agreed to ask Magnard for a retraction. Magnard refused, not surprisingly, denying any connection between the story and the couple's interpretation of it.

Montifaud believed that she and Léon had no choice but to take the matter into their own hands. The next day, they purchased tickets to the premiere of the Comédie-Française (also known as the Théâtre-Français), knowing Magnard would be there. At the end of the third act, they waited for him to come out of his box. Léon leaned forward and tried to slap him, but another man immediately intervened, pushing the angry husband back. As others focused their attention on Léon, Marc stepped closer to Magnard. "You are a coward and a wretch!" she shouted. "In the name of my revolted conscience I have come to say this to your face." Gripping the newspaper with the offending article, Montifaud rammed it against his nose with a violent slap. "I slapped him *in the middle of his face*, and not from the side," she later reported, lest there be any confusion about the precise nature of the gesture.[30]

There's another important detail to this story: when Magnard encountered the angry Montifauds at the theater, he might not have recognized Marc. She was very different from both the figure described in *Le Figaro* and the way she had appeared at her last trial. In "Madame de Sade," the diminutive Valérie Milotte, like Montifaud herself initially, did not at all match the public's fantasies about what the "Marquise de Sade" would look like. "The troubling androgyne that one pictured, the audacious woman who had mixed dirt with ink . . . was only this. A simple storekeeper type, someone you might see on the street in a regular neighborhood."[31] Reporters at Montifaud's trial had described the petite young woman lifting her veil (a fashion accessory in vogue at the time) to speak.[32] The last time anyone had seen Marc de Montifaud in public, she had appeared definitively as a "madame" and not a "monsieur." The figure that slapped Magnard, on the other hand, was impeccably clad in a tailcoat and white tie, with her hair cropped short like a man's.

The newspapers, gleefully reporting on this bit of unexpected entertainment, confirmed the shocking effect of Montifaud's new look: "It was hard to recognize her sex, because she has such an unfeminine face," reported *La Lanterne*.[33] *Le Matin* described Montifaud—"the author of several smutty stories for which she was condemned by the police"—as "wearing men's clothing since her return from Brussels, and no one knows why."[34] Also reporting on the incident, *Le Gaulois* noted that during the play everyone was looking at Montifaud, "dressed as a man, her hair cut short," and that she didn't seem troubled by it in the slightest. She also did not appear uncomfortable in a suit and tie. "In fact, it would be impossible to know that she was a member of the fair sex."[35]

Montifaud had certainly not come back to town quietly, then. Now she knew that she would not be able to stay, a fact she faced with resignation and frustration at once. The same week of the slap, Montifaud went to another premiere with Léon, this time a vaudeville, and noticed a writer from *Le Figaro* eyeing her suspiciously. Seeing this "individual whose blood rose to his face in looking at us made me shiver," she wrote. "His lips trembled, as if in epileptic seizure; his hands paled. I understood that Magnard's subordinated rage had reached its height."[36]

The next day, a pair of theater tickets was delivered to the Montifaud residence as a gift to the couple, supposedly from *L'Evénement*, a newspaper with whom they had friendly relations. But Marc had already fled to Brussels and did not even have a chance to fall for the ruse. The unsuspecting Léon took the other Marc to the theater. Those who had hoped to arrest the writer in an entertaining, if vengeful, public display were infuriated when instead they saw the father and son enjoying an evening out.

ANGER AS A DECLARATION OF SELF

Montifaud's open letter to Delhasse was signed in October of 1882, a month after she slapped Magnard at the theater. This timing gives context to its urgent description of her repeated victimization by the press and the courts. It's true that the censors had pursued her relentlessly. But Montifaud was driven from the country for assaulting a well-known public figure at the theater in front of a crowd of onlookers, and not for criticizing the church or writing salacious tales. From this perspective, the slap begins to look like part of a pattern of provocation, a repeated effort to antagonize certain powerful figures. Montifaud did this sort of thing in her writing too. In *Madame Ducroisy*, she taunted her detractors, daring the censors to come after her. She introduced her protagonist Aloysius Brandt in this way:

> On January 17, in the morning, Mr. Aloysius Brandt's door opened suddenly . . . Ah! Excuse me, a parenthesis. Let us be quick to say that if the door opened this way, it's not because it was built without locks. Heaven forbid! Don't believe it! That would be a true indecency, to have a door in a novel with no lock; indecency of form, indecency of intent; indecency that relates necessarily to morals. Ergo, for having spoken about doors without locks, and as a result having hugely offended morality, we condemn the publisher to a five-hundred-franc fine and three months in prison.[37]

The authorities accepted the dare: five hundred francs as Montifaud predicted and four months in prison, with an extra month thrown in for good measure.

Montifaud's outrage was always accompanied by a sense of imperviousness. The insults lobbed by her detractors couldn't quite reach her, because they simply did not apply to her. "I don't invent anything, and I don't exaggerate," she wrote. "The dishonor that you seek to impose on me cannot reach me because, by definition, it doesn't stem from any of my acts."[38] This was true in so many ways. Montifaud hardly recognized herself in the person being attacked and was genuinely baffled by the criticism each time. Perhaps this is why she was able to do it again and again.

By the time she confronted Magnard at the theater, Montifaud had been gearing up for a fight for a long time. "I never received boxing lessons," she wrote in her 1879 defense of *Madame Ducroisy*. "I admit that my education was horribly neglected." Boxing would have been useful, she went on, "in the midst of this society in which I've been called to live." Her parents were naïve, she noted, in thinking that grammar and dialectics would be enough to protect her from the words of her enemies.[39] She had tried logic and rhetoric for years—to no avail. The tone was wry, but Montifaud was not quite joking.

She had not avoided other opportunities to fight: Montifaud was so incensed by Chapron's description of her as a *bas bleu* that she challenged him to a duel. In reporting this, the press seemed confused about the gendering of the couple and identifying who was who: "Following an article published by Monsieur Léon Chapron on Monday, May 21, [1877] . . . in which the statements emitted in several works by Madame Marc de Montifaud were the object of severe criticism," *Le Gaulois* reported, "Monsieur Marc de Montifaud charged Monsieur Jules Maurie and Monsieur Eugene Gallice with asking Monsieur Léon Chapron for reparation through arms."[40] But if "Madame" Marc de Montifaud was the author of the works, who was "Monsieur" Marc de Montifaud, who had requested the battle? In any case, the request was denied, as Montifaud's writings had landed her in prison for eight days. Chapron's misogynistic vitriol was therefore deemed justified.

This wasn't the only instance. In 1880, *La Justice* reported on a dispute between a certain "M. F." and Léon de Montifaud, who was upset that M. F. had defamed his wife. In response, M. F. left town, having refused Léon's invitation to a duel.[41] Shortly after his return, Léon and Marc tracked him down, once again demanding a duel. He refused, so Léon slapped him while Marc yelled insults.[42] And that was the end of that.

But there was likely a psychology to Montifaud's puzzling behavior, to her seeming provocations, even as she knew the probable results: she was addicted to that danger inherent in her refusals to conform because it was a way to acknowledge an existence that could not otherwise be articulated. In writing provocatively and in seeking out conflict—even of the physical variety—Montifaud seems to have solicited outrage and punishment as a way for her difference to be affirmed. In that light, when she slapped Magnard in her tailcoat and tie, it was less an act of aggression than a declaration of self. This incident was a crucial moment in her gender story—perhaps even what we might now call a "coming out." After that night at the theater, she would only wear men's clothing for the rest of her life.

15 CLOTHING STORIES

OVER THE COURSE OF HER LIFE, Montifaud shared very little about her transition to men's clothing. She mentioned it only once, in her letter to Delhasse, in the story of the slap. Like Dieulafoy upon her return to Paris, she spoke of wearing pants only indirectly, in the ephemeral past perfect tense, thus presenting it as something that she *had been* doing, rather than as a habit with a clear beginning: "I had already been wearing—in several circumstances when I had ventured to far-off neighborhoods to study behaviors—men's clothing," she explained.

The syntax of Montifaud's normally straightforward prose is notably contorted in this moment such that "men's clothing" is the last part of the sentence that the reader takes in. Her explanation for this behavior follows: "In these sorts of places, a self-respecting woman couldn't show her skirts." Notably, she echoes the logic that Dieulafoy offered in her Persian travelogues: to wear pants was to ensure her femininity as a "self-respecting woman" rather than to compromise it in these "outlying neighborhoods," just as for Dieulafoy in Persia, wearing pants was also presented as a way to preserve her status as a proper French woman.[1] With the mention of skirts, the fancy dress that required removal also comes to mind. Pants could not be worn, and masculinity could not be embraced, until skirts were removed. And as with Dieulafoy, the logic ultimately redounds upon itself: Montifaud assures readers that she had to dress as a man to maintain her respect as a woman, because women were not allowed in such milieus. What both really meant was that wearing pants was a way of staying true to themselves.

Montifaud also describes in this passage her discovery that she was "perfectly incognito dressed as a man" in Paris. It was for this reason, she wrote, that she put on men's clothing as a disguise when she was on the run in Belgium, in order to "watch over my child in full security."[2] She could thereby pass as his tutor. She cut her hair and began wearing a man's suit. They must have been a jarring sight, this threesome: Léon, Marc, and Marc, Jr.

Montifaud spoke often of her concern for her son: it was for him that she needed to protect her reputation following the "Madame de Sade" episode, and she presented her change to men's clothing as a gesture of maternal protection. It seems that he spent some time with her in Brussels but that he was often left in the care of his grandmother and aunt while his mother was in exile. In one letter from around 1880, Marc's mother wrote of how happy she was that Montifaud could stay in Belgium safely. "We devoured your letter to your dear little one. Rest assured, dear child, we are taking good care of him."[3]

In the letter to Delhasse, Montifaud explained that when she returned to Paris, she simply continued to wear the attire out of habit: "I adopted the suit that I still wear."[4] If one stops to think about it just a bit longer, though, many questions present themselves. It's a significant number of leaps from the occasional, unspecified "study of behaviors" to passing as her son's tutor and then to taking on this dramatic—and illegal—change as a permanent practice. To explain why she was dressed in formal wear at the theater, she offered: "It wasn't in order to slap a wretch that I put on a tuxedo and a white necktie." Rather, once she began wearing men's clothing, she adhered strictly to "all the clothing etiquette necessitated by the places where I went"—as any member of the nobility would.[5] Once again, the fact of dressing in men's clothing is already established, so that the baseline of assumptions has already shifted. Montifaud uses that fait accompli to emphasize the accompanying detail: that she wore men's clothing in adherence to requisite French etiquette and tradition. It was no matter that to wear men's clothing at all was to break with tradition in the first place. This logical fallacy is particularly striking given that an attack on logical fallacies was the centerpiece of many of her essays. In lengthy manifesto-like pieces, Montifaud would disassemble her critics' arguments bit by bit, revealing their inconsistencies. Dialectics was the one useful subject she credited her education with; she wouldn't likely fall for an improper transposition like this one. Rather, the evasiveness of her account underlines the connection of the clothing shift to another, more private dimension of Montifaud's sense of self, outside the bounds of what she wanted to share with the public. Perhaps it was also outside the limits of language itself.

The story of passing as her son's tutor was not the only anecdote that Montifaud would tell about dressing as a man. In 1922, writer Jane Misme published an essay about cross-dressing in her feminist newspaper *La Française*. Describing Montifaud as a colleague—notably "our *confrère*" rather than "our *consoeur*"—she told of having met the writer late in her life. Montifaud shared with her "the origins of her disguise"—linking them in this instance to her run-ins with the courts "for books that were too frank." Montifaud told Misme that, impoverished by her legal troubles, she had taken to wearing pants so that she could secretly remain in Paris. In order to make money, she worked in a ceramics factory as a man, painting dishes and vases, without anyone recognizing her.[6] Since Rachilde referred to "Madame de Montifaut" in *Why I Am Not a Feminist* as "the one who worked in a glass factory," it seems likely that she had heard some version of this story as well.

Several other questions arise with this story, not the least of which is that Misme dates Montifaud's masculine attire to the Second French Empire of Napoléon III, before Montifaud was ever indicted. Misme might have confused the repressive regime of the empire for that of MacMahon. Or perhaps Montifaud kept casting the the story further back into the past, into the past perfect tense of what had been, mythologizing the origins of her fashion choices to throw interlocutors off the scent. In any case, it's not much of an explanation, making no effort to justify the continuation of the practice long after the "disguise" was no longer necessary. This version of the story, as well as the Belgian one, resembles Dieulafoy's: dressing like a man was a habit that, once begun, whether in war or under another kind of duress, simply could not be broken, regardless of the social pressure to the contrary. Not satisfied with these explanations, those who wrote about them often added that men's clothing was simply easier and more natural for these women who couldn't be bothered with corsets. No one ever bothered to explain the man's haircut.

Montifaud never wrote again publicly about her decision to wear men's clothing. She did write about the cross-dressing Abbé de Choisy, and a few of her fictional characters dress as women in order to disguise themselves, but there is no sustained meditation on the psychology of such choices. In her novels, cross-dressing is disguise, usually as a means toward a sexual end.[7]

In Montifaud's archives, however, there is a letter from a certain Mr. Sauvé from the Accounting Office of the Bureau of Foreign Affairs, dated November 30, 1896. Sauvé reports that he has visited the Prefecture of Police and can confirm for Montifaud the following: "Having the habit of wearing men's clothing for such a long time, and having received from Mr. Grugnon even if just verbally from one of his agents the authorization to wear them, there is no further need to make this request today." Montifaud had apparently been seeking information about whether not having an official pants permit would put her at risk in certain public venues. Sauvé assured her that, based on this information, she could now proceed to give her speeches without worry.[8] From this we learn that Montifaud did not have an actual pants permit, as was widely reported, that is, she did not possess a document granting official authorization but rather had obtained permission by oral agreement, most likely when she returned from Belgium in 1883.

The lack of a permit may have been one of the reasons that Montifaud was so quick to flee in the first place. When she appeared at the Comédie Française in men's clothing and slapped Magnard, she drew these questions into the spotlight momentarily, inspiring some rather predictable misogyny. Fouquier—the writer who would rebuke Rachilde in 1884—did not hold back in his screed for *Le XIXe Siècle*: "Already not a fan of the *bas bleus*, I have even less taste for women writers who don't hide behind the clothing of their sex, and who, already speaking too much like men, dress like them."[9]

Thus, an unintended consequence of Montifaud's public confrontation with Magnard was a renewed focus on the question of pants permits. Shortly after the incident, *La Lanterne* reported that the prefect of police intended to revise the ordinance requiring the permit "that prohibits women—except during Carnival—to dress as a man without permission from the prefect." Readers were reminded that such an authorization is only given with a "certification from a health professional, approved by the police commissioner, stating that transvestism is necessary for health reasons." Any infractions would be sent to police tribunals, as with any other legally problematic behavior, and two infractions in the same year could result in fines or even imprisonment. This particular writer was sympathetic to the cause, however, noting that, had George Sand been born forty years later, she'd have been subject to the same fate: "Sad!"[10]

Interestingly, the law—and the public—seemed to cling to a fragile distinction between those who wore pants out of necessity and those who wore them for other reasons. In discussing the Montifaud incident, Fouquier commented, "If, for reasons that I don't know, Madame de Montifaud is authorized by the prefect of police to run through the streets and the theaters as a young man, I have nothing to say." On the other hand, he noted, "If she is simply following a 'whim,'—one that is not pleasing to decent people who go to the theater," then he felt that the police should "immediately put an end to it."[11]

The letter from Sauvé gives us direct access to Montifaud's sense of vulnerability around the legality of it all—evidence of the personal toll wrought by the public policing of gender roles and their sartorial exigencies. The letter suggests that wearing pants was never a performance and never, for her, a revindication—unlike some of her other defiant acts. Dressing this way was a part of Montifaud's identity: by a certain point, she could not appear in public otherwise. Navigating these choices required a secretive discussion that took place without her being present and that she apparently took pains to hide. In his letter, Sauvé—a personal friend—assures Montifaud that her name was not used, and then passes along regards from his wife and daughter.

THE PHOTO NEVER LIES

In Montifaud's writing, the clothing shift is emotionless: fact, detail, past tense. But as we have seen, the photographs offer more of the missing emotional resonance to the story, in addition to a sense of her journey. Not long after the Nadar photograph of Montifaud wearing a dress, Montifaud posed in a photo studio again (figure 55). This time, there's an end table behind her and a damask curtain pulled to the side, in addition to an upholstered chair. These objects all seem like props suggesting domesticity, arranged rather haphazardly behind Montifaud as if to imply their ancillary nature. Here she stands facing forward, her hands comfortably in her pockets. It's

FIGURE 55. Photograph of Montifaud from the early 1880s, offered to Marguerite Durand by Montifaud's son.

Source: Pierre Petit / Bibliothèque Marguerite Durand / Roger-Viollet.

hard not to tie her visible ease in this portrait to the change in wardrobe; rather than the heavy fabrics that seemed to weigh her down in the sitting pose, she wears lighter materials that drape her body comfortably: loose-fitting wide-legged pants and a matching button-down blazer. Only the top button is closed, underneath a white collar adorned with what looks like a Victorian scarf crossed with a cravat. She looks not only comfortable but quietly powerful.

Montifaud's son Marc, in offering this photo to her dear friend and mentor Marguerite Durand, described it as "the last feminine portrait of his mother," which dates it to sometime around 1880.[12] But Montifaud's clothing defied all the unspoken rules of female attire during that time. To modern eyes, she looks quite the modern woman; in fact, the outfit is downright prescient, the sort of suit a well-dressed woman might happily wear to the office in 2020. But for Montifaud to have worn it outside the house, she needed permission from the prefect of police.

Though her casual comfort has an easeful, off-the-rack feel—especially compared to the earlier photo by Nadar—it would have been anything but usual in 1880. Women around her were wearing corsets and crinolines, bustles and boots. Her silhouette is unburdened here from the dictates of both female and male fashion—hardly the strict obligations of etiquette that dictated her outfit, as she would claim, at the premiere of the Comédie Française in 1882. Neither male nor female, she nods to both masculinity and femininity. The loose fabrics and floppy tie suggest a young boy's sailor outfit, the kind that her son may have been wearing at around the same time. Did she dress to match young Marc, whom she adored, fretted over, and perhaps overly identified with? Or to harness the genderless quality that young boys could enjoy in the fashion practices of the nineteenth century, during the years before adolescence set them on other paths?

The similarity in hairstyle to the Nadar photo suggests that this image was made not too long after the photograph in the dress but before 1882, when she fled to Italy and cut her hair. The pantsuit does not appear to fit the description of the men's clothing that she wore to disguise herself when "visiting outlying neighborhoods"; it was hardly a way to pass as a man. Instead, it suggests that just as she experimented with writing styles, she also experimented with clothing.

The photographic record thus tracks a developing confidence, as well as a merging of the "male wrapping" of Montifaud's literary identity with her physical presence. Montifaud had moved slowly over a few short years from hiding from the camera and refusing its power over her—witness her cold evasiveness in the first image (figure 52)—to engaging it directly and harnessing its power for her own pleasure.

Photographs of Montifaud in men's clothing after her ultimate return to Paris in 1884 reveal the full extent of her transformation during those years in exile. The false pretenses of the nonchalant haircut and men's suit as simple acts of self-preservation and practicality are immediately belied by these images. In one (figure 53), she sits, cheek against arm, leaning on a desk, a notebook open below her; the casual signs of female domesticity are replaced with those of masculine intellect. She is at ease in a black ascot, vest, and tuxedo jacket over men's slacks. Once again, her silhouette appears more natural in these fabrics. In a later photograph by Eugène Pirou (figure 3), her hairline recedes.

The writer Laurent Tailhade produced a volume of portraits of various public figures at the turn of the century, offering among them a profile of Montifaud, whom he knew as a fixture at the Bibliothèque nationale. It was there that she spent most of her days in the early 1900s. Tailhade noted how much she resembled a schoolboy (*un collégien*)—a term often invoked to describe Dieulafoy as well. Tailhade wondered why Montifaud had received permission to wear pants. "Her explanations were muddled on this point," he noted. "She would end any discussion of it as soon as it was politely possible to do so." As a result, "nobody, not even those close to her, knew the answer to the question, which remained a secret."[13]

16 LOVE STORIES

WHAT WE NOW TEND TO SEPARATE as gender expression and sexual inclination was not so clearly demarcated in nineteenth-century France. As a freethinker with little need for gender categories, Montifaud could not understand why she would be sent to a women's prison and not a writers' prison. She seemed to look for reflections of her self in many places, not expecting to find them in a single place, as one kind of person. She moved between masculine and feminine associations, and male and female pronouns; and she seems to have loved both men and women.

Léon truly seems to have been "the most loyal of men," as Montifaud described him in her letter to Delhasse. He was oblivious to his wife's faults—and also to the lovers she may have pursued. Indeed, his correspondence suggests that he was blissfully unaware that Montifaud had an affair with the writer Villiers de l'Isle Adam, a friend the couple had helped during a low point in his life. Villiers credited the Montifauds with the "flash of inspiration" that had led to the ultimate success of his *Cruel Tales*. He had intended to dedicate those stories to Marc but the slap put an end to that: Magnard threatened to withdraw his financial support of Calmann-Lévy, Villiers's publisher, if the dedication was allowed to stand. The books were already printed, and so the dedication pages had to be manually excised. Villiers promised to dedicate one of his other works—perhaps *Future Eve* (1886) or *Axel* (1890)—to Marc, to make up for this unfortunate effacement.

Villiers failed to keep his promise, however. At some point after July 1883 he cut off their romance, not wanting to betray two people: his future wife, whom he still hoped to meet some day, and Léon, whom he considered a friend. Letters from Léon to Marc in Belgium confirm Léon's admiration for Villiers, whose play was opening in Paris while Marc was hiding out, post-slap, in Brussels. Léon recounts with delight the dinner following the dress rehearsal, at which Villiers insisted that they should sit next to each other. "Dear friend," Léon writes (addressing his wife in the feminine, as his *chère amie*), "my letter will seem to you like a ray of sunlight across the somber clouds of these past days." Léon goes on to describe to Marc how, after the rehearsal, Villiers "threw his arms around me and kissed me, saying how happy he was to have met us." What's more, the gesture was made right in front of the theater, "in front of two hundred people." Then they went to dinner, along with Catulle Mendès and some others, and Villiers told him, "Montifaud, you're going to sit right next to me." One can sense the pride that Léon felt at having been singled out in this way. Villiers told the others that Léon was the one "who gave me the impulse, who saved me." Monsieur and Madame de Montifaud, "his worthy wife," Villiers went on, "roused me from my torpor." Villiers then raised a glass to Madame de Montifaud in absentia. Léon was elated.[1]

A few months later, in July, Léon wrote to his wife that "arriving at home, this morning, I learned that Villiers was staying in the house now."[2] He recounted going to the laundry down the street to find a clean shirt, implying, then, that Villiers had helped himself to clothing as well. On his way back, he told Marc, he ran into Villiers. In the exchange, Villiers's news of Marc seemed more recent than her husband's. "Villiers told me about the disappointment that all of his friends felt about you when they saw that you wouldn't be able to get back to France as quickly as anticipated," he wrote. Were Villiers's friends also Marc's, one wonders? In that light, the toast offered a few months earlier to Léon might have served as a wink to those same fellow writers, knowing that the "worthy" woman in question was Villiers's lover. Villiers's reference to an impulse and a sudden *éclair* was precisely the kind of double entendre Montifaud relished in her own writing.

An undated fragment of Villiers's letter to "Marie, my dear good friend," is all that remains of his rupture with Montifaud. Like her husband, he addressed her by her Christian name. "Listen, I have loved enough. I am incapable of caprices, and if I love again, I only want to love my wife," he wrote. There was no wife yet, but the romantic Villiers wanted to preserve this possibility for the future. It was a difficult time for both of them, Villiers offered, perhaps alluding to Montifaud's years of exile and her betrayal by so many others.

Traces of Montifaud remain in certain of Villiers's stories as André Lebois has noted. In "Modern Idyll" (later published as "The House of Happiness"), Paule de Lucanges and the duke Valleran de la Villethéars are soulmates:

> Paule, svelt in her beauty as a Christian Hypatia, was of the race of those *mondaines* [an allusion to Montifaud's status] with the heart of vestal virgins [an allusion to her first work] who, more than the Sands, the Saphos, the Sévignés or the Staels [the female literary tradition], are spared the vanity of writing, and share the virgin light of their inspiration for one soul only.[3]

Montifaud also communicated with Villiers through her published works. Writing under the name Erasme for *L'Evénement* in 1890, she titled one column "Our Future Eves," a reference to Villiers's famous novel. After contemplating the advantages and risks of different kinds of modern women populating Parisian circles, Montifaud ended the long essay with a direct address to her former lover: "You knew something about it, my dear Villiers," noting that he had depicted his future Eve "with such wonderful mastery."

Léon seems never to have suspected. Years later he wrote to Villiers asking for a favor for a young friend who needed help launching his theatrical career. "Madame de Montifaud is whispering in my ear the friendliest words for you and sends you the most cordial handshake."[4]

MADAME OLYMPE A

Montifaud had no shortage of enemies. But among the litany of names to whom she directed her outrage, all of whom, she feared, had colluded against her at one point or another, one stands out: Olympe Audouard, loosely veiled as "Madame Olympe A . . . " in the letter to Delhasse and "la femme Olympe A" in the preface to the memoirs of the Abbé de Choisy, and viciously caricatured as Thérèse Massicourt in the novel *Madame Ducroisy.* Audouard was a writer as well, about twenty years older than Montifaud. In some ways, she seemed a kindred spirit, outspoken and independent minded. When Barbey d'Aurevilly condemned her as a *bas bleu*, she famously challenged him to a duel. (He declined.) At first, Audouard and Montifaud had gotten along, mingling in overlapping worlds. Audouard wrote for many of the same publications, including Montifaud's own short-lived journal, *L'Art moderne*, which she had launched with Léon in 1875.

But by the time the authorities came after Montifaud's writing in 1876, her friend had turned on her. Montifaud claimed that Audouard's own doctor had been introduced into her home to spy on her. Feigning an interest in her son ("He got me where you could get most women, I believe: through maternal love," she reported), "Doctor L de M" insinuated himself into the household, so that he "came to know what happened in my life on pretty much a daily basis." In the end, he convinced others that her home was unrespectable, so that many of her friends would never again "cross the threshold of my house." Montifaud claimed that the only way she prevented Dr. L de M from testifying about her before a disciplinary committee was "in giving the kind of services that I don't wish to detail here."[5]

Something had clearly shifted for Audouard to betray Montifaud in such an extreme way. In *Madame Ducroisy,* written only a few years after the events in question, Montifaud suggests that it was the desire to preserve her own reputation. In the novel, when the female protagonist Raymonde is about to be revealed as an adulteress, Thérèse Massicourt is concerned only with preserving her own carefully cultivated alliances. What's more, Thérèse is depicted as a heartless vixen, who slept around so much that she became "a path too worn for the horseback-rider," while Raymonde's only crime was to fall in love with a man who was not her husband.

Several of the eleven citations for obscenity the novel received referred to passages describing Thérèse. In them, Montifaud openly taunted Audouard, who she claimed was in league with the authorities. In portraying Thérèse, Montifaud often broke with novelistic conventions, addressing the reader directly as she commented on her own description. "To take up a metaphor that won't get us thrown into jail, let's say . . . how shall we say it?" she asked, thereby underlining the rising insult. "That at the time, one could explore

Thérèse—like those grassless paths in the Bois de Boulogne on which one walks without resistance—[and] several had risked taking this road."[6]

There was likely more behind Montifaud's animosity toward Audouard than the loss of a friendship. Thérèse, much older than Raymonde, is depicted as a woman of irresistible beauty despite her age. In another passage cited for affronting public decency, Montifaud describes Thérèse's body, emerging perfumed from the bath, as a "nakedness meant to be inhaled." The passage continues: "Her arms, her hands, her breasts inspired sudden embraces, prolonged pressures, extravagant kisses. Even women felt unexpected raptures when faced with this physical perfection which offered itself willingly, during a friendly visit, to the touch of men."[7]

This tacit acknowledgment of Montifaud's own attraction to Audouard puts their relationship in a new light. Perhaps Montifaud had acted on these feelings, but Audouard had rejected the physical relationship. Or perhaps Audouard only turned on her once the authorities pursued Montifaud because of her writing, and then she, like Thérèse, sought to protect her reputation. In either scenario, it is easy to imagine that this betrayal would lead to acrimony on both sides—with Audouard determined to peg her friend as a deviant to protect herself and Montifaud profoundly wounded and angry.

The story concerning Audouard's doctor, Dr L de M, was retold in *The Perverts*, the sequel to *Madame Ducroisy*, which follows Monsieur Ducroisy's second wife, Renée de Sérigny, after Raymonde has died of heartache. "Dr. D de C" is sent to shadow Renée, searching for information to implicate Ducroisy, the real target of his plot. Montifaud describes how the doctor's job was to insinuate himself into the homes of unsuspecting women, gaining their trust while spying on their every move on behalf of an evil network of newspapers, politicians, and police, all working together.

What evidence did Dr. L de M find in Montifaud's home, and what "services" did she render in order to suppress his testimony? The euphemism suggests that she slept with him in order to preserve her reputation and that of her family. Of course, she may have been referring to a financial arrangement instead. Either way, it's a stunning admission, one that Montifaud knew the accused doctor would never counter, for to do so would incriminate him. She left it to her reader's imagination to fill in the blanks.

In December of 1880, with Montifaud in exile following her condemnation for *Madame Ducroisy*, Camille Delaville reported in *La Presse* that a certain "Madame A" had been visited by a suspicious character wanting to know what she thought of Marc de Montifaud. It's not hard to connect the dots. When Madame A professed to have no thoughts on the person in question, the visitor berated and threatened her. Weeks later, Madame A received a series of mysterious letters from Brussels repeating these insults and accusations. She took the letters to the minister of interior to complain. In response, he went to a back chamber and returned with a pile of letters just like the ones that she had brought. Montifaud's enemies were numerous, it seems. Even so, Audouard—"who sells her nights, instead of her books"—held a special place in Montifaud's heart, where perhaps love, or at least desire, had once been.[8]

RHYMING FOR MARGUERITE

When Léon died in June 1901, Montifaud wrote to Marguerite Durand, the director of the feminist newspaper *La Fronde*. Durand was a popular figure among accomplished women of the time. She managed to marry her feminism—long associated with drab blue stockings and frightening suffragettes—with femininity, and she was admired for her wisdom and beauty. Durand was bold and eccentric without exactly being strange. She owned a pet tiger named Lionne.

Montifaud had by then been writing for *La Fronde* since its inception in 1897. The most famous women writers of the day worked there, many of them both novelists and journalists like herself: Séverine, Marcelle Tinayre, Gyp. Montifaud wrote about international news and politics, signing her work with either "IBO" or Erasme. Montifaud's letters to Durand, held in Durand's archives, are the only personal correspondence we have from her directly.

The purpose of the letter in 1901 was to inform Durand that Montifaud wouldn't be able to make it to work that day. "Today and tomorrow I must allow myself to send my article in without coming," she wrote. Léon had died unexpectedly, just as they had taken him to the hospital. "The day after tomorrow, I will be back at the newspaper," she promised, explaining that work was her only source of comfort.

It wasn't quite feminism that Montifaud enjoyed at *La Fronde*—a paper not so nicely nicknamed "*The Times* in skirts."[9] That was never a lens she adopted in order to contemplate her own gender story; its mention is utterly absent in her writings. A photograph of Montifaud at work for the journal shows her sitting at a table of women, the only one in a man's suit.[10] Despite her apparent awkwardness in the image, she may have had more of a sense of belonging in this community of working women than she felt elsewhere. The most compelling aspect of this work, however, was likely proximity to Durand herself.

In 1903, Montifaud wrote to ask Durand to ask if she would consider her for upcoming projects. "Dear and beloved Madame," she began, "would you allow me to ask if, among the projects that you are considering, I might hope to have a small place, however modest it might be?" Working in Durand's office apparently allowed Montifaud access to certain books, "more manageable than elsewhere." But Montifaud was also desperate to stay in Durand's "sphere of sunlight" instead of having to become the secretary for a politician, a job that she had apparently held before. This letter offers a certain window onto Montifaud's later years and perhaps her earlier ones as well: money was an issue, and she was a breadwinner from the start.

Durand was more than just a trusted colleague and mentor. Montifaud appears to have been quite smitten with her. In 1902, on the feast day of Sainte Marguerite, Montifaud offered the famously beautiful Durand two poems, in which she promised to "rhyme for the blue eyes of Madame Marguerite." She addressed the "dear eyes for whom all the azure of the sky lives" and praised the "honey-colored hair in waves / of which everyone is enamored / by the amber reflections in which gold quivers." The second poem was titled "Because"—an answer to an unspoken question. "Because you are the divinely charming fairy / and the winged Spring that frames the gold of sunshine / which makes life smile in the midst of dark waves." The poem continues with several more, no less adulatory reasons. She signed the poems "Marc" and her letters "Marie."[11]

"NO MATTER THEIR SEX"

Despite her affair with Villiers, it is easy to imagine, based on her writing, that Montifaud was attracted chiefly to women. But she nearly always situated that desire in male narrators and male fictional characters. Early evidence of this can be found in a three-part study of the female nude that she wrote for *L'Art moderne*, the journal she had created with Léon. In these essays, Montifaud was interested in how artists arranged clothing on women's bodies. In the third installment, she argued that the obligatory drapery over nude figures should reflect life rather than the academic rules of portraiture: "The charm that drapery should exert is perhaps comparable," she mused, "to the idea that comes to mind when a beautiful woman is dressed in a way that allows for the suggestion that the clothing only happens to be there, and will not remain for long."[12] In other words, clothing should only be present on a partially clad female figure for the suggestion that it may readily be removed. Later, when she was tried for obscenity, she noted the hypocrisy that no one had objected to her art criticism, which was far more lascivious. She was not wrong. This statement was one of many strikingly overt references to the sexual availability of the female nude in her writings about art.

Similarly, in the first essay of the series, Montifaud gave voice to a sexualized vantage point as she quoted the art critic Thoré. She meant to defend his endorsement of a realism that sought beauty wherever it could be found: "What is there more beautiful in the world than a young and beautiful woman?" she wrote. "Two young, beautiful women?"[13] Ventriloquizing the male artist, she alluded to same-sex *eros* between women. But there is also compelling evidence in these essays that her erotic investment in the nude was tied to her own identification with masculinity. While Montifaud may have loved women, she may have also, like Rachilde's fictional Raoule de Vénérande, loved them as a man.

By the time she published these essays in *L'Art moderne*, Montifaud had also already addressed similar themes in an 1873 reedition of the letters of the star-crossed medieval lovers Abelard and Héloïse. In this volume, the fiercely intelligent Héloïse finds in the philosopher Abelard the only tutor who can match her wit with wisdom. Soon their spiritual connection leads to a passionate, physical one. In Montifaud's preface, she imagined for Abelard a perspective like that of the male artist. She noted that he admired in Héloïse "what the drapery of her clothing revealed to the eye."[14] But it was the job of the historian, argued Montifaud, using the same term with which she had announced her masculine writerly identity in 1870, to remove Héloïse's clothing "as did her master Abelard, in order to admire her hidden beauties."[15] The scholar's job, like the artist's, was to undress the female object of his scrutiny.

Montifaud proceeded to do just that, revealing Héloïse's body to the reader in a way that is never quite as direct in other versions of the famous epistolary exchange between these medieval lovers. In Montifaud's terms:

> One sees that slightly downy line of the back, sculpturally traced between the two shoulders, whose route her lover would trace lower than the waist; the vast spread of the hips, the shiny chest whose ardent pulses would later split open her nun's habit. If there's a woman whom we can depict without any veil, it is most certainly the one whose most hidden shapes will always present themselves in the way that her lover placed her in order to castigate her.[16]

A review in *La Bibliographie contemporaine* confirms that nineteenth-century readers assumed they were reading from a male perspective: "The author has an absolute realism: he says everything that he knows, and the reader has no difficulty 'guessing the rest.'" In addition, the critic noted, one should certainly not "put it before young female eyes."[17]

Montifaud's sustained description of Héloïse put the so-called historian directly in the position not just of the artist but of the lover, deriving erotic pleasure from his visual encounter with the female body. This is what Freud would later call scopophilia, sexual pleasure derived from looking. In its direct discussion of the work of the historian, the passage allows us to see that Montifaud was doing the same with her art criticism. Both forms of writing, it turns out, were ways of undressing women.

This fascination with the female nude carried through in Montifaud's novels and historical works, where the male artist and the male writer exhibit similar sexual attractions. In *Madame Ducroisy*, the words of the artist and architect Aloysius Brandt (with whom Raymonde has her adulterous affair) also directly echo Montifaud's art criticism, similarly collapsing the boundaries between *eros* and representation.[18] Like Montifaud, Brandt criticizes the academic convention of draping the nude: "When I think that there are animals that twist drapery around a model," he laments, "ignoramuses who would go right past this kind of movement without seeing it!"[19] Brandt's speeches to Raymonde as she models for him read as dramatizations of

Montifaud's descriptions of nude portraits. Brandt's contention, like Montifaud's, was that women's clothing got in the way of truth in painting. Art, he claimed, should aim to show "flesh falling out of its envelope, jumping out of its contours." It should show "the tempestuous, the boiling-over of the surface underneath which muscles writhe, full of desire."[20]

In her first essay on nude figures, Montifaud had applauded the painter Jean-Louis Charbonnel for throwing himself into his art in similar terms: "Style will come later; what does it matter?" she imagines him thinking. "What it was about, for him, was attacking the breathless nature of reality, to translate it as the spasm of the skin that makes the hairs of the thighs and belly stand on end."[21] In other words, art should be a sensual experience of arousal inspired by the female form. In *Madame Ducroisy*, Montifaud made clear that it was the artist himself who was aroused. "Doesn't it make your skin shudder?" the fictional Brandt asks in the middle of his excursus on draping the female body, evoking the physical response in creating art and in experiencing it in the same terms—*un frisson*, a shuddering or spasm—as Montifaud had in her comments about Charbonnel. Her fictional artist takes it a step further: for Brandt, the terms of painting and sculpture merge around the nude, "as he wanted to see, penetrate, translate, and feel the object fully."[22] Art and sex become one and the same. As an avatar, Brandt allowed Montifaud to embody the position of both male artist and lover, so that she too could see and feel fully.

The gender and sexual dynamics of this novel are still more complex than they might appear. As Raymonde Ducroisy descends into madness after Brandt abandons her, she composes a piece of music based on the death of Sappho. The only hint of lesbianism in the novel, on the other hand, can be found in the passage cited above, where the narrator acknowledges that even women found themselves attracted to Thérèse. By dedicating Raymonde's music to the death of Sappho and repeatedly referencing this work when it is her male lover who has left her, Montifaud unsettles the gendered poles of this romance. Part of the pathos of the novel's ending is that Thérèse has abandoned Raymonde as well, that she has lost the friendship of this woman whom she loved. While there are no other explicit sexual references, Raymonde's emotions were invested in both Brandt and Thérèse, rather than her well-meaning but oblivious older husband. Perhaps there was an autobiographical thread there as well.

Sappho was a frequent figure in Montifaud's writing. In the fourth edition of *The History of Mary Magdelene* (in expanded form under the original title, *The Courtesans of Antiquity*), Sappho's verse appears as the epigraph: "Love destroys my soul, just as the wind overthrows oaks on the mountains" (fragment 47). Montifaud recognized in Sappho both a writer and lover: she celebrated her natural passion for poetry combined with her actual passion for love, wherever she found it. She admired her "divine fury for passion and love"—the very thing, she explained, that allowed Sappho to have a personality of such "impetuous and terrible beauty."[23]

In a chapter devoted to the poet, Montifaud puzzles over the nature of Sappho's attractions, which were not limited to women. Sappho was married with a child and had the "kind of lifestyle" that earned her her famous reputation either during her marriage or after—no matter. Montifaud describes reading a poem by Sappho to an unnamed friend, concluding, "It's impossible that the woman to whom she was addressing these verses didn't take up a large place in Sappho's life: it's the very paroxysm of passion."[24] In other words, Sappho must have loved men and women. "Yes," she continues, "Sappho loved any object that seemed to her worthy enough of love to want to savor in it the intoxication of possession, no matter their sex."[25]

The modern term for this inclination is pansexuality: being attracted to others for themselves rather than according to their gender. This indirect definition of sapphism contradicts the discourses of same-sex female desire circulating widely in nineteenth-century erotic literature. Montifaud would have been quite familiar with these discourses, but for the most part she did not choose to reproduce them in her own work. The most famous of these was Adolphe Belot's hugely successful 1870 *Mademoiselle Giraud, ma femme*, the story of a man who discovers that his wife loves women. "All told," concludes Gretchen Schultz in her comprehensive study of men writing about lesbianism during the nineteenth century, "male authors invested the tribade with meaning having very little to do with the lives of the kinds of women they ventured to portray."[26] Unlike these authors, however, Montifaud was interested in understanding Sappho, as the bearer of a message that reverberated in many of Montifaud's works and in her life as well: the notion of love "no matter their sex."

"I AM ME"

We gain some insight into Montifaud's complex gender identifications when she describes the source of her artistic inspiration to Delhasse, the Belgian lawyer. Montifaud explains that she had long believed in the motto, "Show your writing, not yourself" (which accounts for the difficulty of reconstructing her biography).[27] She was resistant to defending herself by offering her own version of the story, because "the me, the I, so frequent among the novelists who are my contemporaries, was not as familiar to me as it was to them."[28] Montifaud wasn't one for navel-gazing, she avowed, issuing a rebuke to her fellow writers in the process. This was always her way: to point outward rather than looking inward. But having been so "cruelly slandered" for years, she was in extremis,[29] and wanted desperately to be left alone. Perhaps offering her own version of the story, she reasoned, would finally put an end to the matter.

At the end of her autobiographical sketch, Montifaud appeals to Delhasse's understanding of the literary enterprise. You can imagine, she writes, what it's like to inhabit "the skin of an artist overcome with male literary spasms [*frissons*]."[30] It's a striking statement, indicating not only that her writing was characteristically masculine—she compared herself to Balzac, Zola, and Hugo earlier in the essay—but also suggesting that Delhasse might be able to imagine himself in her skin, for it was one that experienced male sensations.

The formulation shows that for Montifaud, as for Rachilde, writing was a visceral process over which she had little control. Her "male spasms" were precisely that: a natural bodily response. But while she explicitly described her spasms as masculine, they were the result of what she called "laborious childbirth."[31] Montifaud's male response was imagined, then, as the work of a female body. The imagery is curiously similar to Dieulafoy's description of Brother Pelagius, whom she imagined as the male ancestor to Joan of Arc through the spilling of his seed. Both representations construct a body that did not quite correspond to the given terms, through metaphors that regender their subject without entirely renouncing femininity. The namesake of Brother Pelagius, incidentally, was also that of the writers' prison, Sainte-Pélagie. Surely the erudite Montifaud understood the allusion. Would she read Dieulafoy's novel with self-recognition in 1893, long after her own struggles with the authorities?

While Montifaud constructed a male vantage point for her erotic descriptions, she might not have identified exclusively with masculinity or with the male body. In the case of Abelard and Héloïse, for example, Montifaud seems also to identify with the object of Abelard's affections, whose homeliness she related to and whose sensual passion derived from her intellect more than a traditionally feminine beauty. While Héloïse was "the last of her sex in terms of beauty," she was "the first in erudition,"[32] with her brilliant mind compensating for her awkward appearance. Montifaud insisted on this point: admiring "this beauty that has nothing slim or refined in her lines, but who holds, in a large and harmonious package, a powerful, vigorous character."[33] Héloïse's body, like Montifaud's, did not conform to traditional standards of beauty, but it belonged to one of the most famous lovers of all time. Categories, rules, and boundaries were meaningless when it came to gender and sexuality, Montifaud demonstrated again and again; when they were imposed, they were products of culture, of constructed moral orders rather than a more enduring force.

Montifaud articulated her philosophy most succinctly in an essay she wrote in 1879 defending *Madame Ducroisy*. It was a watershed moment for her: she was fed up with being the target of personal attacks but not quite ready to indulge her readers in some of the more sordid details that she would share in the letter to Delhasse three years later. "Madame Ducroisy, the Press, and Justice" was more of a literary treatise, but it began with a personal reflection. She defended the fact that she had written *Madame Ducroisy* from her own vantage point, and not as a loose adaptation of the work of others, as was alleged by some critics. She also pushed back against the attacks on her reputation. Summarizing these two contradictory criticisms, she noted that if she were the "monstrosity, the literary aberration" that one critic had called her, it would be of no consequence to anyone but herself: her monstrosity simply proved that she had borrowed from no one but herself: "I am myself, myself alone," she wrote. "Ultimately, I am me."[34] It was in many ways the fullest explanation she could offer.

17 THE RIGHT TO DIFFERENCE

WHILE BOASTING OF HER ACT OF REVENGE against the editor of *Le Figaro*, Montifaud would deny that her reaction was anything but appropriate and natural. "What woman who loved her husband, upon seeing him treated this way, would not have acted as I did?" she asked.[1] This was not facetiousness: substitute "man" for "woman" and "wife" for "husband" and her question makes more sense. Montifaud's iconoclastic beliefs extended beyond gender: she almost always spoke from her own deeply held belief in the universal values that she often found to be in direct and maddening opposition with those upheld by French society. When this happened, she believed it was essential—and natural—to follow belief rather than custom. "There are times when the impulses of the conscience and the inspirations of the heart defy the rules of discipline or social propriety," she continued, offering this explanation for her physical attack on Magnard.[2]

This belief in one's own sense of right and wrong, above and beyond the rules of social propriety, was at the heart of many of Montifaud's works. Because of this philosophy, those seeking to understand Montifaud—to find some external, preexisting explanation—were destined to be frustrated. She was not concerned with defining herself according to prevailing terms or questions. The explanations, she believed, did not lie elsewhere, and she was infuriated when such pronouncements were made. In her letter to Delhasse, she cited two different articles from the same newspaper on the question of women writers, with "totally contradictory ideas, from one day to the next."[3] What angered her most was that the newspaper was discussing the topic in the first place.

While Montifaud deferred to her own internal logic, she was deeply interested in those who shared her fidelity to an internal compass, even when they were punished for it. Sometimes that compass led them to love unwisely, whether this meant loving the wrong person or in the wrong way, according to society's measure; at other times it led them to write about those who had loved differently. For Jane Dieulafoy and Rachilde, writing was a way of formulating theories of what we might now consider gender and sexual identities. Dieulafoy's primary theory was gender-crossing in the service of heroism, while Rachilde imagined herself a double being and tried to understand the relationship between soul and body. Montifaud's writings, especially her early histories, function differently. Her work was about an undoing.

If Montifaud's writings held a message about how sexuality works, it was one of individualism: sex is different in every time and place. Thus there is little we can say definitively about sexual practices. But it was also a message of universalism: sex is everywhere; it is natural; and it is a way to access meaning and is therefore a legitimate focus of art. In removing the fancy dress to unveil "the fully naked Truth," Montifaud, as critic, historian, and novelist, established that nudity, and sex too, were direct vehicles of meaning.

Contemporary critics and modern scholars have generally classified Montifaud's nonfiction writings as a secular history of Christianity, and Montifaud herself was content to promote that interpretation. But the thematic unity of Montifaud's historical writings lies not in her interest in history per se, nor in the origins of Christianity or its relationship to paganism. Instead, Montifaud was interested in the history of sexuality, and her work demonstrated that morality was culturally determined. With *The Courtesans of Antiquity* and *The Vestal Virgins of the Church*, she offered a history of sexual practices. In this respect, she was not so far from Dieulafoy, whose travels in Persia allowed her to document the way in which gender expression was culturally determined: Persian women wore veils but exposed their breasts, while the more "liberated" Western women were corseted, with their faces exposed. For Montifaud, on the other hand, the distant past revealed that heterosexual norms and moral prudishness were simply a reflection of nineteenth-century culture. Sex itself—the habits of marriage, of clerical celibacy, of monogamy—followed rules that were arbitrary, subject to time and culture. In other words, it hadn't always been thus.

Montifaud was perhaps best known at the time for her defense of Blessebois, "one of the most persecuted writers of his time," a kindred spirit who was also punished for writing illicit tales.[4] Her publication of his *Alosie* in 1876 was one of her first offenses. The rebuke that followed, like the others, seemed only to embolden Montifaud: she published another of his works, *Le lion d'Angélie*, not long after, along with a preface defending him—and implicitly herself. "There could not therefore be offense to morals, to morality, to religion, to politics," she wrote, "since these offenses change in character according to the period that they come from, and stem only from a question of period, time, and place."[5]

The preface was a defiant minitreatise on the right to publish the work that inspires you. Blessebois was persecuted because intellectual brilliance was seen as an enemy of despotism, she argued. "Any intellectual force that tends to define itself individually rather than remain commingled with the collective forces of what we call society, becomes the enemy of that society."[6] Anyone who writes with originality, argued Montifaud, would come under attack in an authoritarian regime. Conflating causation with correlation, she characterized persecution as a sign of originality. The autobiographical implications were clear.

Blessebois was similar to Montifaud in his choice of subject matter—they shared a fascination with erotic tales—and both of them were famously eccentric. While her defense of his work appears to have been based on their shared effort to defy the rules of *bienséance*—that which is collectively deemed appropriate in proper society—Montifaud asserted too that to defend Blessebois was to defend the right to difference. His was a brilliant mind; he lived his life differently than those around him and by his own rules. Condemning such an author for writing about "certain sensual situations" was a way of asking humanity for "a unity of conception, inspiration, color, warmth," wrote Montifaud. But this critique of subject matter was also a critique of the artist: it asked one to overlook "our varied organisms."[7] Those who are condemned by others for their writing know the most about humanity,

Montifaud argued. "Literary pariahs" are those "who know how to tap into the humanity in those who are condemned to disappear."[8] They know how to recognize other literary outcasts and redeem them. People like Blessebois were able to reach a certain kind of reader at risk of being forgotten by society. In other words, defending Blessebois offered an implicit argument for Montifaud's own self-preservation.

Blessebois was not the only writer in whom Montifaud recognized her own difference reflected back as a kind of greatness. In her 1875 edition of the *Travels of Cyrano de Bergerac*, she wrote that she admired Cyrano precisely because he was subjected to ridicule by his peers. She identified with him in other respects, too—not least of which was the awkward appearance that belied both genius and passion—which had also forged for her a common bond with Abelard's Héloïse. Montifaud insisted on this point, repeatedly stressing the disjunction between external appearance and interiority—the nature of feelings.

As with her defense of Héloïse and Blessebois, Montifaud's case for Cyrano was a defense of his genius, mistaken as it sometimes was for madness. Most of all, it was a defense of the right to be oneself. What other choice does a person have? she asked. "You grow like a tree in one direction, and nothing can make you grow to the right if your direction is to grow to the left."[9] She conflated physical growth—which all could agree was outside of the tree's control—with writing, which she saw as another involuntary act, like the "male spasms of literary production" described in her letter to Delhasse. "Everyone writes in their own style," she concluded, and it was through no fault of their own.[10] For the writer, there was no distinction between life and authorship: "My life as a writer is so connected to my private life," she wrote to Delhasse, "that it would be impossible to separate them in two."[11]

As it happens, Montifaud's comments reflect a certain nineteenth-century perception of respected female intellectuals. Some critics were willing to acknowledge that certain women were different from others through a kind of accident of nature. In a profile of Montifaud for the photographic collection *Galerie contemporaine*, Paul Hippeau noted that Montifaud had the right to be upset with nature, "which, in not being content to put in her the qualities that usually distinguish women, gifted her with all the dispositions that make an erudite or a savant."[12] In other words, it was nature that had given her the qualities that one would normally expect to find only in men.

Hippeau then waxed poetic in her defense: "Is it her fault if, after all, instead of a Sévigné or a Madame de Stael, thankless Nature made of the Countess de Quivogne a female bibliophile Jacob"—a reference to the man who had been such a help to Montifaud's research. "Is it her fault if, giving herself over to the current in which she was caught, she treated subjects that should have stayed foreign to a woman's pen and which put her in the rank of writers targeted by the corrections police?" Finally, Hippeau made the same argument as Montifaud about writerly inclination as a fact of nature: "One doesn't criticize the hunchback for the deviation in his spinal cord; should one thus make a crime of the irresistible penchants that brought Madame de Montifaud to hold a monopoly on depicting certain dubious situations?"

But a few paragraphs later, Hippeau seemed to have forgotten his own logic. He went on to question why Montifaud was driven to write about such unfortunate topics, to waste her great intelligence on these particular questions. What had first been described as a natural inclination was now characterized as a choice. Other critics asked similar questions, just as so many who had initially defended Montifaud wondered why she continued to publish books of this kind.

Between the lines of these commentaries is a familiar debate about human nature and the drives that compel us. Almost everyone seemed to recognize that Montifaud was different through no fault of her own. Many critics were willing to acknowledge that she was born into this difference and even that her illicit writings were a product of it. But what remained at issue was whether to fault her for expressing that difference rather than trying to suppress it.

Montifaud offered an answer to this question in 1882, while defending her *Droll Stories* against the critics. "Well, why wouldn't I just admit it?" she wrote in her letter to Delhasse. "There are times in the day when you just want to unwind for a minute, take a break from serious studies. In every man, there's a little bit of the eternal child."[13] With this telling statement, offered casually in her autobiographical letter, Montifaud seems to have temporarily forgotten—once again—that others did not consider her to be a man; that, culturally speaking, she had no right to such a break and that such stories posed a threat, coming from her. And yet, her instinct was always to situate herself outside of gender conventions.

"What can I tell you? At the end of the day," Montifaud continued, "I thought I could allow myself what Mr. Maizeroy from *Le Figaro* allowed himself"—referring to the author of the short story that had enraged her and of many other far more sordid tales.[14] And there, again, was the rub. Just as she fumed that she had not been sent to the men's prison of Sainte-Pélagie, she could not imagine that she should not be allowed to write the same kind of bawdy stories as a male writer. Her mind simply could not accept this logic.

Montifaud's comment is telling in other ways as well: revealing writing as a compulsion, a part of herself that had to be released—as a spasm, perhaps. But this relief that she permitted herself in writing the *Droll Stories* was no small effort. Montifaud published hundreds of these tales, in many volumes, totaling well over one thousand pages. Writing was living, for Montifaud, and it seemed she could no more stop it than she could stop breathing. One could only do it in one's own style, growing to the left or to the right, or in a crooked line. This was nature, this was life.

THE ABBÉ DE CHOISY, GENDER OUTLAW

Montifaud's final historical publication was a revised edition of the memoirs of the Abbé de Choisy, the seventeenth-century abbot who famously passed as a woman for much of his life. Jane Dieulafoy had also planned to publish a biography of him, along with other early gender-crossers. Montifaud had included a chapter on Choisy in *The Vestal Virgins of the Church* in a bold move toward nonbinary gender *avant la lettre*; all the other chapters were devoted to women. Not surprisingly, this distressed many and was one of the reasons that she was obliged to publish his memoirs in Belgium instead of France.

In the early edition of his memoirs, the abbé had voiced a libertine devotion to pleasure in the name of God, together with a fidelity to selfhood. In the expanded version, the abbé reflected on his difference, wondering "where this bizarre Pleasure came from." He had puzzled out that God's work was to be loved, adored, and that humanity's work was the same. He discovered that dressing as a woman enabled this adoration. As a result, "I tasted in myself a Pleasure so great that it can't be compared to anything." The abbé insisted that the pleasure he experienced *en femme* was akin to no other: "Ambition, wealth, even love cannot equal it," he asserted. It also allowed him to love himself as someone extraordinary and unique, "because we love ourselves better than we love others."[15] This defiant self-love was another point of contact with Montifaud. Of course, life was not easy for Choisy. "The world is so cruel," he wrote, "and it's a rare thing to see a man wish to be a woman, so that one is often exposed to terrible jokes."[16]

In her lengthy introduction to the revised edition of Choisy's memoirs, Montifaud ends the first section by directly quoting a long tribute from Jean-Baptiste-Henri de Valincour, a distinguished man of letters and nobleman, on the occasion of the death of Choisy, his fellow academician. "There are extraordinary men who are born with such a natural inclination for writing, and with such singular talents to succeed in that domain, that one believes that nature has uniquely destined them to be the masters and the models."[17] Valincour's words anticipate Montifaud's tributes to Blessebois and Cyrano, crediting "nature" and "inclination" as the source of their singularity. But Choisy's story was different: he had been accepted and celebrated.

Valincour went on to explain that these extraordinary people are able to break the rules. As a result, what was first seen as a rupture in style becomes a new aesthetic norm. Such was the case for Choisy's writing, and it served as the reason, Valincour argued, why we must clear the way for people like him to carve out their own paths: "Let us allow these minds of the first order, when the heavens have caused them to be born, to trace themselves particular paths, and to follow the spark that leads them beyond the common path."[18] In these remarks from 1704, Valincour offered a case for nonconformity, for difference, and for freedom of expression, from the halls of the Académie française, one of the most conservative institutions of French patrimony.

In quoting Valincour's remarks, Montifaud made it impossible for readers to dissociate her own life from that of her chosen subject. She broke from her subject (Choisy) to discuss her own situation directly, specifically why she was obliged to publish the memoirs in Belgium and not in France. "Those who have power in our day use it against those whom they dislike," she proclaimed, describing the repeated counts of censorship against her and the history of her persecution.[19] She told with particular relish of the "flagrant cruelties" of the judiciary and its abuse of power, embracing the kind of gory analogy that Michel de Montaigne used in his essays to evoke the Wars of Religion, which tore Catholics and Protestants apart.[20] She described the legal authorities who had condemned her as follows:

> They take us, and they eat us in little bites, the shreds of our flesh fall from their mouths, our blood squirts from their lips; their ruthless hands rip us apart, rip us unceasingly. They provoke us, they make us—if we want to use an apt image—tie up our hands in order to tickle us, pull our hair and prevent us from removing ourselves from this kind of torture. They inject their saliva in us, they make us gag; and when we declare their treachery, they say that we have lied. They are the masters, do you understand? The masters, the masters, the masters!![21]

Even for Montifaud, this was a particularly emotional rant.

She then calmly returned to the subject at hand: "Now I have explained why this honest preface did not appear in Paris."[22] She couldn't publish it there because it was a subject that "had widely displeased."[23] Acknowledging that she was writing once again about a topic she knew would provoke, she offered a reason for doing so: the abbé was inherently interesting, and people wanted to know more about him.[24] But thanks to her many essays defending Blessebois, Sappho, and Cyrano, one can discern another reason for Montifaud to publish this work: because she had to. Writers do not choose their subject; it chooses them. Her branches were leaning a certain way, and they led her to Choisy.

Montifaud's tirade reveals the extent to which she was tortured by her inability to publish in France, and tortured to succumb to the pressures of her adversaries—to be lessened by them in this way. Now she was doing what everyone begged her to do: avoiding putting herself deliberately in harm's way. In doing so, she likely felt diminished. It was against her principles, and not just because writing as she pleased was a part of who she was. Writing about Choisy—perhaps more than any subject she had broached before—was a way of writing more directly about herself. The Abbé de Choisy was a member of the nobility remembered for both male and female assignations, a lover of both men and women, brilliant and beloved. This was personal.

In Montifaud's salacious stories—her *Droll Stories*, "drolatiques," if not quite "diaboliques," but surely a reference to Barbey d'Aurevilly's earlier collection—she plays with euphemism and meaning, creating humor from the incomprehension of her characters, for the most part young women. When a young provincial woman travels with her parents on her first trip to Paris, she is sent out to buy a hanging lamp for her church—*une suspension*—but ends up asking for *un suspensoir*—a jockstrap. The same young woman, leafing through a catalogue of Parisian curiosities, wonders what a hermaphrodite is; her aunt's embarrassed answer about a kind of fish leads to her ordering "hermaphrodite" on the menu later that evening. Sexual curiosity is perpetually thwarted by naïveté and lack of vocabulary.[25]

In confronting her own difference, Montifaud played a similar literary game. She seemed to know what could be said directly and what could not: how to say just enough to enrage certain readers while leaving them unable to fully account for their response. Knowing this, we can read Montifaud's volume on the abbé as another confession of sorts, another way of taking off the fancy dress. With the Abbé de Choisy, she offered readers a certain version of herself: a coded tale—her own, not exactly dirty, joke.

There's no evidence that Choisy meant more to Montifaud than the other figures to whom she had devoted historical research: Sappho, Blessebois, Cyrano, and Héloïse. Aside from Sappho, they were all versions of the same person: memorialized for being different and for expressing that difference in writing. But Choisy is the only one for whom gender was at stake. And ultimately, Choisy was not punished. He was celebrated and embraced as a hero. And he's the one that she ends with.

"Thus lived and died François Timoléon de Choisy," Montifaud concludes, after citing a series of excerpts from his contemporaries. "Thus departed the one who had been exiled repeatedly as *a girl*, and who was celebrated later as a hero."[26]

Montifaud, like Dieulafoy, may have wished the same for herself: to leave as a girl and return as a hero, as she defiantly made her way back to France, committed to masculine attire. In writing about the gender-crossing Choisy and inserting her own story in the center, she makes her case apparent. How many times had she been forced to leave, hoping to return as another? If the Académie française had been able to recognize and celebrate the Abbé de Choisy, was it so unreasonable for Marc de Montifaud to ask the same of her peers? In the plaintive, defensive, angry recriminations, a rare vulnerability comes through in this narrative—the reverse side of her rage.

18 GENDER EXILE

IF DRESSING IN MEN'S CLOTHING had started out as a disguise for Montifaud, a way to protect her identity in exile, by the time she returned to France in the mid-1880s it had clearly taken on a different meaning. Being on the run offered a convenient pretext for exploring gender expression. As Dieulafoy learned as well, travel to another country allowed for this freedom, and there was no returning to femininity afterwards. Dressing as a man seemed to have made Montifaud feel less embattled. She was able to stay out of trouble, and almost entirely out of the spotlight, for the next decade. But although she avoided writing on scandalous subjects, she still felt the need to reassert her masculinity, as she had so many times before. Perhaps too many now knew her as "Madame" Marc de Montifaud. Within a few years of returning to Paris for good, it was time for a change.

In 1890, Montifaud launched a new column for *L'Evénement*, which was edited by her friend Edmond Magnier. She signed it "Erasme." Later, when Montifaud signed this name to novels and plays, the first name "Paul" accompanied it. To those who knew Montifaud, the name may have been fitting, suggesting a blend of Christian doctrine with Erasmus's belief in independence and free will. In addition to his proverbs, the prolific early modern thinker had exposed the hypocrisy of the church while seeking reform from within the institution.

The new moniker did not have a feminine correlate. In letters to Montifaud, friends switched to calling her Erasme, as if it was a nickname, and always in the masculine. Magnier was delighted with Montifaud's new iteration. "You, know, dear and glorious master," he wrote in an undated letter, "that I find Erasme's article very good, eloquent, truthful. . . . All my compliments to Erasme, whom I confuse with his rightfully famous inventor."[1] In Montifaud's archives, there are several letters from a friend, Mademoiselle de La Tour du Pin Chambly de La Charce, that begin with "my dear Erasme" and address Montifaud as "dear friend" only in the masculine; others wrote to Erasme as "dear *confrère*," "dear master," or simply "monsieur."[2]

Erasme's column did nothing to suggest that its author was not a man. Written in the first person, the author's statements were always gendered in the masculine (*je suis content*, etc.). What's more, Erasme did not shy away from commenting on gender. Erasme wrote columns from this masculine vantage point—"Our Future Eves," "A Woman's Honor," and "Women's News"—in which the author dropped lightly misogynistic comments and referred to women as "the other sex."[3]

Montifaud may have enjoyed the newfound anonymity of this masculine persona; many unsuspecting fans wrote to "Monsieur Paul Erasme," admiring *his* writings. In 1893, Montifaud wrote as Paul Erasme to the queen of Spain, Isabella II, offering Her Majesty his tickets for the theater. She received in return a letter from the queen's emissary, the Duke of Castro, explaining that the queen did not go out at night.

It's impossible to know what prompted the generous offer, but one wonders if Montifaud thrilled at the response, in which Her Majesty thanked "Monsieur Paul Erasme" for his generosity. "Receive, I pray of you, Monsieur, the assurance of my most distinguished sentiments, with the gratitude of the Queen," the duke signed.[4] It was the same gender play that Montifaud had enjoyed at the beginning of her career as an art critic: writing in such a way as to ensure that readers would view her as a man. Did each address to Erasme in the masculine quiet a certain storm within, offering an affirming sign that Montifaud could be seen, at least in writing, as she (he?) wanted to be seen?

It's unclear under what circumstances Montifaud might have been revealed as the person behind Paul Erasme and whether she took any pains to keep the information hidden. In some newspaper reviews of her plays, the author Paul Erasme's name would be accompanied by "Marc de Montifaud" in parentheses; others made no mention. In 1896, *La Justice* reviewed a play by Paul Erasme, "The Convict." The performance was warmly received. The journalist noted that the author's name was received with "true enthusiasm" at the curtain's close. The applause for Paul Erasme was met, he noted, with a warmth equal to that of the very talented actors.[5] Montifaud's manner of dressing allowed her to appear in public without being recognized as a woman, and at any rate, no one seemed to care. A few years earlier, the same newspaper had reported on Erasme's one-act play "Aristotle's Law," noting that "Mr. Paul Erasme is, it seems, a woman," before offering: "Madame Erasme (what a name for a woman!)."[6]

As Paul Erasme, Montifaud published several "patriotic fictions" that seemed vastly different from the sexually themed works for which the author was already so well known. Critics have puzzled over these later works, mentioning them without commentary, as an aberration occurring at the end of Montifaud's career.[7] But Montifaud's patriotic voice can be traced to a much earlier period. In fact, her first patriotic writing dated from 1870, the year of the Franco-Prussian War, when she published a pamphlet titled *Hymn to Death: A Patriotic Song*. In these few pages, Montifaud described death as the realization of "a sacred ambition" that was part of citizenship and part of a greater destiny, "in the great day of history."[8] It was also distinctly male.

The patriotic poem was addressed to France in the first person, as if from a soldier. "Leave death to us, death with the mysterious intoxications that it passes on," Montifaud wrote. "In entering into that beyond of life where our fathers are, let's open up this earth that was our homeland with a final gesture. Adieu, France, those who are dying salute you."[9]

In describing the feeling of death, Montifaud wrote that young soldiers "still pale from childhood weakness" felt, as death approached, "a male spasm run through them," the same terms (*un mâle frisson*) she would use in her letter to Delhasse more than a decade later to describe the urge to write: something natural and powerful that could not be controlled or overcome. The repetition suggests that it may have been how she gave verbal shape to the feeling of maleness that had long been part of her.

The Franco-Prussian War was a traumatic, deeply affecting event for the whole nation. The patriotic song suggests that Montifaud experienced the trauma as a painful reminder of her sex and of the ways in which she could not be a man and could not serve her country as her male peers were called to. "Adieu, France, those who are dying salute you."[10] With this refrain, Montifaud moved from the "we" (*nous*) of the earlier prose to a casual distancing of her voice with "those" (*ceux*). Moving between pronouns seemed to allow her to imagine herself most fully.

The year 1870 was also the year in which Montifaud published *The History of Mary Magdalene*, her first effort to masculinize herself as a historian. In the preface to the fourth edition of 1876, she noted that the first three editions sold out in a few months, between February and July 1870, before the success of the book was interrupted by the war. Thus, by the time Montifaud started writing patriotic fictions by Paul Erasme, this was hardly a new preoccupation. But in these works, the old themes encompassed her more recent experiences in new ways. In 1890, Montifaud published *Our Petty Officers*, the story of the Alsacian Léon Keyser and his "brother-in-arms," Jacques Morin. Jacques and Léon sneak into Alsace in order to retrieve a French flag stolen by the Germans during the Franco-Prussian War, during which Keyser's father had been killed. Their friend, Vicomte Louis de Rivesalte, who enlisted in the army after a failed suicide attempt following an unhappy love affair, stays behind and guards their secret.

The novel, which harnessed the tension between France and Germany for its setting, turned out to be another iteration of the fiction that Montifaud had written throughout her literary career, as it was shot through with the anger that defined so much of her writing. For Montifaud, writing had long offered a form of revenge. In *Madame Ducroisy*, she had expressed her anger at Olympe Audouard. In the sequels, she had turned to her other detractors. Her letter to Delhasse, on the other hand, was an excuse to take down Maizeroy, Magnard, and others; in it she described "la jouissance"—the pleasure—of revenge. But these were personal vendettas known to few. They didn't provide the satisfaction that she sought. She still remained alone with her feelings, discontented and unavenged.

Our Petty Officers was revenge fiction of a different order, as Germany represented a common enemy—a perfect target for all her anger, at last. In the dedication to this novel, Montifaud quotes the nationalist poet Paul Déroulède, who had taken a hard right turn after the Franco-Prussian War.

"O my cavalry / the journey is long," he wrote. "We need to travel as far as my hatred will go." Déroulède—and Montifaud's fictional characters—was as driven by anger and a sense of justice as she was.

Jacques Morin describes the nature of this impulse, as he and Keyser come closer to their goal of retrieving the French flag: "REVENGE" is a "gigantic jewel, which you have to set at some point or another."[11] It's a strange metaphor: the raging, destructive emotion as a beautiful object that one carries around, searching for the right setting in which to place it so that it will be properly appreciated. But this one phrase explains much of Montifaud's psychology. She cultivated and guarded her anger for years, waiting for the moment in which to make it visible to the world in dramatic fashion. She seemed to associate the dark, destructive, and private with that which should be beautifully displayed. It's a fitting metaphor, perhaps, for the repression of gender identity over a lifetime.

Montifaud's own experiences are woven throughout the novel in subtle ways, so that no one character represents her, though her feelings are refracted throughout. One recognizes glimpses of her in the aristocratic Louis de Rivesalte, who longs to go to battle but must remain behind. He can never quite be the "brother-in-arms" that Léon and Jacques so naturally embody; unlike Dieulafoy, Montifaud was unable to imagine this for herself. We glimpse Montifaud again in Jacques's loyal friendship with Léon: of foreign blood, but an ally, like Montifaud's husband by the same name.

One of the most dramatic moments in *Our Petty Officers* takes place as Léon and Jacques slip into Alsace without passports. A female friend named Margot helps them by offering them her suitcase. She advises them to tell the border officials they are salesmen traveling to Alsace to sell their goods to department stores. They could then show the silks and fabrics in the suitcase as proof. Following her advice when questioned later, Jacques confidently offers that they are employees at the Bon Marché department store.

In 1876, when Montifaud was first sentenced to prison, she published a letter in *Le Figaro* describing her narrow escape as she crossed the border without a passport, terrified. "It's evening. I'm on the train. . . . I don't know anyone in Brussels," she wrote. The conductor enters, and as Montifaud mutters monosyllabically, he wonders why she has so few bags with her. She recounts her quick response: "'Well,' I offered, with *superb aplomb*, 'I am traveling for a department store. I'm going to sell . . . some muslins.'"[12]

Clothing is an emotionally resonant motif throughout *Our Petty Officers*, a direct link to patriotism and its risks, and to that possibility of the male spasm. The flag that Keyser and Jacques retrieve is described as "France's gown." Muslins and silks are both the tools of their passage and the clues that reveal their ruse: when they nervously offer the silks that Margot has given them to their Prussian hosts, the hosts become suspicious that these strangers should offer them presents supposedly meant for commerce and cousins. The mission is eventually a success, but Jacques is captured and executed. Keyser, on the other hand, comes home, the French flag wrapped secretly around his torso, under his clothing—a soldier in a dress, as it were.

On the other side of the border, Rivesalte eagerly pays extra money to have his new uniform ready as soon as possible. Montifaud describes vividly the emotional resonance of this sartorial shift: "Everyone knows that the blue dolman jacket, fitted well, in officer's fabric, and the red pants, a little finer and tighter-fitting, are the dream of any young person in the military," she writes. "Some would risk two weeks of prison to wear this uniform" (as it was illegal to do so when off duty).[13] Montifaud imagined that despite the threat of prison, the pleasures and rewards of this ensemble were too great to resist.

Montifaud's descriptions of clothing recall Dieulafoy's emotional scenes in *Volunteer* around the soldier's uniform—inspired by her actual experience in the Franco-Prussian War. For both of these writers, the war was a time in which their gender difference seems to have caused them much pain, which their writing helped them overcome by embodying the male soldier they longed to be. The uniform was a particularly poignant symbol for both writers: they recognized how profoundly it was invested with meaning for their male peers, how it served as the means of transformation from young man to soldier. It seems also to have been suggestive, for both, of the possibility of their own transformation, the possibility of being this kind of man, too. Rivesalte doesn't go to battle, but he becomes a hero of sorts, protecting Léon and Jacques's secret, and earning the trust of his fiancée's family. The uniform transforms him from a suicidal, effete aristocrat into a respected soldier, a man among men.

Julia Serano has described her early struggles with gender dissonance and the varied emotions that it would trigger in terms that seem particularly relevant to understanding Montifaud: "Sometimes it felt like stress or anxiousness," she notes, "which led to marathon battles with insomnia. Other times, it surfaced as jealousy or anger at other people who seemed to enjoy taking their gender for granted. But most of all, it felt like sadness to me—a sort of gender sadness—a chronic and persistent grief."[14] Others have described a sensation akin to homesickness, a feeling of longing for a place where one belongs but can somehow never get to. Jack Halberstam has described himself as a gender "refusenik"—perpetually in motion—like Bartleby in his refusal of answers, fixity.[15]

In French the word for homesickness is to be "dépaysé"—literally *de-countried*. This was a feeling with which Montifaud—the perpetual exile, the staunch patriot—was quite familiar. Perhaps the reason that she was willing to endure it so often had something to do with her sense of already being *dépaysé/e*, even when she was in her homeland. Alsace—with its fluid identities, its multiple languages and iterations—provided a fitting symbol for this conflict: a place both home and not-home, its poles of orientation shifting like her own.

In other texts, Montifaud, like many later transgender writers, seeks the farthest reaches of the earth: the Orient, "this country of avatars" as one character puts it in *The Perverts*.[16] In other words, a place—as Dieulafoy had already discovered, as Jan Morris later would—where the cultural differences are so vast that the gender differences recede to the background in comparison. But the travel itself becomes a fitting metaphor for a sense of gender exile. "Surely they had me in mind when they sang about having to leave the land of one's birth," writes Jennifer Finney Boylan of the epic tales she was drawn to teach as an English professor before making her transition. "Making a difficult ocean crossing. Arriving at last in a new world, the land of promise, the land of freedom. But never quite fitting in, in the new land, always speaking with a trace of a foreign accent. Sometimes I think the best way to understand gender shift is to sing a song of diaspora."[17]

In *Our Petty Officers*, with its border crossings and clothing changes, the hiding, disguises, and the sense of being split in two, Montifaud seemed to be seeking a resolution of her painful exile years—channeling the feelings of loss and vulnerability into a more accessible plot, with heroes and villains more clearly defined. This plot allowed her to have France as her home, while allowing Montifaud to visit Alsace, that place of ambiguity and conflicted selves.

Keyser had his revenge, and it was sweet. It was shared by the regiment and the nation. He returned a hero, just as Montifaud had always wanted to (and as Dieulafoy managed to—bringing the differences of Persia, and the privileges of having gone to battle, with her at every step). The anger that Keyser had carried his whole life was finally released.

Of all the works she had written, this novel brought Montifaud closest to fame, earning accolades and a certain kind of quiet renown when it was performed as a play. When Hans Ryner wrote a profile on her in 1890, she insisted that he only read *Our Petty Officers* in addition to one of her histories and ignore the rest.[18]

It's difficult to know whether the anger finally subsided. Montifaud had frustrated at least some of her pacifist friends with her militant views and her desire to keep revisiting this conflict. Alsace, the contested, plural territory, continued to resonate with her. In 1904, Montifaud/Erasme tried to publish a short play in verse titled *Alsace*, in which she had found a new villain: French natives too quick to forget this particular loss, alongside Alsatians with French roots who had assimilated to German identity. For some, this play crossed a line, implicitly attacking certain French politicians. *La Justice* wryly reported that Erasme's new play had been closed "for its overly francophilic verses."[19]

From Montifaud's perspective, however, something about Alsace was quintessentially French and resonated deeply with her own sense of Frenchness. "France alone is there," declares Fritzel, her protagonist and the voice of this patriotic fury, in the closing verse. "As a right she *is*, because she *is*." This was the aspect of French Alsace that Montifaud could relate to—she *is* because she *is*—just as Montifaud saw herself—*but ultimately, I am me*: tautological, self-referential, fated.

"Was it that the box was too small, with its preposterous expectations of what women are, or was it that I didn't fit?" asks Olivia Laing in her recent memoir of loneliness. "I'd never been comfortable with the demands of femininity, had always felt . . . that I inhabited a gender position somewhere between the binaries of male and female, some impossible other, some impossible both." Laing comes to realize that "trans" was the category that she fell into, "which isn't to say I was transitioning from one thing to another, but rather that I inhabited a space in the centre, which didn't exist, except there I was."[20] Was the feeling Laing describes something like what Montifaud felt as she sought to lay claim to a space that wasn't there but which she knew existed? Perhaps Alsace grew larger in her imagination with the years because she was frustrated that others were willing to forget the hard-fought battles and because she did not want to forget so quickly the contested territory and tortured history of her own bifurcated past. The battle was not yet won, she wanted to remind her compatriots. Did some part of her still feel abandoned in exile, wearing the French gown under her men's suit?

GENDER FAILURE

In 1920, the writer Laurent Tailhade offered a portrait of Marc de Montifaud in his collection "Phantoms of Yesteryear." He had come to know Montifaud from their days at the Bibliothèque nationale, which he described as itself a relic of an earlier time: "a picturesque place, undeniably unique," that was a rarity in modern Paris, a city "that changes and becomes uglier every day, more Americanized, with a furious haste to plunder whatever is left of its old beauties." The library stood apart, wrote Tailhade, "in the Paris of the automobile, the telephone, the crowds and the pavement," by maintaining "its affable, provincial calm." In this quiet refuge, the author appreciated a colorful cast of characters: "journalists, onlookers, students, translators, highschoolers, *bas bleus*, compulsive old men, astrologers and those who simply needed to stay warm."[21] But Montifaud could not be described by any of these terms. Tailhade's portrait of her offers more complexity and more color than any other image that we have.

> Imagine for yourself a student, done up in style, like those wax figures that high-end tailors use to display their wares. Complete with spring season nuances, hat the color of turtledoves, with a rainbow of ties—pale pink, floral linen, Nile river, bit of lilac, thigh of nymph, daffodil, touch of gold. A complementary-colored scarf gracefully falls over her outside pocket, on the left side of the jacket. A round head, washed out hair, cut in a "half-Capoul" on a face without beauty, with a chubby nose, pale eyes, thin lips, painted with makeup, covered with powder—all of this together made for a troubling look.[22]

This Montifaud, of the late 1890s and early 1900s, cuts a striking figure: youthful in her men's suits, accessorized to the hilt (figure 56). Her colorful ties and matching pocket scarves make her something of a dandy—a term used to describe fashionable men of the time. But she also wears jewelry—in addition to the rings, "all sorts of gaudy jewels" and makeup. The result

A la Bibliothèque Nationale, on remarquait souvent avant l'autre guerre, un « petit vieux » qui, non seulement compulsait les ouvrages littéraires ou historiques, mais demandait souvent les œuvres de la comtesse de Ségur. Ce vieux monsieur dont Fernand Fau dessina un jour le portrait ci-dessus, n'était d'ailleurs qu'une femme, et une femme de lettres encore. Mme Marc de Montifaud qui fut collaboratrice de Marguerite Durand lorsque celle-ci fonda la Fronde, avait adopté le costume masculin qu'elle ne devait jamais quitter jusqu'à sa mort pour pouvoir d'abord travailler dans une verrerie.

FIGURE 56. Sketch of Montifaud at the Bibliothèque nationale, from a feature on Belle Epoque women writers in the newspaper *La Marianne*, January 1940.
Source: Bibliothèque nationale de France.

is unsettling. "What could be her place in the world?" asks Tailhade, not unkindly, of this "whippersnapper with wrinkles." "If this were a student, in what time period had he embarked on his studies?"[23]

Like Frédéric Loliée's description of Dieulafoy and the portraits of Rachilde by so many of her peers, Tailhade's image of Montifaud captures the way in which she escaped categories: an excess of adjectives and details all working against each other. In her men's suits, Montifaud resembled Dieulafoy in some ways. On more than one occasion, they were confused for one another, and from the black-and-white photographs, one can see how that might have happened.[24] But Tailhade's colorful description allows us to see the ways in which Montifaud's persona was uniquely striking. It is a reminder that the whole was so much more than the sum of the parts.

A letter of condolence to Montifaud's son upon her death in 1912 further demonstrates the way in which Montifaud's gender difference was recognized and respected by many of those who came into contact with her. "Believe, dear friend, that the great soul of Paul Erasme will manage to survive all events and will conserve the precious and imperishable memory of the Countess de Montifaud," Mr. Fresquel wrote, signaling the subtle relationship between Paul Erasme and Montifaud, who shared a soul, if not a sex. The rest of the letter carefully avoids gender markers, referring to the "spirit" of Marc's mother, calling Montifaud "a being" whom he had had the pleasure of hearing speak and the "exquisite author" (m.) who had autographed copies of her works for Fresquel.[25]

We might think of Montifaud (and perhaps those around her as well) as having accepted, rather than begrudged, her "gender failure," to take up Rae Spoon and Ivan Coyote's turn of phrase. Like these two modern storytellers, she didn't fit into the available categories or the models for masculine and feminine behavior. Rather than attempt to make sense of her complex, gender-variant self, as Dieulafoy did through feminist theories and stories that championed gender-crossing, or as Rachilde did through an obsessive focus on her relationship to the category of woman, Montifaud seems to have dispensed with categories entirely. Her powerful self-determination, captured in her confident declaration of selfhood, exhibited her decidedly modern deference to internal logic above all else.

Replace all the "buts" with "ands": in this worldview, you can be wife and mother *and* identify with masculinity; you can be attracted to women *and* to your husband or other men.[26] You can wear men's suits, sport a man's haircut, *and* also wear makeup, jewelry, and heels.

"I am not trapped in the wrong body," explains Ivan Coyote. "I'm trapped in a world that makes very little space for bodies like mine."[27] Montifaud might have agreed with this sentiment. While she looked to models from Héloïse to Blessebois to the Abbé de Choisy, she did not seem to puzzle over herself or allow herself to acknowledge the particular pain of her difference from those around her. Instead of self-loathing, she loathed others and eternally plotted her revenge. She looked outward, not inward. This, in the end, was the most prescient thing about her: she understood that the problem was not with her but with everybody else.

CONCLUSION

IN THE SUMMER OF 2018, I stumbled into Jane Dieulafoy's living room. I was in Paris, conducting some final research for this book during a sweltering heat wave in late June. Temperatures were making their way to the upper nineties as I faced off against a list of still-needed sources. The hunt took me far from the modern comforts of the French national library, which had air conditioning but required room reservations and long waits. Instead, I was scrambling around the city to smaller, older venues that, even in the heat, were more pleasant to work in. At the Bibliothèque historique de la Ville de Paris, for example, I could peruse the pages of certain rare editions of newspapers and magazines that the national library would only offer in microfilm, if at all. What's more, the BHVP was housed in the former home of Diane de France, daughter of Henri II. It's a gorgeous, sixteenth-century mansion nestled among the winding streets of the charming Marais neighborhood—the Paris of Balzac and Hugo.

I needed to go to the BHVP to find the limited-issue folio *Galerie contemporaine*, featuring a profile and portrait of Marc de Montifaud. Once there, I plugged Dieulafoy's name into the library's search engine. It was more of a whim than anything else; I was always looking for an excuse to stay in their lovely reading room. The BHVP had recently gone digital, causing new treasures to reveal themselves. I was surprised to discover that the library held two letters from Jane to Marcel: her last will and testament. Soon I was flipping through a thick album filled with nineteenth-century correspondence that had apparently come into the hands of a single collector. When I found my way to the Dieulafoy page, it wasn't too hard to make out the cryptic scrawl: "My beloved," Jane wrote to Marcel. "Not one beat of my tender heart, since we met, has not been for you." My trip was already paying dividends.

I had also been to the library of the Institut de France, the seat of the Académie française. In the nineteenth century, the institute, which houses the French academies of arts, letters, and sciences, was known metonymically as La Coupole: its famous cupola stands directly opposite the Louvre Palace, on the other side of the Seine, connected by the Pont des Arts. Official entry into La Coupole marks the highest form of intellectual achievement. One doesn't enter La Coupole, it is said, but is rather received there: only when one member dies can another be elected to join its ranks.

Because, remarkably, Marcel Dieulafoy had been selected for this honor, both Jane's and Marcel's archives are there. He had become an *immortel*—an immortal one—as members are dubbed, together with the Abbé de Choisy of long before. So it was something of a coup to get to work in their library, since to be admitted one needs permission from a living *immortel*—something I had improbably secured. It was always a thrill to breeze through the entrance gates on the Quai de Conti and make my way to the nineteenth-century reading room, even if it was stifling indoors, in the summer heat.

While the official archives are at the institute, I had known for a while that Marcel bequeathed the Dieulafoy home to the Red Cross organization and that it served as some sort of headquarters. I had heard that the 1870 portrait of Jane as a soldier was still hanging there. But I wasn't sure that a trip to the Passy neighborhood, near the Eiffel Tower, was worth my precious research time, especially in the relentless heat. I had photographs of the painting, after all.

I couldn't reach anyone on the phone when I tried to call, just one of those maddening phone trees. The hours weren't posted anywhere. But since many of the smaller archives didn't open until the afternoon, I decided to take my chances one morning. It seemed at least worth a shot.

I found a bus that took me directly from where I was staying in central Paris to the 16th arrondissement and found the building easily—a squat, stand-alone structure, magisterial all the same. Entrance seemed doubtful at first: I rang the bell, and an answering machine picked up. I tried again, reasoning that the trip would have been worth it just for having seen the outside of the house and taken a photo of the small plaque that marked it as a "patriomonial site."

But then someone answered. "I'm an American scholar, working on Madame Dieulafoy," I offered. I was ushered in immediately, directed to the second floor. A door opened, and there was Jane Dieulafoy's living room. Not just the painting of her, but much of the décor: the wallpaper, the ceiling, the cornices, the fireplace.

In some ways, it was just as I had seen it in photographs; I recognized the dramatic chimney in front of which she sometimes posed for pictures, tiny beneath the sweeping heights of the floor-to-ceiling fixture (figure 57; cp. figure 29). But the black-and-white reproductions had not done it justice. I had to catch my breath to take it all in, this coming together of the image on my computer and the reality in front of me. There's something especially powerful about this kind of unmediated contact with the object of your research. I felt as though I'd walked into a time capsule, even though there was also plenty of modern clutter—plastic conference tables and chairs, papers lying around. In the back stood a red-and-gold breakfront stuffed with bits of colored pottery. Apparently not all of their finds ended up in the Louvre.

I looked closer at the fireplace, the focal point of the room. It was indeed "a veritable marvel," as the women's magazine *Femina* had described it in 1902; the engravings that embellish the mantel were painted in startlingly vibrant colors, which I had never before appreciated. The scene depicts the mythological story of Perseus slaying the Gorgon. Surely they must have chosen that scene in honor of Persia's namesake.

The whole room is a blend of Persia and Paris, signaling the Dieulafoys' double alliances. The scene of Perseus on the mantel is crowned by a series of fleur-de-lys, those flowers long associated with the French throne, and dotted with daisies like those found on the Persian archers now on display in the Louvre, which Dieulafoy called the *immortels*, as well as her "sons." Did she

suspect their discovery would guarantee Marcel entry into that illustrious academy, making him an *immortel*? Did she realize they would secure her legacy as well?

The colors decorating the fireplace—and the fact that it was colored at all—evoke the greens and blues that the Dieulafoys had discovered in their excavations, some of which were held behind the glass doors of the cabinet on the other side. In addition, the high, vaulted ceilings are fitted with elaborate, temple-like cornices, painted with wine-colored Middle Eastern swirls, gesturing toward the palaces the Dieulafoys had unearthed. Painted mosaics fill the ceilings in between planks of dark wood, while the walls are lined with thick sheets of the velvet floral wallpaper that was very much in vogue in late nineteenth-century Paris.

It was against this backdrop that I took in the portrait of young Jane after the war. There she stood, in cummerbund and riding boots, leaning confidently against a rock (figure 6). Her hair is cropped in short waves, a man's hat and cloak lying nearby. The colors were more vibrant in person, even though the painting had been damaged by the glaring light of the Parisian sun. But there was another portrait too, also of young Jane, that was unfamiliar (figure 58). In this painting, Dieulafoy wears a white dress, with a blue silk ribbon tied in a bow around her waist. A wedding dress, perhaps? It is possible that this portrait—similar in size—was meant as a corollary to the other one, from the same post–Franco-Prussian War period, when Jane had tried her hand at being a wife. It is the only image that I've ever seen of her in women's clothing. I was stunned.

In this second portrait, Dieulafoy's left hand holds a rose that seems attached to a large bouquet, arranged in an urn to her side. We see only a fragment of those flowers, though; they are part of some other domestic space, suggested but not quite depicted. On the right side of Dieulafoy another suggested, fragmented background presents itself: an open landscape of green and sky, which illuminates her face with reflected light. Dieulafoy stands awkwardly before a damask drape, between the cut flowers and the shining world beyond. We can't quite tell if she's inside or outside.

Looking at that painting, I found myself thinking of the photograph of Montifaud *en femme*—the one I'd just seen at the BHVP (figure 52). Dieulafoy

< **FIGURE 57.** The fireplace in the Dieulafoy salon today (cp. figure 29). Photograph by author.

FIGURE 58. Portrait of Jane Dieulafoy in the Hôtel Dieulafoy, Paris. Photograph by author.

looks similarly uncomfortable. With her hair parted in the middle, pinned back in two loose chignons, her elongated forehead is awkwardly exposed. Her expression is somber, unhappy—so different from the pleasant calm depicted on the opposite wall, not to mention the photographs that would follow. Was it just hindsight that made me see her as a man in women's clothing, just as the reporter from *Le Figaro* had described Montifaud in 1878 as having the "look of a man dressed as a lady"?

For a moment I was puzzled as to why Dieulafoy would have hung this portrait in her living room, side by side with the one of her as a soldier that always made her so proud. But then I realized that she hadn't, in fact. There were no paintings on the wall in the photographs of Dieulafoy that I had seen. Someone had made this decorating decision after she was gone.

"You know, I always thought that these paintings were of Madame and Monsieur," the caretaker tells me. "But then I found out that they were both Madame!" His name is Michel, and he is eager to share these forgotten artifacts with me. Michel looks to be in his midfifties and clearly has been working here for some time. There aren't many visitors, and he is excited about a promised restoration that's under way. He tells me about the days when the Iranian embassy held events in this room. There's a pause. "Do you happen to know why she wore pants?"

Michel offers his own reasoning: that Dieulafoy traveled a lot, so it must have been more comfortable. That she was some kind of early feminist. But his question lingers. "She identified with masculinity," I offer. "It's complicated. That's what my book is about."

Does Michel understand what I'm getting at? It's unlikely that he knows much about trans identity, or that he would think of using that word in relation to these portraits. Trans hasn't quite made it into mainstream culture in France as it has in the United States, where, even so, most people haven't really taken the time to try to understand it unless they have some personal reason to do so. But like so many of Dieulafoy's peers, Michel intuits that there's more to the story. It wasn't just about her wearing comfortable clothing.

Like me, Michel feels protective of Jane Dieulafoy and also proud. We agree that she is a national treasure. He introduces me to the Red Cross receptionist, who tells me there are others researching these materials and takes my name, promising to put me in touch with these *French* researchers (she never does). I am used to these kinds of gatekeepers, having wrangled with so many librarians in this country who are inexplicably reluctant to share their collections.

Michel sneaks me past her, up to the attic. He shows me the boxes of Dieulafoy's books and notes. There's another portrait of Dieulafoy that I've never seen before, hidden away in a corner: a small black-and-white pastel on canvas by the female artist Amélie Baury Saurel, dated 1887. Saurel has given Jane a little shadow above her lip and adorned her lapel with the red Legion of Honor pin that she'd earned for her sharpshooting (see figure 8). In another fraying cardboard box, there are more Persian shards. Michel encourages me to look inside and touch them.

I don't tell Michel that I'm interested in Dieulafoy because I'm writing a book about gender identity in nineteenth-century France, nor do I tell the librarians at the Institut de France. The stated function of the French Academy since 1634 has been to protect the French patrimony. When I was there a few days before my visit to the Dieulafoy house, the agenda for the day was posted outside on a whiteboard: "Dictionary," then "Prizes." The members of the Academy—the *immortels*—would be deciding that very day which new words to let into the French language; then they would vote on their annual literary prizes. The year before, in 2017, that same group of people (four women and thirty-three men) had decided that gender-inclusive language—*l'écriture inclusive*—was a "mortal threat" to the French language, which must be preserved for the sake of future generations. It was a devastating blow to feminists and transgender activists.

All of this had seemed sadly ironic to me as I made my way past that whiteboard into the privileged space of the library reading room. In order to gain entrance to the collection, I had told the *immortel* whom I'd solicited (there have only been six *immortelles* to this day) that I was writing about Jane in the context of my work on Belle Epoque women writers. What would have happened had I told him that I was interested in her in the context of modern notions of transgender identity?

This question is particularly relevant in considering Dieulafoy, Rachilde, and Montifaud and their legacies. In some cases, the fact that their difference was never defined has preserved a certain status for them. Dieulafoy remains a French hero, her legacy protected by the ironclad firewalls of the French academy. But she also remains underexplored and often misunderstood.

In the United States, we are living through what has been described as a "transgender moment" or a "transgender tipping point," in reference to the increased visibility of the past decade.[1] The category of trans and its terminologies have expanded dramatically and will likely continue to do so as we become more aware of gender diversity. As I began this research, I was hesitant to invoke this language in speaking about Dieulafoy, Rachilde, and Montifaud. I did not want to impose modern sensibilities on a very different time and place. I soon realized, however, that the modern framework was crucial. Without recourse to an expansive notion of gender identity, scholars are inclined to see these figures as feminist. Feminism has proven to be an important historical lens through which to recognize resistance to gender norms in nineteenth-century France, despite the anachronistic nature of the term. I believe we need to articulate the possible dimensions of trans history in a similar fashion, so as to better distinguish it from what it was not.

Despite evidence of these figures' gender nonconformity, scholars have been understandably reluctant to make claims about identity as it relates to them. But to not make these claims, even if only tentatively, is to make a different kind of claim, leaving unquestioned the assumption that they were gender normative, that is, that they saw themselves as women in a binary structure. A host of other assumptions flow from that reflexive categorization, limiting our ability to understand their lives in all their particularities. Recovering gender variance in the past is not a simple affair, and the evidence is not always direct or conclusive. This difficulty is why José Muñoz described queer history as requiring scholars to redefine what counts as scholarly rigor, directing us toward "ephemera as evidence" in order to discern what has, by necessity, been transmitted covertly. Relying on traditional scholarly methods too often means denying gender variability as a historical possibility and thus burying an important thread of the past and its multiple dimensions.

Dieulafoy, Rachilde, and Montifaud are often mentioned together, in a list, as women who, along with George Sand and Rosa Bonheur, wore pants in nineteenth-century France.[2] To group them together in this way implies that they came to men's clothing from the same starting point. The sartorial affinities are relevant, as is the fact that they were considered women; but this doesn't mean that they thought of themselves as women, or that they understood that category the way we do now or the way their peers did. That's why to examine these figures productively requires feminist and trans studies approaches working together, in order to account for both the affinities and the differences, and to allow for depth instead of mere lists.[3]

This book makes a case, then, for pushing feminist history beyond the gender binary so that we can better understand the full array of challenges to patriarchal structures in earlier times.[4] It makes a case not for trans history in place of feminist history but for trans history as a facet of feminist history for masculine-identifying figures.[5] A trans-feminist history can help us to define hidden dimensions within earlier acts of resistance to the patriarchy and to parse the role of gender identity in acts such as wearing pants and taking on masculine roles. Trans-feminist history recognizes that challenges to gender norms in the past were not always about advocacy for or on behalf of women; rather, they are sometimes better characterized as a fight for independence and freedom from gender determinacy more completely. Trans-feminist history also allows for the intersection of gender nonconformity and alliances on behalf of women as a group. Such points of contact make it possible to understand Dieulafoy's unique brand of feminism, which was predicated on *not* identifying with the women of her time. Trans-feminist history doesn't mean "losing" certain figures to trans history, then. It means recognizing that those who were considered women but may not have seen themselves as such shared certain circumstances with other women of their time while also facing different sets of challenges.

Those different sets of challenges require their own historical work, in part because there are likely connections to be drawn between those who may not have seen themselves as women and those who may not have seen themselves as men. The relationship between trans-masculine and trans-feminine identities in the nineteenth century is beyond the scope of this book but it was an issue that seems to have preoccupied Jane Dieulafoy. She researched several figures who had been designated male at birth but later lived as women, suggesting that she felt a sense of connection with others who had departed from their assigned gender. During my research, I was struck by one of the pages in her history of the eighteenth-century Chevalier d'Eon, in which Dieulafoy had transcribed a letter from the Marquis de l'Hôpital. Dieulafoy had underlined the female pronouns with which the marquis addressed his friend, apparently taking note of the ways in which the chevalier's femininity had been affirmed linguistically by those around him. I had done something similar in analyzing Dieulafoy's writings and those of Rachilde and Montifaud.

Dieulafoy left a loose collection of these histories, including essays on d'Eon, Choisy, and several others. But she never wrote an introduction to her anticipated volume or attempted to explain the connection between the figures she had researched. As a result, they remain uncategorized in one of the many dossiers held in the Bibliothèque de l'Institut. It seems to me that Leslie Feinberg's 1996 *Transgender Warriors: Making History from Joan of Arc to Dennis Rodman* is an analog of Dieulafoy's forgotten project. With information gathered on a variety of gender-crossers across time, Feinberg offers a history of "sex and gender rebellions" in which she describes her own identification with these figures. She mentions Joan of Arc and d'Eon and includes an image of Jane Dieulafoy.

In their interest in history as a means of understanding gender variability, Dieulafoy—and Montifaud as well, with her own history of the Abbé de Choisy—began the work of trans history before trans. In this way, they anticipated not only Feinberg but also Jan Morris, who would later describe her lifelong historical work as "disguised autobiography"; Jennifer Finney Boylan, who studied epic literature in ways she later understood as related to her own quest; and even Jill Soloway, who looked to Weimar Germany to tell the story of her family on *Transparent*. All of these modern figures turned to earlier narratives, myths, and histories to work through their own gender stories. Dieulafoy, Rachilde, and Montifaud can thus be seen as the precursors of a genre whose wide parameters are just coming into view.

The expansion of modern terminologies to designate gender variance has led to many sorts of debates within the wider culture, in both France and the United States, about how accommodating our language should be. The inclusive language that was rejected by the French Academy but is increasingly in use employs new gender pronouns, made more complex by the gendered nature of the French language. There have also been debates within the transgender community about the aptness of certain terms. One result of these discussions, in our own country, has been the emergence of the denomination "trans*" to help address the imperfections of the new vocabulary. I have found that the asterisk presents a useful historical tool as well, pointing to the linguistic gap between the nineteenth century and the twenty-first. The asterisk can work against the anachronistic nature of the modern term—the thing that feels wrong about using it—with this symbolic reminder of the imperfection of language. Trans* makes clear that generalizing language will always be insufficient, that there is no way to perfectly designate Dieulafoy, Rachilde, and Montifaud but that we may try nonetheless. At the same time, the asterisk "keeps at bay any sense of knowing in advance what the meaning of this or that gender variant form may be," as Jack Halberstam has put it. In the process, Halberstam explains, the asterisk "makes trans* people the authors of their own categorizations." It's a helpful turn of phrase for this book that has sought to highlight stories rather than terms and labels. It has been my intention to show the various ways in which Dieulafoy, Rachilde, and Montifaud acted as *authors* of their identities over the course of their lives.

It must be also acknowledged, however, that there are those who have objected to the trans* designation and to the asterisk in particular, fearing that the category loses meaning by being *too* expansive. The job of naming, after all, is to designate something specific, exclusive, different from other things. Such objections to the asterisk are also relevant to the work of this book: a reminder that the most basic challenge in discussing gender variance—whether in the present or the past—occurs on the level of language. The language that one person chooses and with which they feel most comfortable may very well make another person ill at ease. And that is precisely the point—the very thing that links past with present. A fraught relationship to certain aspects of language that others take for granted is often a defining feature of trans* identity—one we can recognize in each of the figures in this book.

There were some benefits to being outside of language in the nineteenth century. Rather than search for an identity to claim, Dieulafoy, Rachilde, and Montifaud experienced their gender as a rough and endless terrain to explore, an invitation for a lifetime of stories. Some—but certainly not all—more recent trans writers have signaled their desire for such freedoms, for gender to be a "story that I tell myself," as Rae Spoon puts it, for a way to *not* have to fit it into a language that is always necessarily imperfect even as it tries to adapt.[6]

Halberstam describes the asterisk as that which "holds open the meaning of the term trans* and refuses to deliver certainty through the act of naming." That "holding open" of meaning has become sought after in our new sea of terms, the desire for a language that gestures toward rather than seals in. This is one of the points around which the challenge of gender variance connects with other, more universal challenges: a way in which trans*—in its search for individual truths—refracts and intensifies the human condition itself.

But we still need to name, or people won't really understand what we're talking about. And that's perhaps the most important lesson that trans* teaches us: the possibility of linguistic affirmation—the relief of existing in language—does not mean that language needs to be all-defining. There ought to be enough room in the labels for difference, so that each individual can tell their own gender story without having to fight an army of cultural barriers in order to do so.

Acknowledgments

This project was completed thanks to the support of a National Endowment for the Humanities Public Scholar grant, which enabled me to complete the research and writing; an NEH summer stipend helped me along at an earlier stage. A Chelst, Schweiber, and Zwas book grant covered the costs of reproducing the many images in these pages. Over the course of my research, I was fortunate to benefit from archives at the Bibliothèque Marguerite Durand, the Bibliothèque de l'Institut, the Bibliothèque Jacques Doucet, the Bibliothèque nationale de France, the Archives nationales, and the Institut national d'histoire de l'art; I'm thankful to the many librarians at these institutions who facilitated my work, as well as the Office of the Dean at Yeshiva University for making it possible to travel to them. Special thanks to Michel Lenaerts at the Hôtel Dieulafoy, who granted me access to its many treasures.

An earlier, partial version of Chapters 1 and 5 in Part 1 appeared as "'O my hero! O my comrade in arms! O my fiancée!' Gender Crossing and Republican Values in Jane Dieulafoy's Fictions," *PMLA* 132, no. 2 (March 2017): 314–330.

French scholars are often organized into research teams, even in the humanities, while we Americans tend to toil as individuals. But over the years in which I was piecing together the details of my three subjects' lives, I formed my own ad hoc research team: colleagues who were always willing to lend their expertise and talents, and who made it seem as if they were as invested in this project as I was. Michael Finn fielded endless queries about Rachilde and generously shared obscure documents. Raisa Rexer marveled over Dieulafoy photos with me early on and helped moved the project forward. Heidi Brevik-Zender interrupted her own research to hunt down missing sources at the Bibliothèque de l'Institut. In addition to answering many questions, Margot Irvine accompanied me to Dieulafoy's former residence—what a treat to share that experience with someone who has contributed so much to existing scholarship. Kasia Stempniak scoped out the Montifaud archives for me before I could get there myself. Elizabeth Emery generously offered her research finds whenever they overlapped with my own. Jann Matlock shared her detective-like skills in hunting down sources, in addition to offering a careful reading early on. Seth Whidden helped decipher obscure French inscriptions and cheered me on at each step. Kirsten Ringelberg read many pages and pushed me in important ways. Marni Kessler and Susan Hiner weighed in on nineteenth-century fashions and so much more. Leah Chang was willing to talk about these figures for hours on end, as if they were mutual friends, and inspired me through her own writing to find a new kind of voice. Masha Belenky, dearest colleague and dearest friend, has been there every step of the way—from conference hotels to Paris rentals—ready to read, talk, gripe, and delight over each discovery.

I am deeply grateful to those outside of French studies who have graciously offered their wisdom. Jack Halberstam's generous and incisive reading of the manuscript for Stanford University Press forced me to sharpen my claims and helped me to think more broadly. Joy Ladin, my colleague at Yeshiva University, inspired this project by sharing her own journey in her searing memoir and her public speaking. Josh Tranen read and reread; I am grateful for his sharp mind, endless generosity, and overall delightfulness. Everyone should be lucky enough to have a former student become their editor and dear friend.

I am also immensely thankful for my greater nineteenth-century French studies cohort, whose wisdom, enthusiasm, and intellectual comradery propelled this work and made it that much more pleasurable: Janet Beizer, Patrick Bray, Mike Garval, Andrea Goulet, Nigel Harkness, Cary Hollinshead-Strick, Mary Hunter, Cheryl Krueger, Bettina Lerner, Brian Martin, Cathy Nesci, Gerry Prince, Maurie Samuels, Alex Wettlaufer, and Nick White.

Emily-Jane Cohen was my editor at Stanford University Press until just a few months ago; the shape this book has taken is largely thanks to her. Heartfelt gratitude to Margo Irvin for taking it over so faithfully, and to Faith Wilson Stein, Gigi Mark, and the rest of the SUP team for seeing it over the finish line. Enormous thanks to Peggy Waller and David Powell, who offered crucial comments, to the anonymous readers for the press, and to copyeditors Christine Gever and Susan Johnson.

My children, Abigail, Eliza, and Sammy know more about Jane Dieulafoy, Rachilde, and Marc de Montifaud than do most nineteenth-century French scholars. I hope they also know how much I appreciate their curiosity and patience. Most of all, I am grateful to Eric for his giant role in making possible all of the above.

Notes

INTRODUCTION

1. The French feminist movement was far less focused on suffrage than the British, and suffrage for French women would not be achieved until 1945. On the particular demands of late nineteenth-century French feminism, see Offen, "Depopulation, Nationalism, and Feminism in Fin-de-Siècle France." On the French version of the New Woman and the perceived threats from her, see Roberts, *Disruptive Acts*; and Silverman, *Art Nouveau in Fin-de-Siècle France.*

2. For more on this new female figure known as the politically neutral "femme moderne," see Mesch, *Having It All.*

3. Bard, "Le 'DB58' aux Archives," 1.

4. See, e.g., Rachilde, *Quand j'étais jeune*; *Le parc du mystère*; preface to *A mort*, and her correspondence with Catulle Mendès.

5. Rachilde, *Le parc*, 207–208; Rachilde, *Pourquoi je ne suis pas féministe*, 84.

6. Rachilde, *Pourquoi je ne suis pas féministe*, 69.

7. Guentner, "Translating," 127.

8. Stryker defines transgender as "people who move away from the gender they were assigned at birth, people who cross over (trans-) the boundaries constructed by their culture to define and contain that gender" (*Transgender History*, 36).

9. DeVun and Tortorici, "Trans, Time, and History," 524.

10. Mills, "Visibly Trans?," 542. The asterisk attached to trans* is a way of signaling the expansiveness of the category, not limited to the notion of being assigned the wrong gender at birth and including other departures from binary notions of gender. Some have objected to the asterisk as creating too much expansiveness. "Historicities" rather than "History" reminds of the impossibility of knowing the past and "rejects the imposition of any single narrative of events" (DeVun and Tortorici, "Trans, Time, and History," 535).

11. Agarwal, "What Is Trans History?" As Agarwal notes, the field of trans history is only now emerging, building on earlier work by Meyerowitz (*How Sex Changed*) and Stryker (*Transgender Studies Reader 1* (with Stephen Whittle) and *Transgender Studies Reader 2* (with Aren Z. Aizura); see also Stryker's more recent *Transgender History*. Emily Skidmore's *True Sex* and C. Riley Snorton's *Black on Both Sides* are two recent examples from the new field. Others can be found in part 6, "Timely Matters," in Stryker and Aizura, *Transgender Studies Reader* 2, 317–400.

12. My method is indebted to Jack Halberstam's notion of "perverse presentism," which he defines as a "presentist model of historical analysis . . . that avoids the trap of simply projecting contemporary understandings back in time, but one that can apply insights from the present to conundrums of the past" (*Female Masculinity*, 52). In *How to Do the History of Homosexuality*, David Halperin describes an approach that "foregrounds historical differences, that attempts to acknowledge the alterity of the past as well as the irreducible cultural and historical specificities of the present" (17). My work, while acknowledging these historical differences, is based on a belief that certain modern critical frameworks can illuminate what was not fully articulated in the past, lessening that alterity.

13. In *The History of Sexuality*, Michel Foucault argues that the notion of homosexuality and heterosexuality as distinct identities is a modern construction and that sexual identity is a product of specific social and discursive conditions. The same can be said for gender identity, and it is precisely the project of this book to chart the ways in which Dieulafoy, Rachilde, and Montifaud worked out their gender in relationship to their society and its various discourses (literary, political, sociological, medical, etc.).

14. Throughout this book, I use the term "sex" when I wish to refer to physical and biological markers of identity, and the term "gender" to refer to a sense of self as well as a recognized social category. I also use the term "sex" when translating

nineteenth-century terminology (*le sexe*) and referring to the category of women as a whole. However, the terms are not always totally distinct. Generally speaking, sex refers to a person's biological makeup, usually tied to the reproductive system, while gender is the social role one takes on in reference (or not) to that biological designation. The notion of gender as separate from sex has allowed scholars to comment upon the way in which gender roles are socially constructed rather than biologically determined, and enabled individuals to identify the ways in which their sense of self does not line up with their bodily traits. However, more recent science, along with writings on transgender identity, have clouded any simple distinction between sex and gender, demonstrating that one's sense of one's own gender can also be a function of biology; that the biological distinctions between male and female are not always clear; and that sex and gender are likely both culturally and physiologically determined. One's sense of self as masculine or feminine or neither or both is thus not entirely socially constructed; the distinction between sex as biological identity and gender as social identity is no longer as clear as it once was thought to be. And yet, the difference in connotations between the two terms can still be helpful.

15. As Stryker notes, "historically and cross-culturally, there have been many different social systems of organizing people into genders. Some cultures, including many Native American cultures, have had three or more social genders" (*Transgender History*, 15). For an important contextualization of how Two Spirits are often deployed in discussions about trans identity, see Pyle, "Naming and Claiming."

16. Some are now using the new pronoun *iel* in French to reflect trans and nonbinary identities.

17. Wilchins, *Queer Theory, Gender Theory*, 4.

18. Like Duggan's important work, this book considers the relationships among cultural, social, literary, and medical discourse and the stories people tell about their own lives. See "The Trials of Alice Mitchell," 793, and her related book, *Sapphic Slashers*.

19. Boylan, *She's Not There*, xii.

20. Spoon and Coyote, *Gender Failure*, 239.

21. This project builds on Jay Prosser's notion of the "narrative work" of transgender identity, which "requires remolding of the life into a particular narrative shape" (*Second Skins*, 4). Like Prosser, I privilege the subject's own artic-

ulation of self and bodily experiences, using a literary approach to understand their writings and other modes of self-expression more deeply.

22. Ladin, *Through the Door of Life*, 4.

23. Boylan, *She's Not There*, xii.

24. Feinberg, *Transgender Warriors*, 12. Feinberg's volume includes an image of Jane and Marcel Dieulafoy with the caption "A female-to-male trans person with husband. Are they a heterosexual couple? Two gay men?" (85).

25. While there is overlap, the experience of being trans feminine, which tends to garner more media attention, involves different challenges than that of being trans masculine; race and class also determine how gender variance is experienced. See Janet Mock's memoir *Redefining Realness* and Snorton's work on trans in the context of black identities, *Black on Both Sides*.

26. For more on the development of mass culture in Paris and the creation of urban community, see Schwartz, *Spectacular Realities*. More detailed statistics are offered in Leroy and Bertrand-Sabiani, *La vie littéraire à la Belle Epoque*.

27. On nineteenth-century anxiety about the French family, see Offen, "Depopulation, Nationalism, and Feminism."

28. On the divorce debates, see Pedersen, *Legislating the French Family*.

29. On the anxieties around class mixing in the public sphere brought on through the omnibus, see Belenky, *Engine of Modernity*.

30. On French feminism during this time, see Accampo, Fuchs, and Stewart, *Gender and the Politics of Social Reform in France, 1870–1914*; Forth and Accampo, *Confronting Modernity in Fin-de-Siècle France*.

31. On the *bas bleu*, see Mesch, *The Hysteric's Revenge*, 2–16; on the relationship between the *bas bleu*, the New Woman, and the feminist, see Mesch, *Having It All*, 7 and 19.

32. On hysteria and the female mind, as well as the biological differences linking the female body to hysteria, see Mesch, *The Hysteric's Revenge*, 14–21.

33. For some examples of these categories in relationship to femininity, see Cryle and Downing, "Feminine Sexual Pathologies."

34. See Murat, *La loi du genre*; and Hekma, "'A Female Soul in a Male Body.'" Female same-sex desire was designated alternately by the terms "tribade," "saphist," and "lesbian" in nineteenth-century France, as Schultz has documented. The medical literature was based largely on French fictions. See Schultz, *Sapphic Fathers*, 7. Prosser argues that the nineteenth-century notion of inversion to

describe homosexuality was in fact a precursor to transgender recognition, as it separated sex and gender (*Second Skins*, 140–152).

35. In Case 131 from 1889 (translated into French in 1895), Krafft-Ebing describes "gynandry," in which a woman identifies as a man and marries another woman. See "Selections from *Psychopathia Sexualis*," in Stryker and Whittle, *Transgender Studies Reader 1*.

36. On the relationship between male-authored nineteenth-century sapphic discourses and the history of female same-sex desire, see Schultz, *Sapphic Fathers*, 187–230.

37. Duggan, *Sapphic Slashers*, 24.

38. For discussion of the relationship of doctors and writers in shaping discourse around sexuality, see Beizer, *Ventriloquized Bodies*, 30–54; Mesch, *The Hysteric's Revenge*, 14–21.

39. Scholars do not generally view Sand's cross-dressing as relating to a questioning of gender identity. See Martine Reid's compelling recent biography, *George Sand*, 9–10.

40. The examples of Lorrain and Lôti suggest further paths for exploring nineteenth-century resistance to the gender binary, beyond the scope of this study, in relation to men who identified with femininity.

41. I trace some of these relationships in *The Hysteric's Revenge*, 44–80. Schultz describes the role of this community in shaping both identity formation and lesbian poetics at the turn of the century (*Sapphic Fathers*, 190–193). While Dieulafoy, Rachilde, and Montifaud were all still alive in the early 1900s, they did not interact socially with this community, although Rachilde had professional interactions with Colette and her husband Willy.

42. André Billy coined this term in his book *L'Epoque 1900*.

43. The definitive biography of Dieulafoy describes her as "joining George Sand in provocation as a response to the insulting censure of men" and assimilates her with other female intellectuals of her time (Gran-Aymeric and Gran-Aymeric, *Jane Dieulafoy*, 214, 217). Rossiter reads her clothing as "a claim to equality" (*Sweet Boy, Dear Wife*, 3). Brogniez asks whether Montifaud should be seen as an "insufferable *bas bleu*, militant feminist or a vulgar pornographer hungry for scandal" (*Marc de Montifaud*, 80).

44. In a study of female travel writers, Monicat notes that, of the women writers under review, Dieulafoy makes the least mention of her femininity (*Itinéraires de l'écriture au féminin*, 69). A 2018 article asks whether "Dieulafoy's femininity"

leads to a different treatment of the Muslim veil than that of male photographers, and thus whether "the female photographer in the colonial regime behaves differently than the male photographer" (Ferraris-Besso, "La subversion par l'image," 245). Guentner's otherwise excellent study of Montifaud, "Translating the Aesthetic Impression," refers to her as "Marc" de Montifaud—placing her masculine first name in quotation marks throughout. Dawkins considers Montifaud in light of "structural conflicts between femininity, sexuality, and the spectatorship of the nude" (*The Nude in French Art and Culture*, 135) and concludes that her writing "exemplified Woman . . . as an interlocutor deep in conversation about the female body, passion, art, Catholicism, femininity, and intellectual freedom" (171). Irvine's 1999 article "Jane Dieulafoy's Gender Transgressive Behavior" is an important exception to this trend. Because of the way Rachilde engaged directly with questions of gender and sexuality, Rachilde scholarship is more extensively developed and far more nuanced. Scholars recognize Rachilde's resistance to gender norms but almost always see this resistance as a frustration with the limits placed on women in the nineteenth century rather than as related to her repeated disavowals of female identity. In that sense, trans offers a means of understanding the contradictions that scholars have already noted but for which the framework of women writers fails to account.

45. I made this error in my discussion of Rachilde in *The Hysteric's Revenge*, where I argued that her "resistance to the feminist label" should not prevent us from recognizing her as such, following Roberts's delineation of "disruptive acts" feminism, through which women's subversive behavior can be recognized as feminist (*Disruptive Acts*, 124). Roberts's framework is a crucial expansion of the ways of recognizing feminist resistance in times before feminism existed in an expansive way. However, it fails to recognize resistance to binary gender as distinct from other forms of resistance to gender norms.

46. Bard's *Une histoire politique du pantalon* largely ignores gender variance as a motivating factor; see Bauer's more nuanced *Women and Cross-Dressing in Britain, 1800–1939*. No comparable multivolume study exists for France.

47. Earlier studies have engaged with such figures in different ways. Halberstam laid the groundwork in *Female Masculinity*, where he resists using modern terminology to discuss same-sex desire and other behaviors in women that he considers signs of gender variance, looking instead to terms in use at the time (65–73).

48. French queer history of the nineteenth century has tended toward the binary, with separate histories of male and female homosexuality or little engagement with questions of gender identity. Literary scholars have disproportionately focused on Dieulafoy's photographs of female subjects during her travels to Persia, even though she was far more preoccupied with images of masculinity. Boer reads "a displaced erotic fantasy" (*Uncertain Territories*, 95) in Dieulafoy's visit to the harem. There are numerous readings of Rachilde's writings in a queer context, although Downing distinguishes between Rachilde's "proto-queer writing" and what she views as her "heteronormative lifestyle." See also Gantz, "The Difficult Guest." Both Downing's and Gantz's readings acknowledge Rachilde's challenges to gender normativity. It is possible that some of what they recognized as queer or "proto-queer" in 2011 and 2005 they would now understand as anticipating trans. Despite Montifaud's descriptions of same-sex desire, the limited scholarship on her life ignores her own sexuality, even as it relates to her gender expression.

49. There has been one biography of Jane Dieulafoy in French, Gran-Aymeric and Gran-Aymeric, *Jane Dieulafoy: Une vie d'homme*, and a recent retelling of her travelogues in English, Rossiter's *Sweet Boy, Dear Wife*. She has also been covered widely in anthologies of female explorers: Bird, *Travelling in Different Skins*; Cohen and Joukowsky, *Breaking Ground*; Adams, *Ladies of the Field*. Rachilde has received far more critical attention, especially in Anglophone scholarship over the past thirty years. At least three biographies have appeared in English following Dauphiné's two biographies. See Finn, *Hysteria, Hypnotism, the Spirits, and Pornography*; Hawthorne, *Rachilde and French Women's Authorship*; and Holmes, *Rachilde*. There is no full-length biography of Montifaud in English or French. Guentner has done the most extensive scholarly work in her edited volume *Women Art Critics in Nineteenth-Century France*, which includes a chapter on Montifaud and a thorough biographical essay. Dawkins also devotes an impeccably researched chapter to Montifaud, her criticism and novels, and her fascination with the nude, in *The Nude in French Art and Culture*. See also Brogniez, "Marc de Montifaud"; and Morgan's study of her humor in "De 'la plaisanterie meurtrière' à la comédie contemporaine."

50. Muñoz, "Ephemera as Evidence," 6.

51. Halberstam describes how the language can be both liberating and constraining: "Until the middle of the last century, countless transgender men and women . . . found themselves stranded in unnameable realms of embodiment. Today we have an abundance of names for who we are, and some people actively desire that space of the unnameable again" (*Trans**, 4).

52. "Leslie Feinberg, writer and activist, dies at 65." *New York Times*, November 25, 2014.

53. Emily Skidmore uses male pronouns to refer to the subjects of her recent book on trans* men in turn-of-the-century America. However, unlike Dieulafoy, Rachilde, and Montifaud, her subjects lived their public lives as men and took on a masculine identity more fully and permanently. See Skidmore, *True Sex*, 10–11.

54. Serano, *Whipping Girl*, 212.

CHAPTER 1

1. See, e.g., the comprehensive biography by Eve and Jean Gran-Aymeric, *Jane Dieulafoy: Une vie d'homme*.

2. Summer, "Quelques femmes écrivains," 130.

3. DA, MS 2685–2690.

4. In her essay "Concerning the Historical Novel," which appeared as a preface to her historical novella *Rose d'Hatra*, Dieulafoy acknowledges that some reviewers of her previous work, *Parysatis*, found it "tiring, academic, good for the scholars; in other words: boring" (2).

5. For more on Paule Mink, see McMillan, *France and Women, 1789–1914*. Mink had a relationship with the anarchist writer James Guillaume, who shares a name with Paule Magre's own love interest, suggesting that Dieulafoy had also done her research.

6. Eve and Jean Gran-Aymeric state, without clarification, that "by virtue of the hazards of physiology, Jane could not have children" (*Jane Dieulafoy*, 239).

7. Dieulafoy, *Volontaire*, 77. All translations are mine unless otherwise indicated.

8. Ibid., 76.

9. Ibid., 30–31.

10. DA, MS 2685.

11. Ibid., dossier titled "Théories féministes."

12. On the French version of the New Woman and the "disruptive acts" feminism with which she was associated, see Roberts, *Disruptive Acts*.

13. For more on the modern woman promoted by the Belle Epoque women's press, see Mesch, *Having It All.*

14. Dieulafoy, *Volontaire*, 31.

CHAPTER 2

1. In his influential 1978 work *Orientalism*, Edward Said argued that the nineteenth-century European Orientalist enterprise was an effort to establish Western imperial superiority and intellectual dominance over Eastern cultures. In light of this, I use the terms "Orient" and "Oriental" only to refer to the Dieulafoys' way of thinking about this part of the world.

2. DAL, INHA, Album 4 PHOT 18 (5) 92.

3. Gran-Aymeric and Gran-Aymeric, *Jane Dieulafoy*, 35.

4. Dieulafoy, *La Perse*, 2.

5. See, e.g., Adams, *Ladies of the Field*; and Bird, *Travelling in Different Skins.*

6. "The Replacement of Men," *Daily Mail.* This article is found taped into Dieulafoy's notebook, DA, MS 2685.

7. For previous studies of Dieulafoy's travelogues, see Rossiter, *Sweet Boy*; Irvine, *Pour suivre un époux*; Bird, *Travelling in Different Skins*; and Monicat, *Itinéraires.* These studies tend to see her as a proto-feminist, seeking equality by dressing in men's clothing.

8. Montesquieu, *Les lettres persanes*, Letter XXX, 67–68.

9. Dieulafoy, *La Perse*, 56 (April 16, 1881). I have included the dates of the entries so that one can find the same passages in the *Tour du Monde* or other editions of the travelogues with different pagination.

10. Ibid., 68 (April 22, 1881).

11. Ibid., 149 (June 7, 1881).

12. Ibid., 651 (January 13, 1882).

13. Ibid., 655 (January 13, 1882).

14. Ibid., 194 (July 31, 1881).

15. See, e.g., Boer, *Uncertain Territories*, 96.

16. Flaubert writes of being shocked that women lift the veils covering their breasts to hide their faces when they see men. See Rexer, "Sex Education." Dieulafoy, *La Perse*, 268 (September 2, 1881).

17. Dieulafoy, *La Perse*, 654 (January 13, 1882).

18. Ibid., 653 (January 13, 1882).

CHAPTER 3

1. MDA, AN.

2. Ibid.

3. *A Suse*, 228 (March 15, 1886).

4. Dieulafoy, *A Suse*, 181 (May 14, 1885).

5. Ibid., 182 (May 14, 1885).

6. On the importance of trans photography, see Prosser, *Second Skins*, 207–236.

7. These photos constitute a stunning corpus that merits further exploration in the context of Orientalist visions. See the catalogue from a recent exhibit featuring one of Dieulafoy's images, Galifot, Pohlmann, and Robert, *Qui a peur des femmes photographes?*

8. The Gran-Aymerics write, for example: "Throughout the travels, Jane pays a special attention to the women that she encounters" (Jane Dieulafoy, 69). Boer focuses on Dieulafoy's "repeated interest and concern with the position of Muslim women, and her photographs of these women" (*Uncertain Territories*, 88–103).

9. Dieulafoy, *A Suse*, 183 (April 20, 1885).

10. Ibid., 151 (March 29, 1885).

11. See, e.g., entries from December 3, 1884; January 1, 1885; and April 4, 1886.

12. See, e.g., "Attaque de la tranche des immortels," Dieulafoy, *A Suse*, 289 (December 31, 1885).

13. Ibid., 248 (December 5, 1885).

14. Ibid., 255 (December 13, 1885).

15. 5 MDA.

16. Dieulafoy, *A Suse*, 288 (December 31, 1885).

17. Marcel confirms Jane's role in this regard in letters to Ronchaud detailing their discoveries. MDA.

18. Dieulafoy, *A Suse*, 289 (December 31, 1885).

19. Ibid., 290 (December 31, 1885).

20. Ibid., 295 (December 31, 1885).

21. Letter to Ronchaud, February 1, 1886. MDA.

22. Letter to the Comtesse de Castiglione, undated, AN.

23. Dieulafoy, *A Suse*, 289 (December 31, 1885).

24. Ibid., 293 (December 31, 1885).

25. Dieulafoy was said to share a striking resemblance with Lôti. For more on their relationship, see Noblet, "Une correspondance exhumée," 66.

26. Dieulafoy, *A Suse*, 335 (March 29, 1886).

27. Ibid., 353 (May 26, 1886).

28. Van Slyke, "Sexual and Textual Politics of Dress," 327.

29. Letter from Louis de Ronchaud, undated, DMD.

30. "Madame Dieulafoy," *Le Monde Illustré*, November 20, 1886, 319.

31. Dieulafoy, *A Suse*, 258 (December 13, 1885).

32. "Courrier de Paris," 370.

33. Newspaper clipping, MDA.

34. "Au Musée du louvre" newspaper clipping, MDA.

35. "La Salle Dieulafoy au Louvre," 378.

36. Tailhade, *Petits mémoires*, 37.

37. Brisson, *Portraits intimes*, 130.

CHAPTER 4

1. Summer, "Quelques femmes écrivains."

2. Gran-Aymeric and Gran-Aymeric, *Jane Dieulafoy*, 29.

3. Dieulafoy, *Frère Pélage*, 319–320.

4. Ibid., 73.

5. Ibid., 201.

6. Ibid., 74.

7. Crane, "Clothing and Gender Definition."

8. Dieulafoy, *Frère Pélage*, 75.

9. Ibid., 80.

10. When Fortunat does not recognize her, she says, "Marguerite is indeed dead . . . dead forever." Ibid., 269.

11. These plays included Emile Augier's 1876 *Madame Caverlet*, Paul Hervieu's 1895 *Les tenailles*, and Paul Bourget's 1908 *Un divorce*. See Pedersen, *Legislating the French Family*, 13–102. For more on the divorce debates, see Berenson, *The Trial of Madame Caillaux*.

12. DA, MS 2682.

13. Dieulafoy, *Déchéance*, 277.

14. DA, MS 2682.

15. Dieulafoy, *Frère Pélage*, 319.

16. Ibid., 310–312.

17. Ibid., 319.

18. "La femme roi aux temps historiques," Conférence No. 16, speech given at the Horticultural Society, rue de Grenelle, 1910. DA, MS 2685.

19. Quoted in Noblet, "Une correspondance exhumée," 67.

20. DA, MS 2685.

21. Dieulafoy, *Frère Pélage*, 285.

22. Ibid., 288.

23. Ibid., 260.

24. Dieulafoy, *Volontaire*, 77.

25. What Dieulafoy describes here anticipates Jennifer Finney Boylan's writing about her gender transition: "Above all, I wanted my friends and family to know that Jenny was not a stranger, that she was someone they already knew." Boylan wanted them to understand that she could be "both unambiguously female and, at the same time, the person they had always known." This seemed impossible, she writes, "yet it was an impossibility that was largely true" (*She's Not There*, 153).

26. Dieulafoy, *Frère Pélage*, 199.

CHAPTER 5

1. Uzanne, *Figures contemporaines.*
2. Feinberg, *Transgender Warriors*, 85.
3. *Femina*, November 1, 1902, 248.
4. MDA.
5. Dieulafoy scrapbook, DA, MS 2685.
6. Ibid.
7. Jane and Marcel Dieulafoy, *Le théâtre*, 7.
8. Ibid., 11.

CHAPTER 6

1. Tailhade, *Petits mémoires*, 35.
2. Ibid., 35–36.
3. Ibid.
4. "The Replacement of Men by Women," *Daily Mail*, October 30, 1905.
5. Summer, "Quelques femmes écrivains," 130.
6. The text of her speech can be found in *Eschyle: Les Perses*, a publication of the *Revue bleue* from 1896.
7. Loliée, "Madame Jane Dieulafoy," 690.

8. An article from 1894 found in Dieulafoy's scrapbook notes that her permission to wear pants followed "scrupulous inquiry" by the police and distinguishes her behavior from that of women who wear pants in their homes. DA, MS 2685.

9. On the pervasiveness of the "intellectual man at his desk" as a visual trope, see Emery, *Photojournalism*.

CHAPTER 7

1. On Rachilde's Spiritism and its influences, see Finn, *Hysteria*, 119–156.
2. David, *Rachilde*, 9–10.
3. Rachilde, *Le parc*, 166.
4. Rachilde, *Pourquoi je ne suis pas féministe*.
5. Rachilde, *Le parc*, 166.
6. Rachilde, *Quand j'étais jeune*, 149.
7. Ibid., 136–144.
8. Finn situates this gesture of "a male spirit [inhabiting] a female body" in the context of nineteenth-century Spiritism and possession, whose broad influence on her work he explores in *Hysteria*, 119–156.
9. Ibid., 41.
10. Dauphiné, *Rachilde*, 25.
11. Pommerade, "Le sol et le sang de Rachilde," 803–804.
12. Rachilde, *Le parc*, 182. Rachilde explores the affinity of humans with the animal species in several of her novels, including *Minette*, *L'animale*, *La princesse des ténèbres*, *Le meneur de louves*, and *Les Rageac*.
13. Rachilde, *Quand j'étais jeune*, 7.
14. Soulignac, "Ecrits de jeunesse," 195.
15. Rachilde, *Quand j'étais jeune*, 13.
16. Ibid., 15.
17. Ibid., 49.
18. Ibid., 12–13.
19. Ibid., 8.
20. Ibid., 9.
21. Ibid., 52–53.
22. Rachilde, *Le parc*, 31, 207.
23. Rachilde, *Quand j'étais jeune*, 86.

24. Ibid., 164.

25. Later she describes him in slightly more flattering terms: "Physically, he was tall and strong, a little heavy. . . . Very handsome." *Les Rageac*, 194, 228. Rachilde describes him in a letter to Catulle Mendès: "A fat thirty-five-year-old man; I was fourteen!" Letters to Catulle Mendès, RA, BJD, MS 9930.

26. Rachilde, *Les Rageac*, 217.

27. In the preface to *A mort*, Rachilde describes these efforts: "They tried to save her, naturally, and she hated the human race for that. She became a lunatic, tiresome, speaking only of Paris. They tried to marry her, and she wholeheartedly refused. This one was too fat, that one too thin, or she wanted to become a nun, or she wanted to visit China. In other words, madness, and which madness? . . . every kind" (xii). In the scene based on these events in *Les Rageac*, Magui's jump into the pond is described not as a suicide attempt ("It was not an effort to commit suicide") but as a way to retrieve her beloved animals (217). Finn argues that "the idea of suicide is . . . central to Rachilde's fictional *imaginaire*" (*Hysteria*, 31).

28. A Jacques-like character appears in the autobiographical novel *Les Rageac*, the novel *The Marquise de Sade*, and the short story "The Wolf-Catcher's Daughter." Rachilde retells the story in the autobiographical preface to her early novel *To the Death* and in her letters (housed in the BJD) to Catulle Mendès when she first arrives in Paris. See also Finn, *Hysteria*, 46.

29. Finn, *Hysteria*, 46.

30. Rachilde, preface to *A mort*, x.

31. Hawthorne writes that the drowned man represented "all that is rejected . . . as well as the potentially terrifying consequences of rejecting others' demands. He personifies guilt and conscience while also threatening self-realization" (*Rachilde and French Women's Authorship*, 61).

32. Rachilde, *Quand j'étais jeune*, 47.

33. Ibid., 78. David refers to "beautiful eyes that inspire poets" in his biography, 7.

34. Rachilde, *Quand j'étais jeune*, 79.

35. Ibid., 85.

36. Ibid., 86.

37. Ibid.

38. Ibid., 7.

39. Dauphiné, *Rachilde*, 30. In *Quand j'étais jeune*, she describes her age as fifteen at the time, linking the episode more directly to her rejection of marriage.

40. Rachilde, *Quand j'étais jeune*, 53.

41. Ibid., 9.

42. Auriant, *Souvenirs.*

43. Rachilde, *Quand j'étais jeune*, 19.

44. Ibid., 19.

CHAPTER 8

1. On Rachilde in the context of late nineteenth-century erotic literature, see Finn, *Hysteria*, 157–185.

2. Rachilde, *Monsieur Vénus*, 72.

3. Colombine [Henry Fouquier], *Le Gil Blas*, September 29, 1884, 1.

4. On the hysteria diagnosis in *Monsieur Vénus*, see Beizer's important reading in *Ventriloquized Bodies*, 227–260, and my own in *The Hysteric's Revenge*, 124–140.

5. Beizer, *Ventriloquized Bodies*, 240.

6. Montapic [Dubut de Laforest], "Fille d'Hermès et d'Aphrodite," *L'Evènement*, June 18, 1886, 2.

7. Ibid.

8. Villatte, review of *Monsieur Vénus*, *Le Décadent*, February 15–28, 1889, 59.

9. Montapic, "Fille d'Hermès et d'Aphrodite."

10. For more on Gisèle d'Estoc, pseudonym of Marie Paule Alice Courbe, see Hawthorne, *Finding the Woman Who Didn't Exist.*

11. D'Estoc, *La Vierge-Réclame*, 36–37.

12. David, *Rachilde*, 22.

13. Finn, *Hysteria*, 54.

14. Rachilde, *Portraits*, 21–40.

15. David, *Rachilde*, 31.

16. Barbey d'Aurevilly, *Bas bleus*, 342.

17. David, *Rachilde*, 32–33.

18. Barbey's *Les diaboliques* was found guilty of "offenses against decency" in 1875.

19. David, *Rachilde*, 32.

20. Auriant, *Souvenirs*, 61.

21. Rachilde describes her transformation in *Pourquoi je ne suis pas féministe*, 69.

22. March 27, 1885; Vallette, *Le roman*, 8.

23. Finn, *Hysteria*, 49.

24. Rachilde, *Pourquoi*, 69.

CHAPTER 9

1. Auriant, *Souvenirs*, 30–31.

2. Soulignac, *Ecrits de jeunesse*, 196.

3. On the possible origins of the novel, see Sanchez, "Rachilde ou la genèse."

4. Sanchez, *Lettres de Camille Delaville*, 112.

5. David, *Rachilde*, 30.

6. Rachilde, *Monsieur Vénus*, 69.

7. See Hekma, "'A Female Soul in a Male Body.'" On inversion as it pertains to nineteenth-century understandings of sapphism, see Schultz, *Sapphic Fathers*, 158–159.

8. Rachilde, *Monsieur Vénus*, 75.

9. Ibid., 73–74.

10. See my own analysis in *The Hysteric's Revenge*, 132. Other Rachilde scholars who cite Butler include Lisa Downing, Dominique Fisher, and Rita Felski (*Hysteric's Revenge*, 232n55).

11. Rachilde, *Monsieur Vénus*, 77–78.

12. Valentine, "PC Language Changed My Life," *New York Times*, January 3, 2018.

13. Rachilde, *Quand j'étais jeune*, 117–118.

14. Rachilde, *La souris japonaise*, 6.

15. Rachilde, *Jeux d'artifice*, 9.

16. Peyrebrune, *Correspondance*, 50.

17. Ibid., 43.

18. Ibid., 50.

19. Finn, *Hysteria*, 46.

20. Rachilde, *Monsieur Vénus*, 62.

21. Ibid., 98.

22. Ibid., 184.

23. In her 1974 memoir, Jan Morris describes prayers of a similar nature:

"I began to dream of ways in which I might throw off the hide of my body and reveal myself pristine within. . . . I prayed for it every evening. A moment of silence followed each day the words of the Grace. . . . Into that hiatus, while my betters I suppose were asking for forgiveness or enlightenment, I inserted silently every night, year after year throughout my boyhood, an appeal less graceful but no less heartfelt: 'And please, God, let me be a girl. Amen'" (*Conundrum*, 19–20).

24. Finn, *Hysteria*, 65–66.

25. See Prosser, *Second Skins*, 75–77. Of course, these experiences are particular to each individual.

26. Méténier, *Décadence*, 74.

27. RA, BJD, MS 9930.

28. Rachilde, preface to *A Mort*, xvii.

29. Finn, *Rachilde–Maurice Barrès*, 92; Finn, *Hysteria*, 57.

30. Scholars have thus far been unable to track down Mendès's essay. See Finn, *Hysteria*, 234n54.

31. RA, BJD, MS 9904.

32. Finn, *Rachilde–Maurice Barrès*, 122.

33. Ibid., 123.

34. Rachilde, *Monsieur Vénus*, 143.

35. Peyrebrune, *Correspondance*, 48.

36. Villatte, review of *Monsieur Vénus*, *Le Décadent*, February 15–28, 1889.

37. Rachilde, *Monsieur Vénus*, 133.

38. See in particular Gayle Salamon, *Assuming a Body*.

39. Prosser, *Second Skins*, 73.

40. Morris, *Conundrum*, 20.

41. Thompson, *What Took You So Long?*, 26; qtd. in Prosser, *Second Skins*, 73.

42. Halberstam, *Trans**, 20.

43. Prosser, *Second Skins*, 68.

44. Hall, *Well of Loneliness*, 138. There has been much debate about whether Stephen should be considered transgender, as Prosser does (*Second Skins*, 135–170) in the context of body narratives and Halberstam does not (*Female Masculinity*, 75–110) in the context of contemporary sexological discourse. Regardless of how one understands this protagonist, the compassionate treatment of gender nonconformity is what I mean to highlight here.

45. Auriant, *Souvenirs*, 61–62.

46. Prosser, *Second Skins*, 68.

47. Ibid., 73.

48. Rachilde, *Monsieur Vénus*, 68.

CHAPTER 10

1. Ernest-Charles, "'Bas-bleus,'" 227–231.

2. D'Estoc, *La Vierge-Réclame*, 19.

3. Ibid., 30, 47.

4. Lorrain, *Dans l'oratoire*, 220.

5. Finn, *Rachilde–Maurice Barrès*, 72–73.

6. Barrès, *Sous l'oeil*, 6.

7. Verlaine, *Lettres inédites*, 260.

8. Méténier, *Grâce*, 100.

9. Barrès, "Mademoiselle Baudelaire," *Le Voltaire*, June 24, 1886; in Finn, *Rachilde–Maurice Barrès*, 175.

10. Lorrain, *Dans l'oratoire*, 206, 213.

11. Ibid., 215.

12. Rachilde, *Quand j'étais jeune*, 146.

13. Rachilde, preface to *A Mort*, xxi.

14. Ibid., i.

15. Finn, *Rachilde–Maurice Barrès*, 115.

16. Peyrebrune, *Correspondance*, 52–53.

17. D'Estoc, *La Vierge-Réclame*, 10.

18. Rachilde, *La Marquise de Sade*, 214.

19. Rachilde, *Pourquoi je ne suis pas féministe*, 69.

20. Quoted in Finn, *Hysteria*, 143.

21. Rachilde, "La joie d'aimer," in Finn, *Rachilde–Maurice Barrès*, 149.

22. Ibid., 151.

23. Ibid.

24. RA, BJD, LT MS 1017.

25. RA, BJD, LT MS 10526–10528.

CHAPTER 11

1. Rachilde, *Pourquoi je ne suis pas féministe*, 71.

2. Vallette, *Le roman d'un homme sérieux*, 11.

3. Ibid., 15.

4. Ibid., 18.

5. Ibid., 63, 71, 113.

6. Ibid., 65.

7. Ibid., 86–87.

8. Ibid., 88.

9. Ibid., 111.

10. Ibid., 119.

11. Ibid.

12. Ibid.

13. Peyrebrune, *Correspondance*, 77.

14. Ibid., 67.

15. Finn, *Hysteria*, 67.

16. Peyrebrune, *Correspondance*, 67.

17. Ibid., 71.

18. Ibid., 67.

19. Ibid.

20. Ibid., 121.

21. Ibid., 67.

22. Rachilde, *Pourquoi je ne suis pas féministe*, 70–71.

23. Rachilde, *Monsieur Vénus*, 91–92.

24. Gounaridou and Lively, introduction to *Madame La Mort and Other Plays*, 38.

25. Rachilde, *Madame Adonis*, 127.

26. Rachilde, *La jongleuse*, 172.

27. Rachilde, *La princesse de ténèbres*, 270. Quoted in Finn, *Hysteria*, 281.

28. Finn suggests as much in ibid.

29. Peyrebrune, *Correspondance*, 77.

30. Auriant, *Souvenirs*, 38.

31. Ibid., 9.

32. Ibid., 40.

33. Gounaridou and Lively, introduction to *Madame La Mort and Other Plays*, 11.

34. Ibid., 9.

35. Auriant, *Souvenirs*, 40.

36. Ibid., 41.

37. Letter from Aurel, papers from Alfred Mortier et d'Aurel, MSS of the Bibliothèque nationale de France.

38. Auriant, *Souvenirs*, 41.

39. Rachilde, *L'animale*, 144. Finn makes this connection in *Hysteria*, 142.

40. Rachilde, *Duvet-d'ange*, 120–122.

41. Ibid., 128.

42. Ibid., 130.

43. Ibid., 40.

44. David, *Rachilde*, 55.

45. Auriant, *Souvenirs*, 52.

CHAPTER 12

1. Rachilde, *Pourquoi je ne suis pas féministe*, 67.

2. Rachilde, *Le parc*, 165.

3. Peyrebrune, *Une décadante*, 18.

4. RA, BJD, MS 8024–8292.

5. Choisy, *Sur la route*, 106, 112, 113, 138.

6. Rachilde, *Pourquoi je ne suis pas féministe*, 84.

7. Quoted in Gounaridou and Lively, introduction to *Madame La Mort and Other Plays*, 7–8.

8. Rachilde described this style in *Portraits d'hommes*: "A masculine fedora hides short hair, an originality at the time, and, also anomalous, a little white veil, pulled down over the face" (22).

9. Rachilde, *Le parc*, 207–208.

10. Hawthorne makes this observation in *Rachilde*, 140.

11. Pierre Philippe, "Rachilde saisie par la débauche," *Le Monde*, August 21, 1998.

12. Rachilde, *Pourquoi je ne suis pas féministe*, 72.

13. Auriant, *Souvenirs*, 27, 57.

14. Rachilde, *Duvet-d'ange*, 131.

15. Auriant, *Souvenirs*, 27.

16. Rachilde, *L'animale*, 143.

17. Hayward and Weinstein, "Introduction," 196, 201.

18. Deleuze and Guattari, *A Thousand Plateaus: Capitalism and Schizophrenia*, 27; quoted in Hayward and Weinstein, "Introduction," 197.

19. Rachilde, *Duvet-d'ange*, 161.

20. Rachilde, *Le parc*, 58.

CHAPTER 13

1. Her official funeral announcement (BMD) in September 1912 lists her age as sixty-seven, making her year of birth 1844 or 1845. Nineteenth-century biographical accounts emphasized Montifaud's youth and described her as having married at sixteen, including the entry from the *Dictionnaire Larousse* that she appended, along with other positive "excerpts from different newspapers," to *Marc de Montifaud devant l'opinion publique*, 108–110. Another appended article, from the newspaper *L'Eclair*, states that she was twenty-seven in 1877 and reports that she married "very young" (ibid., 105–106). Much later, Laurent Tailhade commented on Montifaud's obsession with age in the early 1900s: "She would whine, lamenting the fact of aging, of having entered her 'forties'—which her son had already passed through a while ago!" (*Quelques fantômes*, 181–182).

2. Delaville, "Chronique parisienne," *La Presse*, December 5, 1880.

3. In official documents from *L'Artiste*, Léon's name is listed as "Léon de Montifaud." MA.

4. MA, BMD, M8.

5. Montifaud, "Salon de 1865 II," 224.

6. Ibid.

7. See Guentner, *Women Art Critics*.

8. Montifaud, "Portraits," 318–331.

9. Montifaud, *Marc de Montifaud*, 8.

10. Montifaud, "Portraits," 318.

11. Montifaud, *Marc de Montifaud*, 43.

12. Montifaud, "Exposition," 307.

13. Ibid., 313. See Dawkins, *The Nude*, 148–152.

14. Marc de Montifaud, *fils*, wrote admiringly of Houssaye in a lengthy tribute found in Montifaud's archives at the BMD.

15. Quoted in Montifaud, *Les courtisanes*, 2.

16. Ibid.

CHAPTER 14

1. Twenty-six literary works were prosecuted by the French government between 1821 and 1892. Montifaud appears to have been the only female author among them. For more on the history of censorship in France and the trials of Baudelaire and Flaubert, see Ladenson, *Dirt for Art's Sake.*

2. Montifaud, *Les dévoyés*, 309.

3. "Letter from Madame de Montifaud," *Le Figaro*, December 27, 1876.

4. Ibid.

5. Ibid.

6. Montifaud, *Marc de Montifaud*, 9–12.

7. Ibid., 10. On Barbey and censorship, see Ladenson, *Dirt for Art's Sake*, 6–7.

8. Montifaud, *Aventures de l'abbé de Choisy*, xliv.

9. Ibid., xlii.

10. Ibid., xliv.

11. Montifaud, *Marc de Montifaud*, 27.

12. Ibid., 34.

13. Ibid., 26.

14. Ibid., 36.

15. Ibid., 57.

16. Ibid., 13.

17. Ibid., 18–19.

18. Ibid., 15.

19. As recent scholars have demonstrated, departures from the gender binary can trigger other people's sense of fragility and insecurity around their own identities, and these feelings often emerge as misdirected rage. Julia Serano writes: "All forms of gender entitlement and gender anxiety are, at their core, expressions of insecurity. After all, people who are truly comfortable with their own desires and expressions of gender and sexuality do not have any need to be bothered or concerned by dissimilar expressions and desires in others" (*Whipping Girl*, 90–91).

20. Louis de Villote [Octave Uzanne], "Un curieux procès (20 décembre 1876)," *Conseiller du Bibliophilie*, January 1, 1877.

21. Chapron, "Le cas de Madame de Montifaud."

22. Chapron, "Chronique parisienne," *Le Gaulois*, May 21, 1877.

23. Ibid.

24. Rodaya, "Gazette des tribunaux," December 15, 1878.

25. "Gazette des tribuneaux," *Le Figaro*, May 24, 1878.

26. Bataille, "Gazette des tribuneaux," *Le Figaro*, December 1, 1880.

27. Montifaud, *Marc de Montifaud*, 24.

28. Ibid., 22.

29. Ibid.

30. Ibid., 50.

31. Frescata [René Maizeroy], "Madame de Sade," *Le Figaro*, September 10, 1882.

32. See Chapron's account from 1876, reported in "Le cas de Madame de Montifaud."

33. "L'affaire Montifaud," *La Lanterne*, September 17, 1882.

34. "Faits divers," *Le Matin*, September 16, 1882.

35. Choufleuri, "Soirées parisiennes," *Le Gaulois*, September 12, 1882.

36. Montifaud, *Marc de Montifaud*, 71.

37. Montifaud, *Madame Ducroisy*, 9.

38. Montifaud, *Marc de Montifaud*, 29.

39. Ibid., 15.

40. "Echos de Paris," *Le Gaulois*, May 25, 1877.

41. "Gazette du jour," *La Justice*, October 1, 1880.

42. "Nouvelles diverses," *Le Figaro*, September 29, 1880.

CHAPTER 15

1. Montifaud, *Marc de Montifaud*, 43.

2. Ibid.

3. MA, BMD M8. Montifaud's worries surfaced once again when her son joined the military as an adolescent in 1889. The young Marc, often sickly as a child, seems to have become ill right away. Letters from Sister Saint Basile detail the progress of his health in a local hospital, far from Paris. Like Montifaud's mother, the nun commented on the "very touching" letters from Montifaud to Marc and promised to do all she could to restore him in health. MA, BMD, M29.

4. Montifaud, *Marc de Montifaud*, 43.

5. Ibid., 49.

6. Misme, "Le précieux déguisement," *La Française*, September 16, 1922.

7. The novel *Sabine* opens with Henri shaving his beard and disguising himself as a woman in order to sneak into a harem and abscond with a woman with

whom he has fallen in love. Before fleeing together, Henri begins to make love to her, still dressed *en femme*.

8. MA, BMD, M19.2.

9. Henry Fouquier, "Chronique," *Le XIXe Siècle*, September 17, 1882.

10. "Paris," *La Lanterne*, September 20, 1882.

11. Henry Fouquier, "Chronique," *Le XIXe Siècle*, September 17, 1882.

12. MA, BMD.

13. Tailhade, *Quelques fantômes*, 179.

CHAPTER 16

1. MA, BMD, M72.

2. "Two Letters from Léon de Montifaud to Marc de Montifaud," Archives de Melun, Melun, France.

3. See Lebois, "Deux amours," 76.

4. Bollery, *Correspondance générale de Villiers de l'Isle Adam*, vol. 2, letter 438, 197.

5. Montifaud, *Marc de Montifaud*, 15.

6. Montifaud, *Madame Ducroisy*, 77; suspension points in original.

7. Ibid., 182–183.

8. Montifaud, *Aventures de l'abbé de Choisy*, xlv.

9. Montifaud's affiliation with *La Fronde* may be one of the many reasons that the few modern critics who have attempted to write about her tend to misinterpret her. In an article from 2007, Eric Dussert concluded: "Marc de Montifaud demonstrates that even before the suffragettes, some women imagined their total emancipation. If Louise Michel opted for socialism and revolution, Marie-Amelie Chartroule, wife of Quivogne, seems to have not proved unworthy in provocation." Dussert, like other critics, saw Montifaud as a kind of "disruptive acts" feminist, to take Mary Louise Roberts's term for women who rebelled against gender norms rather than fight for legislative change—and for which Durand herself served as a formidable example. Dussert, "Quiquengrogne," 49.

10. The photograph from *Le Monde Illustré*, January 11, 1936, is too dark to reproduce here.

11. BMD, Montifaud dossier. Originals may be found in the Durand dossier at the BMD.

12. Montifaud, "Du style III," September 1875, 19.

13. Montifaud, "Du style I," July 1875, 6.
14. Montifaud, *Histoire*, 3.
15. Ibid.
16. Ibid.
17. Gabriel Demarne, *La Bibliographie contemporaine*, May 1, 1873, 63.
18. See Dawkins's astute treatment of this parallel in *The Nude*, 148–152.
19. Montifaud, *Madame Ducroisy*, 157; Dawkins, *The Nude*, 149.
20. Montifaud, *Madame Ducroisy*, 158–159.
21. Montifaud, "Du style I," July 1875, 7.
22. Montifaud, *Madame Ducroisy*, 159.
23. Montifaud, *Les courtisanes*, 80.
24. Ibid., 81.
25. Ibid.
26. Schultz, *Sapphic Fathers*, 188.
27. Montifaud, *Marc de Montifaud*, 5.
28. Ibid., 6.
29. Ibid., 5.
30. Ibid., 36.
31. Ibid.
32. Montifaud, *Histoire*, 2.
33. Ibid., 4.
34. Montifaud, "*Madame Ducroisy*," 16.

CHAPTER 17

1. Montifaud, *Marc de Montifaud*, 51.
2. Ibid.
3. Ibid., 31–32.
4. Montifaud, *Le lion d'Angélie*, ix.
5. Ibid., xii.
6. Ibid.
7. Ibid., xxiii.
8. Ibid., xxi.
9. Montifaud, *Voyages fantastiques*, lxx.
10. Ibid.
11. Montifaud, *Marc de Montifaud*, 13.

12. Hippeau, "Marc de Montifaud."

13. Montifaud, *Marc de Montifaud*, 41.

14. Ibid.

15. Montifaud, *Aventures de l'abbé de Choisy*, 7.

16. Ibid., 9.

17. Ibid., lviii.

18. Ibid.

19. Ibid., xli.

20. Ibid., lii.

21. Ibid., liv.

22. Ibid., lv.

23. Ibid.

24. Ibid., lvi.

25. "Le chocolat de l'amour et la suspension de Saint-Joseph," in *Nouvelles drolatiques*, 3–44.

26. Montifaud, *Aventures de l'abbé de Choisy*, lix, italics in the original.

CHAPTER 18

1. MA, BMD, M40.

2. MA, BMD, M23.

3. Erasme, "Nos Eves futures," *L'Evénement*, October 1, 1890; "Actualité féminine," *L'Evénement*, October 30, 1890; "L'honneur d'une femme," *L'Evénement*, October 17, 1890.

4. MA, BMD, M25.

5. G.L., "Au Théâtre Montparnasse," *La Justice*, September 1, 1896.

6. B. Guinaudeau, "Nos soirées," *La Justice*, May 24, 1893.

7. See, e.g., Guentner: "It was under this last last pseudonym [Paul Erasme] that Montifaud published patriotic texts in a virile register that contrasted with her traditionally lighthearted and suggestive fiction of earlier decades" (*Women Art Critics*, 270).

8. Montifaud, *Hymne à la mort*, BMD.

9. Ibid., 3.

10. Montifaud was echoing a traditional war salute by Roman gladiators, "Qui morituri te salutamus" (We who are about to die salute you).

11. Erasme, *Nos sous-officiers*, 238.

12. "A Letter from Marc de Montifaud," *Le Figaro*, December 27, 1876.

13. Erasme, *Nos sous-officiers*, 164.

14. Serano, *Whipping Girl*, 85.

15. Halberstam, *Trans**, 154.

16. Montifaud, *Les Dévoyés*, 332.

17. Boylan, *She's Not There*, 113.

18. Ryner, *Le massacre des amazones*, 106.

19. "Chronique mondaine," *La Justice*, February 1, 1904, 4.

20. Laing, *Lonely City*, 125.

21. Tailhade, *Quelques fantômes*, 177.

22. Ibid., 177–178.

23. Ibid., 178.

24. An article about the restaurant at the Bibliothèque nationale in *L'Attaque* from June 9, 1910, described Montifaud as "rivaling Madame J Dieulafoy" in her resemblance to men. In 1901, a gossip column recounted spotting Madame Dieulafoy at the theater and then realizing with disappointment that it was Montifaud, who appeared "ridiculous in her men's suit" and who was "horribly older than the famous traveler." *La Vie Parisienne*, March 23, 1901, 165.

25. MA, BMD, M67.

26. I am grateful to my daughter, Abigail Fisher, for introducing me to this concept of using "and" instead of "but." See her "Raised on Intersectionality, What's a Teen to Do?," *Lilith*, February 6, 2019, https://www.lilith.org/blog/2019/02/raised-on-intersectionality-whats-a-teen-to-do/.

27. Coyote, *Tomboy Survival Guide*, 170–171.

CONCLUSION

1. The June 9, 2014, issue of *Time* magazine announced the "transgender tipping point." On some of the potential pitfalls of this visibility, see Nicolazzo, "What's Transgressive about Trans* Studies in Education Now?"

2. See, e.g., Hawthorne, *Rachilde*, 100; Bard places them on a continuum, one "opening the door" for the other (*Une histoire politique*, 183–203).

3. Gretchen Van Slyke's 1998 article "The Sexual and Textual Politics of Dress" offers depth in comparing George Sand's and Rosa Bonheur's sartorial habits in relation to their biographical writings. However, her conclusion—that

Bonheur was a "cross-dresser" but not a "transvestite," because "her dressing habits don't reveal any phallic investment" or fetishism—points to the importance of the modern trans framework in dispelling problematic medical and psychoanalytic narratives.

4. A case could also be made to push queer history further so as to carve out a clearer place for trans history. Queer histories of France tend to be divided by gender and focus on male homosexuality. See Peniston and Erber, *Queer Lives*; and Gunther, *The Elastic Closet*.

5. An example of where feminist history falls short can be found in Mary Louise Roberts's important study of "disruptive acts" as kinds of feminism that put on display multiple, nontraditional modes of enacting femininity. Despite its usefulness in displacing traditional paradigms of what defines feminism, this broad construct erases the role of gender and sexual identity in certain kinds of public acts (think of Montifaud slapping Magnard) and makes it more difficult to see the individual, personal stakes in public behaviors. The study thus points to one area in which a nonbinary reading of history could be quite useful. Some efforts to think through "Transfeminisms" can be found in Stryker and Aizura, *Transgender Studies Reader 2*, 199–258. However, the essays included in the *Reader* do not propose a way to think about trans and feminism together in a historical context.

6. See note 51 in the Introduction.

Bibliography

ARCHIVES

Dieulafoy Albums (DAL), Institut national de l'histoire de l'art (INHA)
Dieulafoy Archives (DA), Bibliothèque de l'Institut
Mission Dieulafoy Archives (MDA), Archives nationales (AN)
Montifaud Archives (MA), Bibliothèque Marguerite Durand (BMD)
Rachilde Archives (RA), Bibliothèque Jacques Doucet (BJD)

SELECTED WORKS BY JANE DIEULAFOY

La Perse, la Chaldée et la Susiane. Paris: Hachette, 1887.

A Suse, journal des fouilles, 1884–1886. Paris: Hachette, 1888.

Parysatis. Paris: Lemerre, 1890.

Volontaire, 1792–1793. Paris: Colin, 1892.

"A propos du roman historique." In *Rose d'Hatra*, 1–10. Paris: A. Colin, 1893.

Frère Pélage. Paris: Lemerre, 1894.

Déchéance. Paris: Lemerre, 1897.

"La femme roi aux temps historiques." Conférence no. 16. Faite à la Société d'horticulture rue de Grevelle. DA MS 2685.

Le théâtre dans l'intimité (with Marcel Dieulafoy). Paris: Ollendorff, 1900.

SELECTED WORKS BY RACHILDE

Monsieur Vénus: Roman matérialiste. Brussels, 1884.

A mort. Paris: E. Monnier, 1886.

La Marquise de Sade. 1887. Reprint, Paris: Mercure de France, 1981.

Madame Adonis. 1888. Reprint, Paris: J Ferenczi et fils, 1929.

Le mordu. Paris: Genonceaux, 1889.

L'animale. 1893. Reprint, Paris: Mercure de France, 1993.

La princesse des ténèbres. Paris: Calmann-Lévy, 1896.

La jongleuse. 1900. Reprint: Paris: Des femmes, 1977.

Le meneur de louves. Paris: Mercure de France, 1904.

Les Rageac. Paris: Flammarion, 1921.

La souris japonaise. Paris: Flammarion, 1921.

Le parc du mystère (with F. de Homem Christo). Paris: Flammarion, 1923.

Pourquoi je ne suis pas féministe. Paris: Editions de France, 1928.

Portraits d'hommes. Paris: Mornay, 1929.

Jeux d'artifice. Paris: Ferenczi, 1932.

Duvet-d'ange: Confessions d'un jeune homme de lettres. Paris: Albert Messein, 1943.

Quand j'étais jeune. Paris: Mercure de France, 1947.

SELECTED WORKS BY MARC DE MONTIFAUD [PAUL ERASME]

"Salon de 1865." *L'Artiste*, May 1, 1865.

"Salon de 1865 II." *L'Artiste*, May 15, 1865.

Les courtisanes de l'antiquité: Marie-Magdeleine. 1870. Reprint, Paris: Librairie André Sagnier, 1876.

Hymne à la mort: Chant patriotique. Trouville-sur-mer: Imprimerie de Charles Trinité, 1870.

Histoire d'Héloïse et d'Abailard, suivie des lettres les plus mémorables des deux immortels amants. Paris: Flammarion, 1873.

"Exposition du Boulevard des capucines." *L'Artiste*, April (May?) 1874, 307–313.

"Du style dans les figures nues." Three-part series in *L'Art moderne*, July–September 1875.

Voyages fantastiques de Cyrano de Bergerac, publié avec une introduction et des notes. Paris: Librairie des bibliophiles, 1875.

Alosie, ou les amours de Mme de M.T.P., par Pierre-Corneille Blessebois. Paris: Debons, 1876.

"Le lion d'Angélie" par Pierre Corneille Blessebois, précédé par une notice sur le style Romanesque et réponse aux attaques contre Corneille Blessebois. Brussels: A. Lacroix, 1877.

Les vestales de l'église. Brussels. Chez tous les libraires, 1877.

Les dévoyés. Paris: Collombou et Brulé, 1879.

Madame Ducroisy. Paris: André Sagnier, 1879.

"Madame Ducroisy," la presse, et la justice. Paris: A. Reiff, 1879.

Nouvelles drolatiques. Paris and Brussels, 1880–1890 (multiple volumes and later editions).

Marc de Montifaud devant l'opinion publique, sa justification: Lettre à M. Félix Delhasse. London, 1882.

Sabine. Paris: Grande Imprimerie, Société anonyme, 1882.

Aventures de l'abbé de Choisy habillé en femme, précédée d'une notice et de documents inédits et d'une eau forte d'Hanriot. Brussels: Charles Gilliet, 1884.

[Paul Erasme]. *Nos sous-officiers.* Paris: A-L Charles, 1890.

[Paul Erasme]. *Alsace.* (Pièce interdite par la censure.) Paris: Albin Michel, 1904.

WORKS CITED

Accampo, Elinor, Rachel Fuchs, and Mary Lynn Stewart, eds. *Gender and the Politics of Social Reform in France, 1870–1914.* Baltimore: Johns Hopkins University Press, 1995.

Adams, Amanda. *Ladies of the Field: Early Archaeologists and Their Search for Adventure.* Toronto: Greystone Books, 2010.

Agarwal, Kritika. "What Is Trans History? From Activist and Academic Roots, a Field Takes Shape." *Perspectives on History,* May 1, 2018. https://www.historians.org/publications-and-directories/perspectives-on-history/may-2018/what-is-trans-history-from-activist-and-academic-roots-a-field-takes-shape.

Auriant. *Souvenirs sur Madame Rachilde.* Paris: A l'écart, 1989.

Bard, Christine. "Le 'DB58' aux Archives de la Préfecture de Police." In "Femmes travesties: Un 'mauvais' genre," ed. Bard and Nicole Pellegrin. Special issue, *CLIO: Histoires, femmes et sociétés* 10 (1999): 1–20.

———. *Une histoire politique du pantalon.* Paris: Editions du Seuil, 2010.

Barrès, Maurice. *Sous l'oeil des barbares*. Paris: Alphonse Lemerre Editeur, 1888.

Bauer, Heike. *Women and Cross-Dressing in Britain, 1800–1939*. Vols. 1–3. New York: Routledge, 2006.

Beizer, Janet. *Ventriloquized Bodies: Narratives of Hysteria in Nineteenth-Century France*. Ithaca, NY: Cornell University Press, 1994.

Belenky, Masha. *Engine of Modernity: The Omnibus in French Literature and Culture*. Manchester, UK: Manchester University Press, 2019.

Berenson, Edward. *The Trial of Madame Caillaux*. Berkeley: University of California Press, 1992.

Billy, André. *L'Epoque 1900*. Paris: Editions Jules Taillandy, 1951.

Bird, Dunlaith. *Travelling in Different Skins: Gender Identity in European Women's Oriental Travelogues, 1850–1950*. Oxford: Oxford University Press, 2012.

Boer, Inge. *Uncertain Territories: Boundaries in Cultural Analysis*. Amsterdam: Rodopi, 2006.

Bollery, Joseph, ed. *Correspondance générale de Villiers de l'Isle Adam*. Vols. 1–2. Paris: Mercure de France, 1962.

Bornstein, Kate. *Gender Outlaw: On Men, Women, and the Rest of Us*. New York: Routledge, 1994.

Boylan, Jennifer Finney. *She's Not There: A Life in Two Genders*. New York: Random House, 2003.

———. "A Twist in Her Plot." *New York Times*, April 6, 2016.

Brisson, Adolphe. *Portraits intimes*. Paris: Colin, 1897.

Brogniez, Laurence. "Marc de Montifaud: Une femme en procès avec son siècle." *Sextant* 6 (1996): 55–80.

Chapron, Léon. "Le cas de Madame de Montifaud." In *Les coins de Paris*, 48–55. Paris: Dentu, 1881.

———. "Chronique parisienne." *Le Gaulois*, May 21, 1877.

Choisy, Maryse. *Sur la route de Dieu on rencontre d'abord le diable: Mémoires 1925–1939*. Paris: Editions Emile-Paul, 1978.

Cohen, Getzel, and Martha Sharp Joukowsky, eds. *Breaking Ground: Pioneering Women Archaeologists*. Ann Arbor: University of Michigan Press, 2004.

Constable, Liz, and Melanie Hawthorne. Introduction to *Monsieur Vénus: A Materialist Novel*, by Rachilde, ix–xxxix. New York: MLA, 2004.

Coyote, Ivan E. *Tomboy Survival Guide*. Vancouver: Arsenal Pulp Press, 2016.

Crane, Susan. "Clothing and Gender Definition: Joan of Arc." *Journal of Medieval and Early Modern Studies* 26, no. 2 (Spring 1996): 298–318.

Cryle, Peter, and Lisa Downing, eds. "Feminine Sexual Pathologies in Nineteenth- and Early Twentieth-Century Europe." Special issue, *Journal of the History of Sexuality* 18, no. 1 (2009).

Dauphiné, Claude. *Rachilde*. Paris: Mercure de France, 1991.

———. *Rachilde, femme de lettres 1900*. Paris: Pierre Fanlac, 1985.

David, André. *Rachilde, homme de lettres: Son oeuvre; Portrait et autographe*. Paris: Editions de la Nouvelle Revue Critique, 1924.

Dawkins, Heather. *The Nude in French Art and Culture, 1870–1910*. New York: Cambridge University Press, 2002.

D'Estoc, Gisèle. *La Vierge-Réclame*. Paris: Librairie Richelieu, 1887.

DeVun, Leah, and Zeb Tortorici. "Trans, Time, and History." *Transgender Studies Quarterly* 5, no. 4 (November 2018): 518–539.

Downing, Lisa. "Notes on a Proto-Queer Rachilde: Decadence, Deviance, and (Reverse) Discourse in *La Marquise de Sade*." *Sexualities* 15, no. 1 (2012): 16–27.

Dubut de Laforest, Jean-Louis [Montapic]. "Fille d'Hermès et d'Aphrodite." *L'Evénement*, June 18, 1886.

Duggan, Lisa. *Sapphic Slashers: Sex, Violence, and American Modernity*. Durham, NC: Duke University Press, 2000.

———. "The Trials of Alice Mitchell: Sensationalism, Sexology, and the Lesbian Subject in Turn-of-the-Century America." *Signs: Journal of Women in Culture and Society* 18, no. 4 (1993):791–814.

Dussert, Eric. "Quiquengrogne, femme libre." *Le matricule des anges: Le mensuel de la littérature contemporaine* (April 2007).

Ernest-Charles, Jean. "Les bas-bleus et la littérature féminine." In *Les Samedis littéraires*, 2:234. Paris: Sansot, 1905.

Emery, Elizabeth. *Photojournalism and the Origins of the French Writer House Museum (1881–1914): Privacy, Publicity, and Personality*. Burlington, VT: Ashgate, 2012.

Feinberg, Leslie. *Transgender Warriors: Making History from Joan of Arc to Dennis Rodman*. Boston: Beacon Press, 1996.

Ferraris-Besso, Caroline. "La subversion par l'image: *La Perse, la Chaldée et la Susiane* de Jane Dieulafoy." *Women in French Studies* 7 (2018): 241–258.

Finn, Michael. *Hysteria, Hypnotism, the Spirits, and Pornography: Fin-de-Siècle Cultural Discourses in the Decadent Rachilde.* Newark: University of Delaware Press, 2009.

———, ed. *Rachilde–Maurice Barrès: Correspondance inédite, 1885–1914.* Brest: Centre d'étude des correspondances et des journaux intimes, 2002.

Forth, Christopher E., and Elinor Accampo. *Confronting Modernity in Fin-de-Siècle France: Bodies, Minds, and Gender.* New York: Palgrave Macmillan, 2010.

Foucault, Michel. *The History of Sexuality,* vol. 1: *An Introduction.* New York: Vintage Books, 1980.

Fouquier, Henry (as Colombine). *Le Gil Blas,* September 29, 1884.

Gantz, Katherine. "The Difficult Guest: French Queer Theory Makes Room for Rachilde." *South Central Review* 22, no. 3 (Fall 2005): 113–132.

Gounaridou, Kiki, and Frazer Lively. Introduction to *Madame La Mort and Other Plays,* by Rachilde. Baltimore: Johns Hopkins University Press, 1998.

Gran-Aymeric, Eve, and Jean Gran-Aymeric. *Jane Dieulafoy: Une vie d'homme.* Paris: Perrin, 1991.

Guentner, Wendelin. "The Art Writing of 'Marc' de Montifaud." In *Translation and the Arts in Modern France,* ed. Sonya Stephens, 113–130. Bloomington: Indiana University Press, 2017.

———, ed. *Women Art Critics in Nineteenth-Century France: Vanishing Acts.* Newark: University of Delaware Press, 2013.

Gunther, Scott. *The Elastic Closet: A History of Homosexuality in France, 1942–present.* New York: Palgrave Macmillan, 2009.

Halberstam, Jack. *Female Masculinity.* Durham, NC: Duke University Press, 1998.

———. *In a Queer Time and Place: Transgender Bodies, Subcultural Lives.* New York: New York University Press, 2005.

———. *Trans*: A Quick and Quirky Account of Gender Variability.* Oakland: University of California Press, 2018.

Hall, Radclyffe. *The Well of Loneliness.* 1928. Reprint, London: Wordsworth, 2014.

Halperin, David M. *How to Do the History of Homosexuality.* Chicago: University of Chicago Press, 2002.

Hawthorne, Melanie. *Rachilde and French Women's Authorship.* Lincoln: University of Nebraska Press, 2001.

———. *Finding the Woman Who Didn't Exist: The Curious Life of Gisèle d'Estoc.* Lincoln: University of Nebraska Press, 2013.

Hayward, Eva, and Jami Weinstein. "Introduction: Tranimalities in the Age of Trans* Life." *TSQ: Transgender Quarterly* 2, no. 2 (May 2015): 195–208.

Hekma, Gert. "'A Female Soul in a Male Body': Sexual Inversion as Gender Inversion in Nineteenth-Century Sexology." In *Third Sex, Third Gender: Beyond Sexual Dimorphism in Culture and History*, ed. Gilbert Herdt, 213–40. New York: Zone Books, 1994.

Hippeau, Paul. "Marc de Montifaud." In *Galerie Contemporaine* ser. I, vol. III. Paris: L. Baschet, 1878.

Holmes, Diana. *Rachilde: Decadence, Gender, and the Woman Writer*. Oxford, UK: Berg, 2001.

Irvine, Margot. "Jane Dieulafoy's Gender Transgressive Behavior and Conformist Writing." In *Gender and Identities in France: Working Papers on Contemporary France*, vol. 4, ed. Brigitte Rollet and Emily Salines, 13–23. Portsmouth, UK: University of Portsmouth Research Office, 1999.

———. *Pour suivre un époux: Les récits de voyage des couples au XIX siècle*. Montreal: Editions Nota Bene, 2008.

Krieger, Nick. *Nina Here nor There: My Journey beyond Gender*. Boston: Beacon Press, 2011.

Ladenson, Elisabeth. *Dirt for Art's Sake: Books on Trial from "Madame Bovary" to "Lolita."* Ithaca, NY: Cornell University Press, 2007.

Ladin, Joy. *Through the Door of Life: A Jewish Journey between Genders*. Madison: University of Wisconsin Press, 2012.

Laing, Olivia. *The Lonely City: Adventures in the Art of Being Alone*. New York: Picador, 2017.

Lebois, André. "Deux amours cruelles de Villiers." *Revue d'histoire littéraire de la France* 52, no. 1 (1952): 73–80.

———. *Villiers de l'Isle Adam, revelateur du verbe*. Neuchatel: Editions de Messeiller, 1952.

Leroy, Géraldi, and Julie Bertrand-Sabiani. *La vie littéraire à la Belle Epoque*. Paris: Presses Universitaires de France, 1998.

Loliée, Frédéric. "Madame Jane Dieulafoy." *Revue Politique Et Littéraire, Revue Bleue*, 4th ser., vol. 6 (July 1–December 31, 1896), 690–943.

Lorrain, Jean. *Dans l'oratoire*. Paris: C. Dalou, 1888.

Maizeroy, René (as Frescata). "Madame de Sade." *Le Figaro*, September 10, 1882.

Mancini, Elena. *Magnus Hirschfeld and the Quest for Sexual Freedom: A History of the First International Sexual Freedom Movement.* New York: Palgrave Macmillan, 2010.

McMillan, James. *France and Women, 1789–1914: Gender, Society and Politics.* New York: Routledge, 2000.

Mesch, Rachel. *Having It All in the Belle Epoque: How French Women's Magazines Invented the Modern Woman.* Stanford: Stanford University Press, 2013.

———. *The Hysteric's Revenge: French Women Writers at the Fin de Siècle.* Nashville: Vanderbilt University Press, 2006.

Méténier, Oscar. *Grâce.* Paris: Giraud, 1886.

Meyerowitz, Joanne. *How Sex Changed: A History of Transsexuality in the United States.* Cambridge: Harvard University Press, 2002.

Mills, Robert. "Visibly Trans? Picturing Saint Eugenia in Medieval Art." *Transgender Studies Quarterly* 5, no. 4 (November 2018): 540–562.

Misme, Jane. "Le précieux déguisement." *La Française,* September 16, 1922.

Mock, Janet. *Redefining Realness: My Path to Womanhood, Identity, Love and So Much More.* New York: Atria Books, 2014.

Monicat, Bénédicte. *Itinéraires de l'écriture au féminin: Voyageuses du dix-neuvième siècle.* Amsterdam: Rodopi, 1996.

Montapic. *See* Dubut de Laforest.

Montesquieu, Charles de Secondat, baron de. *Les lettres persanes.* Paris: Alphonse Lemerre, 1873.

Morgan, Cheryl. "De 'la plaisanterie meurtrière' à la comédie contemporaine." In *La littérature en bas bleus,* Tome III: *Romancières en France de 1870 à 1914,* ed. Andréa Del Lungo and Brigitte Louichon, 176–193. Paris: Classiques Garnier, 2017.

Morris, Jan. *Conundrum.* 1974. Reprint, New York: New York Review of Books, 2002.

Muñoz, José. "Ephemera as Evidence: Introductory Notes to Queer Acts." *Women and Performance: A Journal of Feminist Theory* 8, no. 2 (1996): 5–16.

Murat, Laure. *La loi du genre: Une histoire culturelle du "troisième sexe."* Paris: Fayard, 2006.

Nicolazzo, Z. "What's Transgressive about Trans* Studies in Education Now?" *International Journal of Qualitative Studies in Education* 30 (2017): 211–216.

Nelson, Maggie. *The Argonauts.* Minneapolis: Greywolf Press, 2015.

Noblet, Agnès de. "Une correspondance exhumée: Lôti et Madame Dieulafoy." *Revue Pierre Lôti* 9, no. 36 (1988): 56–69.

Nochlin, Linda. *The Politics of Vision: Essays on Nineteenth-Century Art and Society.* New York: Harper and Row, 1989.

Offen, Karen. "Depopulation, Nationalism, and Feminism in Fin-de-Siècle France." *American Historical Review* 89, no. 3 (June 1984): 684–676.

Pedersen, Jean. *Legislating the French Family: Feminism, Theater, and Republican Politics.* Camden, NJ: Rutgers University Press, 2003.

Peniston, William A., and Nancy Erber, eds. *Queer Lives: Men's Autobiographies from Nineteenth-Century France.* Lincoln: University of Nebraska Press, 2007.

Peyrebrune, Georges de. *Une décadente.* Paris: Frinzine, 1886.

———. *Le roman d'un bas bleu.* Paris: Ollendorff, 1892.

———. *Correspondance: De la Société des gens de lettres au jury du prix Vie heureuse.* Ed. Nelly Sanchez. Paris: Classiques Garnier, 2016.

Philippe, Pierre. "Rachilde saisie par la débauche." *Le Monde,* August 21, 1998.

Pommerade, Pierre. "Le sol et le sang de Rachilde." *Bulletin de la Société historique et archéologique du Périgord* 120 (1993): 785–821.

Prosser, Jay. *Second Skins: The Body Narratives of Transsexuality.* New York: Columbia University Press, 1998.

Pyle, Kai. "Naming and Claiming: Recovering Ojibwe and Plains Cree Two-Spirit Language." *Transgender Studies Quarterly* 5, no. 4 (November 2018): 574–605.

Reid, Martine. *George Sand.* Trans. Gretchen Van Slyke. University Park: Penn State University Press, 2018.

Rexer, Raisa. "Sex Education: Obscenity, Romanticism, and Creativity in Flaubert's letters from the *Voyage en Egypte* and *L'éducation sentimentale.*" *Nineteenth-Century French Studies* 44, nos. 1–2 (2015): 95–110.

Richet, Charles. "Les démoniaques d'aujourd'hui." *Revue des deux mondes* 37 (January 15, 1880): 340–372.

Robert, Marie, Ulrich Pohlmann, and Thomas Galifot, eds. *Qui a peur des femmes photographes? 1839–1945.* Paris: Musée d'Orsay, 2015.

Roberts, Mary Louise. *Disruptive Acts: The New Woman in Fin-de-Siècle France.* Chicago: University of Chicago Press, 2002.

Rose, Jacqueline. "Who Do You Think You Are?" *London Review of Books,* May 5, 2016.

Rossiter, Heather. *Sweet Boy, Dear Wife: Jane Dieulafoy in Persia, 1881–1886*. Adelaide, Australia: Wakefield Press, 2015.

Ryner, Hans. *Le massacre des amazones: Etudes critiques sur deux cent bas-bleus contemporains*. Paris: Chamuel, 1890.

Salamon, Gayle. *Assuming a Body: Transgender and the Rhetorics of Materiality*. New York: Columbia University Press, 2010.

Sanchez, Nelly, ed. *Lettres de Camille Delaville à Georges de Peyrebrune, 1884–1888*. Brest: Centre d'étude des correspondances et des journaux intimes, 2010.

———. "Rachilde ou la genèse (possible) de *Monsieur Vénus*." *Nineteenth-Century French Studies* 38, no. 3/4 (Spring/Summer 2010): 252–263.

Schultz, Gretchen. *Sapphic Fathers: Discourses of Same-Sex Desire from Nineteenth-Century France*. Toronto: University of Toronto Press, 2014.

Schwartz, Vanessa. *Spectacular Realities: Early Mass Culture in Fin-de-Siècle Paris*. Berkeley: University of California Press, 1999.

Scott, Joan. "Gender: A Useful Category of Historical Analysis." *American Historical Review* 91, no. 5 (December 1986): 1053–1075.

Serano, Julia. *Whipping Girl: A Transsexual Woman on Sexism and the Scapegoating of Femininity*. Berkeley, CA: Seal Press, 2016.

Silverman, Deborah. *Art Nouveau in Fin-de-Siècle France: Politics, Psychology, Style*. Berkeley: University of California Press, 1989.

Skidmore, Emily. *True Sex: The Lives of Trans Men at the Turn of the Twentieth Century*. New York: New York University Press, 2017.

Snorton, C. Riley. *Black on Both Sides: A Racial History of Trans Identity*. Minneapolis: University of Minnesota Press, 2017.

Soulignac, Christian. "Ecrits de jeunesse de Mademoiselle de Vénérande." *Revue Frontenac* 10–11 (1993–1994): 192–218.

Spoon, Rae, and Ivan E. Coyote. *Gender Failure*. Vancouver: Arsenal Pulp Press, 2014.

Stryker, Susan. *Transgender History: The Roots of Today's Revolution*. Rev. ed. New York: Seal Press, 2017.

Stryker, Susan, and Aren Z. Aizura, eds. *The Transgender Studies Reader 2*. New York: Routledge, 2013.

Stryker, Susan, and Stephen Whittle. *The Transgender Studies Reader 1*. New York: Routledge, 2006.

Summer, Mary. "Quelques femmes écrivains d'aujourd'hui." *La Vie Quotidienne*, October 23, 1898, 130.

Tailhade, Laurent. *Petits mémoires de la vie*. Paris: G. Crès, 1921.

———. *Quelques fantômes de jadis*. Paris: A Messein, 1913.

Thompson, Raymond (with Kitty Swell). *What Took You So Long? A Girl's Journey to Manhood*. London: Penguin, 1995.

Uzanne, Joseph. *Figures contemporaines tirées de l'album Mariani*. Vol. 6. Paris: Librairie Henri Floury, 1901.

Valentine, Giancarlo. "PC Language Changed My Life." *New York Times*, January 3, 2018.

Vallette, Alfred. *Le roman d'un homme sérieux*. Paris: Mercure de France, 1994.

Van Slyke, Gretchen. "The Sexual and Textual Politics of Dress: Rosa Bonheur and Her Cross-Dressing Permits." *Nineteenth-Century French Studies* 26, no. 3/4 (1998): 321–335.

Verlaine, Paul. *Lettres inédites à divers correspondants*. Published and annotated by Georges Zayed. Geneva: Librairie Droz, 1976.

Villatte, Louis. Review of *Monsieur Vénus*, by Rachilde, 1889 ed. *Le Décadent*, February 15–28, 1889, 58–59.

Wilchins, Riki. *Queer Theory, Gender Theory: An Instant Primer*. New York: Magnus Books, 2004.

Index

NOTE: Page numbers followed by *f* refer to figures.

Lightning Source UK Ltd.
Milton Keynes UK
UKHW010656280121
377821UK00008B/77/J